Praise for
The Beyond Access Model

"This is the book every teacher leader, administrator, or school board needs to plan for inclusive schooling and to keep their model fresh, effective, and relevant. Not just a description of state-of-the-art practices or illustrations of 'what is possible' in K–12 schools, but a challenge to the field to pay attention to how practices have evolved and what inclusive education needs to look like today. With its focus on responsive instruction, challenging curriculum, and collaboration, *The Beyond Access Model* is a wake-up call for educators to be reflective about their work, see the potential and complexity in their students, and raise expectations for all. I was hooked from the first story on the first page and kept reading until I had examined every chapter, figure, table, and checklist. If you are looking to engage in school reform that is both thoughtful and powerful, this book is for you."

—**Paula Kluth, Ph.D.**
Independent Consultant and Scholar
Oak Park, Illinois

"Research tells us that a student's presence in the general education classroom is a necessary but not sufficient requirement for true inclusion. Similarly, research suggests that access to the general education curriculum is a necessary but not sufficient requirement for students with disabilities to progress in the general education curriculum. *The Beyond Access Model* provides a systematic means to do just that: go beyond simply access. Jorgensen, McSheehan, and Sonnenmeier have provided a timely, user-friendly text that moves us toward a third generation of inclusive practices that doesn't stop at just presence or access."

—**Michael L. Wehmeyer, Ph.D.**
Professor, Department of Special Education
Director, Kansas University Center on Developmental Disabilities
Senior Scientist, Beach Center on Disability, University of Kansas

"An awesome tool for educators and parents. With the strategies in this book, educators can create classrooms where all children belong, teachers will have the tools to ensure all students learn together, and children with disabilities will receive the strong educational foundation they so richly deserve in order to move on to successful lives as adults."

—**Kathie Snow**
Parent, trainer, and author of
Disability Is Natural:
Revolutionary Common Sense for Raising Successful
Children with Disabilities

"For years, Jorgensen, McSheehan, and Sonnenmeier have been thought leaders in promoting inclusive practices. In this book, they combine their expertise and talents to come up with a framework that can assist any district/school working to actively involve students in the general education setting. *The Beyond Access Model* is a well-thought-out process that goes beyond a student's mere presence in the general education setting and promotes their true membership."

—Cathy Pratt Ph.D.
Director, Indiana Resource Center for Autism
Board Chair, Autism Society of America

The
Beyond
Access
Model

The Beyond Access Model

Promoting Membership,
Participation,
and Learning
for Students with Disabilities
in the General Education Classroom

by

Cheryl M. Jorgensen, Ph.D.

Michael McSheehan

Rae M. Sonnenmeier, Ph.D.
Institute on Disability/UCED
University of New Hampshire

·P A U L·H·
BROOKES
PUBLISHING Cº®

Baltimore • London • Sydney

Paul H. Brookes Publishing Co.
Post Office Box 10624
Baltimore, Maryland 21285-0624
USA

www.brookespublishing.com

Typeset by Matrix Publishing Services, York, Pennsylvania.
Manufactured in the United States of America by
Sheridan Books, Inc., Chelsea, Michigan.

Preparation of this book was supported in part by the U.S. Department of Education, Office of
Special Education Programs, Grant #H324M020067 and Grant# H326X060010 to the University
of New Hampshire, Institute on Disability/UCED. The opinions expressed by this book do not
necessarily represent those of the U.S. Department of Education or the University of New
Hampshire.

Library of Congress Cataloging-in-Publication Data

Jorgensen, Cheryl M.
   The Beyond Access Model: Promoting membership, participation, and learning for students with
disabilities in the general education classroom / by Cheryl M. Jorgensen, Michael McSheehan, Rae M.
Sonnenmeier.
   p.   cm.
   Includes bibliographical references and index.
   ISBN-13: 978-1-55766-717-5 (pbk.)
   ISBN-10: 1-55766-717-9 (pbk.)
   1. Mainstreaming in education—United States—Case studies.   2. School improvement programs—
United States—Case studies.   I. McSheehan, Michael.   II. Sonnenmeier, Rae M.   III. Title.
   LC1201.J6698 2009
   371.9'0460973—dc22

                                                                                    2009017737

British Library Cataloguing in Publication data are available from the British Library.

2013   2012   2011   2010   2009

10   9   8   7   6   5   4   3   2   1

Contents

Contents of the Accompanying CD-ROM

Note: All forms are fillable in the individual folders unless denoted by an *. Forms in tbam.pdf can be printed out for reference only.

About the Authors

Cheryl M. Jorgensen, Ph.D., is Project Director and Member of the Strategic Team at the Institute on Disability/UCED (University Center for Excellence on Disability) at the University of New Hampshire (UNH) and Research Assistant Professor in UNH's Department of Education. She also is the director of the newly funded National Center on Inclusive Education for Children and Youth with Autism Spectrum Disorders and Related Disabilities. Dr. Jorgensen co-coordinates personnel preparation programs in the areas of autism spectrum disorders and intellectual and other developmental disabilities. Since 1985, she has worked on a variety of state- and federally funded inclusive education initiatives through model demonstration, in-service training, systems change, and personnel preparation. She chaired a statewide committee that revised New Hampshire's teacher certification standards in the areas of general special education and intellectual and other developmental disabilities. Dr. Jorgensen serves on New Hampshire's Alternate Assessment Advisory Committee. Her publications include numerous journal articles, book chapters, and policy briefs, as well as three other books, including *The Inclusion Facilitator's Guide* (coauthored with Mary C. Schuh & Jan Nisbet; Paul H. Brookes Publishing Co., 2006). Her research interests include inclusive education, the influence of teacher expectations on student achievement, curriculum and instructional design, and systems change.

Michael McSheehan is Clinical Assistant Professor in the Department of Communication Sciences and Disorders and Project Coordinator with the Institute on Disability/UCED at the University of New Hampshire. Mr. McSheehan is a coordinator of the newly funded National Center on Inclusive Education for Children and Youth with Autism Spectrum Disorders and Related Disabilities. He has worked on a variety of state- and federally funded initiatives to advance research, policy, and practice in inclusive education, alternate assessment, augmentative and alternative communication, autism spectrum disorders, collaborative teaming, and response to intervention. He serves on New Hampshire Department of Education advisory committees, including Alternate Assessment and Response to

Intervention, and consults with other state departments of education on similar topics.

Rae M. Sonnenmeier, Ph.D., CCC-SLP, is Clinical Associate Professor in the Department of Communication Sciences and Disorders and with the Institute on Disability/UCED at the University of New Hampshire and is an adjunct assistant professor of pediatrics with the Dartmouth Medical School. She served as Interdisciplinary Training Director for the New Hampshire Leadership Education in Neurodevelopmental Disabilities (LEND) program at the University of New Hampshire from 1999 to 2009. Dr. Sonnenmeier is an expert in the areas of interdisciplinary practice, augmentative communication techniques, and the inclusion of students who experience significant disabilities, including students with autism spectrum disorders. Currently, she is collaborating on an Office of Special Education Programs project that prepares speech-language pathologists in the area of augmentative and alternative communication to support the academic learning of students with significant disabilities. She regularly presents at state, national, and international conferences and does technical assistance in the New England region.

Foreword

Being invited to write the foreword for *The Beyond Access Model* provided me with an opportunity to reflect on my relationship with the authors over the past decade. I first met Rae at the 1995 Pittsburgh Employment Conference for Augmented Communicators, when she was a doctoral student with Jeff Higginbotham. Over dinner one evening, I gave her advice about her dissertation (which she wisely ignored), and I encouraged her to consider a position at the University of New Hampshire, since I knew that folks there were doing exciting work in the area of augmentative and alternative communication (AAC) and inclusive education. This time, she took my advice, and I met her again, along with Michael, several years later at a conference. I remember being impressed with their joint commitment to providing AAC supports to students with severe disabilities in inclusive classrooms. I also remember wishing that I could have a chance to work with them—although by "work with them" I'm sure I meant "mentor them" since, by that time, I had already coauthored the second edition of *Augmentative and Alternative Communication: Management of Severe Communication Disorders in Children and Adults* (with David R. Beukelman; Paul H. Brookes Publishing Co., 1998) and was no doubt thinking that they could learn a lot from me. Little did I know that it was I who would do the learning, from them.

I first "met" Cheryl vicariously, through a book she wrote in 1998 about inclusive education for students with severe disabilities in high school (*Restructuring High Schools for All Students: Taking Inclusion to the Next Level*; Brookes Publishing Co.). I remember, quite distinctly, reading it and—especially when I got to the chapter in which she advocated for the elimination of community-based instruction in functional skill areas—thinking, "This woman is out to lunch!" Of course, her suggestion that functional skills could easily be taught in high schools in the context of the same educational opportunities that are available to all students eventually proved to be quite accurate, but I and many of my colleagues viewed her suggestion as heresy at the time. At the very least, what this experience taught me was to be on the alert for any project with Cheryl's name attached to it, since it was sure to be interesting, if not controversial!

Although memories of my early history with this team are somewhat foggy, an encounter I had with Michael in 2006 is not: We had an e-mail fight. He, Cheryl, and Rae were writing an article for *Topics in Language Disorders* about the Beyond Access Model and, in one section of the manuscript, they wanted to contrast the use of their model with that of the Participation Model described in *Augmentative and Alternative Communication: Supporting Children and Adults with Complex Communication Needs, Third Edition* (Beukelman & Mirenda, Brookes Publishing Co., 2005). Michael and I disagreed about how he and his coauthors depicted the Participation Model in their article (and, in the end, they were kind enough to change their wording to appease me), but that was not the real point of the exchange, at least for me. What it made me realize was that my thinking about inclusion up to that point had been surprisingly conservative in that I believed that, for some students with significant intellectual disabilities, the goals of instruction in general education classrooms should be primarily in areas such as communication, social, and motor skill development rather than in "academic" areas such as reading, math, or science. Michael challenged this position and noted that, in the Beyond Access Model, "The goals are full inclusion, learning of general education curriculum content commensurate with age-appropriate typical peers . . . and an AAC system that allows any student to communicate about curriculum and other topics commensurate with their age-appropriate typical peers" (personal communication, April 12, 2006). I remember thinking, "What planet does this guy come from, if he really believes that all students—even those with profound, multiple disabilities—can learn academic content?" And I think I even called him an "inclusion ideologue" at one point in our e-mail exchange. But despite my defensive reaction, another part of me was thinking, "If they are really accomplishing this goal with Beyond Access, I need to learn more about what they are doing and how they are doing it." It was an unsettling experience for me, to say the least, and it made me question my own self-perception as a diehard advocate for inclusion. Was I really being too conservative?

The next time we had a chance to talk about this was in 2007, at a "think tank" meeting sponsored by the University of New Hampshire group in Washington, D.C. I was one of the people invited to spend a day talking about inclusion and students with severe disabilities and what each of us who attended the meeting *really* thought about what was possible and how inclusion should look in schools. For me, it was a day that was simultaneously humbling, challenging, and invigorating. I was humbled to hear people talk about instruction in ways that made me realize that (shock!) I *was* being conservative in my assumption that academics were not on the radar screen for some students. I was challenged to consider the implications of presuming competence of all students and its inverse, presuming incompetence, and I was also challenged to self-evaluate my own attitudes in this regard. And, in the end, I was invigorated by student stories and examples that helped me understand that, with the proper supports—not the least of which involve AAC—it might indeed be possible to "leave no child behind" with regard to inclusive participation, even in the academic curriculum of general education classrooms.

Which brings me to this unique and timely book. This book describes the Beyond Access Model, which was developed by the authorship team over a 4-year period as a federally funded model demonstration project through the Institute on Disability at the University of New Hampshire. There are several things that are unique about this model. First, it emphasizes the importance of presuming students' competence and providing them with opportunities consistent with high expectations, in line with noted researcher Anne Donnellan's 1984 principle of the "least dangerous assumption." Second, it focuses on ensuring that all students are granted full membership in general education classrooms so that they can participate and demonstrate learning in the same activities as their peers. Third, it promotes learning of the general education curriculum by students with significant disabilities in inclusive classrooms, through a student and team planning process that is grounded in high-quality professional development. This process organizes recommended practices for students and their teams into a coherent, reiterative, and manageable process of assessment, implementation, evaluation, reflection, and revision that promotes continuous program improvement.

In other words, the Beyond Access Model is not simple; this is not inclusion for people who either want quick fixes or who are squeamish about tackling difficult challenges head-on. Rather, the model acknowledges and systematically deals with the policy, practice, attitudes, knowledge, and skill barriers that often prevent implementation of even the most well-thought-out inclusion plans. It emphasizes the importance of accurate and reliable AAC supports and services that enable students to communicate about academic curricular content and engage in social interactions with adults and age-appropriate classmates. It focuses on the use of authentic, performance-based assessments for individualized student planning and on family and school partnerships that are both equitable and collaborative. And, it includes school administrators as key catalytic agents for aligning general and special education reforms toward the goal of creating communities of learners that are truly inclusive.

One of the things that I especially admire about this book is that the authors are not at all coy about what it takes to implement their model. They acknowledge that implementation requires commitment, time, energy, and expertise from all team members as well as from a Beyond Access facilitator who understands and is familiar with the model. At the same time, they provide a detailed, virtually step-by-step description of the attitudes and skills that are required, along with examples from their own work of how to approach implementation systematically and carefully. Throughout, they also provide student stories that both inspire and motivate while simultaneously providing realistic examples portraying the range of potential outcomes.

I know that some readers will get through this book and think, "No way, not possible"—and for them, it will not be. Others will think, "Well, maybe . . . ," and give the model a try or will think, "It's about time," and embrace the principles and practices described here wholeheartedly. If even a small proportion of readers in the latter two groups succeed in making the Beyond Access vision become a reality in their schools, a significant number of students with severe disabilities will benefit tremendously. Cheryl, Michael, and Rae—thank you for your vision, for this book, and for teaching this old dog some new and very valuable tricks.

Pat Mirenda, Ph.D., BCBA-D
Professor
University of British Columbia

Preface

In this preface, we will describe the origins of the Beyond Access (BA) Model through a story about a student named Stephen. When Michael McSheehan and Rae Sonnenmeier were providing technical assistance to Stephen's team, school, and district in the late 1990s, the elements of a new professional development and team planning process came together in a coherent way for the first time (McSheehan & Sonnenmeier, 2001). When Michael and Rae shared what they were learning with Cheryl Jorgensen, it became clear that many of the issues that she had been thinking about with respect to curriculum modification based on presuming students' competence might well be addressed with teams through the process that Michael and Rae were developing. This led to yet another iteration of the emerging model (McSheehan, Sonnenmeier, & Jorgensen, 2002), a model demonstration project to further refine the model's phases, and an evaluation of the outcomes for students and teams who implemented the model. We will describe what we have learned over the past decade that has led us to the current version of the BA Model. We will then describe the students with whom the model has been used and explain the disability terminology that will be used in the book. We will also provide a brief overview of each chapter and make some suggestions for how different readers might approach the book for optimal understanding. Finally, we will say a few words about the various BA forms, checklists, and templates.

STEPHEN'S STORY

Following a presentation by Michael and Rae in a suburban New England town, Michael received a call from a special education director who attended the session asking if he would consult on "a challenging situation." The situation involved Stephen, a fourth-grade student with multiple disabilities whose team had been attempting to include in general education classes since he enrolled at the school. During his most recent comprehensive reevaluation, evaluators from a center renowned for their expertise evaluating children with significant, multiple disabilities (cognitive, communicative, developmental, and medical) had recommended a full-time residential placement for Stephen, with a program design emphasizing activities of daily living and functional life skills. His dedicated parents, long-time advocates for his inclusion in the neighborhood school, and other members of the individualized education program (IEP) team, began questioning the team's effectiveness and capabilities to educate Stephen. The special education director wondered if there was any way to continue to educate Stephen in the local school and to better support the team (including his family) to design and implement effective supports for him that demonstrated an effective program based in a general education setting.

An initial review of his educational records was conducted in advance of a full-day onsite visit by Michael. During the day at school, Stephen was observed in general education classrooms and in a variety of pull-out therapies with his speech-language and occupational therapists. Team members met with Michael individually to reflect on the supports they had tried over the years with Stephen and the team's dilemma with the recent recommendation for a residential placement. Throughout interviews, it became apparent that Stephen was surrounded by educators who adored him and wanted the best for him. However, the majority of the educators were engaged in practices that they had learned during their own discipline training programs (years earlier) or had learned from a variety of consultants who, over the years, came and went, each consultant with his or her own differing philosophies and priorities for what the team should do to support Stephen. The design of Stephen's educational program and the practices of his team reflected these many disparate perspectives and priorities. No unifying effort was present to focus the team to utilize practices geared specifically to increasing Stephen's participation and communication in class.

At the end of the day's observation, Michael facilitated a conversation with the team, with Stephen present for the report of findings. Michael directed several comments to Stephen and spoke to him as if he understood what was going on. Several team members' nonverbal body language suggested that they were surprised (to put it lightly) that a consultant would speak directly with Stephen and expect that he would understand what was going on. It was interesting to note that Stephen, who was observed throughout the day to give minimal eye gaze to people and to get up and roam around during activities, sat in full attention looking at Michael as he reported his impressions and recommendations.

Over the course of the next year, with consultation, educators at the school and in the district began to adopt different practices that were central to the BA Model. As Stephen entered fifth grade, he was attending and participating in most of the academic instruction in the general education classroom throughout his school day. His team had tirelessly spent hours learning about and trying new ways to support his communication and learning, and it was paying off.

The special education director, after several months of monitoring the consultation and the team's progress, invited Michael and Rae to expand the consultation to other students with intellectual and developmental disabilities in other schools in the district. As they did so, and as they reflected on their consultation, patterns of their consulting and of educators' learning were consistent with literature on "cycles of inquiry" (Keeney, 1998). They began to describe predictable phases of developing supports for students: explore and describe, observe and document, and reflect and recommend. This framework of iterative phases was well received by educators and family members across the district. It seemed to make a series of trials of otherwise complex and technical aspects of communication and instructional strategies more tangible and understandable.

THE BEYOND ACCESS MODEL

The BA Model was further developed, implemented, and evaluated from 2002 to 2006 as part of a 4-year Model Demonstration Project funded by the U.S. Department of Education Office of Special Education Programs. The model was designed to promote learning of general education curriculum content by what we referred to at the time as "students with significant cognitive disabilities." The model has been used with students from the ages of 6 through 18. They have been shy or outgoing, quiet or loud, fast or slow, serious or outrageously funny. They have been interested in airplanes, trains, animals, reading, oranges, the 2004 presidential election, kites, WWE wrestling, and saving the environment. Some have been only children and others part of large families. They have been affected by medical diagnoses including Down syndrome, mitochondrial disorder, spina bifida, autism, Alfi syndrome (9p–), seizures, and visual impairments. Each and every student had been perceived by some members of their educational teams as having a significant intellectual disability, regardless of whether that diagnosis was supported by formal evaluations. All met the participation criteria for New Hampshire's alternate assessment based on alternate achievement standards.

THE STUDENTS

These students had a variety of disability labels mentioned under the Individuals with Disabilities Education Act (IDEA) of 1990 (PL 101-476) and subsequent revisions, such as autism (including pervasive developmental disorder-not otherwise specified [PDD-NOS]), mental retardation, multiple disability, developmental delay, orthopedic disabilities, and other health impairments. None of the students was deaf/hard of hearing or blind/visually impaired *in the absence of* an intellectual and/or other developmental disability. All of the students we have worked with have had complex communication needs, and several have had challenging behavior.

In this book we will use the terms *intellectual and/or other developmental disabilities* (abbreviated IDD) and *complex communication needs* (http://www.isaac-online .org/en/publications/aac_information.html) to describe the students, with two exceptions. When a direct quote from another source uses a different term, we will use the term from the original work, and if research being cited was conducted with students with a specific disability label, we will use the label used by the researchers. We recognize that none of these terms reflects how we really view these students: as competent, engaging learners who make valuable contributions to their classrooms, schools, and communities.

CHAPTER OVERVIEW

Chapter 1 begins with Jay's story, one of many we'll share to illustrate both the challenges of supporting students' membership, participation, communication, and learning, and how the BA Model might support teams to work more effectively to help students achieve those important outcomes. Chapter 2 provides the historical context and the current "state of the state" in the field, focusing on the issues of expectations for student learning, what is deemed appropriate curriculum for students with IDD, communication supports, and the environments in which students with IDD are being taught. The four phases of the BA Model are described briefly in this chapter as is the role of the model's administrative leadership team. Chapter 3 presents an underlying best practice of the BA Model: presuming that, when students are provided with the right supports, they are competent to learn the general education curriculum in the general education classroom and to communicate in a way that is commensurate with same-age peers. Chapter 4 defines membership, participation, and learning and presents observable indicators of these constructs that will be used to measure the efficacy of the BA Model in later chapters. The membership, functions, and skills of the members of a BA collaborative team are presented in Chapter 5. Chapter 5 also describes the critical role of a BA facilitator in supporting a team's use of the model.

Chapters 6–9 describe the purpose, outcomes, and instructions for activities that comprise the four iterative phases of the model. These chapters also present successful examples of real teams using that particular phase of the Model as well as challenges to success.

Chapter 10 describes the essential role of the Administrative Leadership Team (ALT) in the model's start-up and the initial phases of implementation, and in helping to problem solve any difficulties that cannot be managed by the team. The book concludes with an afterword highlighting some insights on the change process by Michael Fullan and featuring reflections on using the model by Laurie Lambert, who was a BA facilitator for several years in an elementary school that implemented the BA Model.

If you like to get the big picture of a new way of thinking or doing before delving into the details, you may want to first read Chapters 1–5, then read *just the examples* that are presented at the beginning of Chapters 6–9. After that, read Chapter 10 and the afterword. Then return to Chapters 6–9 to fill in the missing details.

If your understanding of a new way of thinking or doing is enhanced by knowing all of the details, then by all means, read the chapters in their entirety from start to finish.

CHECKLISTS, FORMS, AND TEMPLATES

Yes, there are a lot of checklists, forms, and templates in this book! Anyone who has ever been in the position of leading a team to include a student with IDD in a general education classroom knows that there is a lot of information to manage, many people to communicate with, stacks of instructional materials, and important team processes and decisions to document. On the one hand, we know that forms created for one student, team, or school almost always need to be adapted for the specific needs of another student, team, or school. On the other hand, we think that these forms may provide a welcome structure for teams when they first begin using the BA Model. You will find copies of the pertinent forms and checklists (some fillable) on the enclosed CD-ROM. (*Please see the copyright page for this book and the software license agreement on the accompanying CD-ROM for information and usage restrictions.*) We encourage you to adapt the forms as permitted to your local needs and make them work for you.

REFERENCES

Individuals with Disabilities Education Act (IDEA) of 1990, PL 101-476, 20 U.S.C. §§ 1400 *et seq.*

Keeney, L. (1998). *Using data for school improvement.* Providence, RI: Annenberg Institute for School Reform.

McSheehan, M., & Sonnenmeier, R. (2001). Developing augmentative communication to support participation in general education classrooms. *2000 TASH Conference Yearbook.* Washington, DC: TASH.

McSheehan, M., Sonnenmeier, R., & Jorgensen, C. (2002). Communication and learning: Creating systems of support for students with significant disabilities. *TASH Connections Newsletter.*

Acknowledgments

Writing the acknowledgment section for a book is somewhat like going through an old photo album. Memories of the students, families, and mentors whom we have known bring smiles, laughter, a few tears, and the occasional pang of regret for not having done something as well as we would have liked. Since each of us has come to do this work through very different life and career paths, each of us would like to acknowledge those individuals who have had the most impact on the beliefs and knowledge that informed the development of the Beyond Access Model. We all gratefully acknowledge Rebecca Lazo's support of our work and that of other authors published by Paul H. Brookes Publishing Co. who contribute to the quality of life of children with disabilities and their families.

As we approached the second year of the Beyond Access Model Demonstration Project in 2003, we had a series of meetings with New Hampshire schools to recruit their participation in the project. Each had positive attributes, but all had one or more reasons for not signing on to the project at that time. Some had too many other school improvement initiatives on their plates, a few were in the midst of administrative turnovers, and others were not ready to make the commitment of time and personnel that the project required.

Just as we were worried that we might not be able to recruit any additional project sites, I received an e-mail inquiry about the project from an excellent inclusion facilitator in a school district just outside New Hampshire's state capital. Vicki Therrien had attended professional development workshops, conferences, and leadership training events sponsored by the Institute on Disability and had heard about the project from a colleague in another district. She set up an informational meeting with the school principal (Mike Reardon), the district special education administrator (Patty Willis), the building special education coordinator (Karen Guercia), a special education teacher (Karen Medeiros), and herself. Michael McSheehan and I were scheduled to do the presentation together, though we were planning to drive to the school separately. In the days before GPS, I got totally lost and arrived at the presentation 45 minutes late. Michael carried on without me, and despite a less-than-impressive showing that day by the Beyond Access Project Director, Pembroke High School (part of New Hampshire School Administrative Unit 53) elected to participate in the project for its second, third, and fourth years. During that time, we worked closely with the same folks who had attended the informational meeting, as well as students with and without disabilities, their parents, general and special education teachers, paraprofessionals, and related service providers.

We are very grateful to Pembroke Academy and our other project sites (Windham-Pelham schools, Three Rivers School in Pembroke, Epsom Elementary School, Maplewood Elementary School in Somersworth, and Lamprey River Elementary School in Raymond) because it is their everyday experience that brings to life the Model's foundational beliefs and practices related to students' membership, participation, and learning. Thank you.

Cheryl M. Jorgensen

The values and knowledge at the heart of the Beyond Access Model are those that I first came to understand and prioritize through the bold mentoring of my University of New Hampshire undergraduate advisor, Steve Calculator, and other faculty, Jan Nisbet and Cheryl Jorgensen. Putting those understandings into practice in public schools is not always easy. The first iteration of the Beyond Access Model emerged in a long-term consultative arrangement with the Old Rochester Regional school district in southern Massachusetts. I am very grateful for collaboration experiences that I had with these students, families, and educators. In particular, Stephen, Ben, and Craig, their families, and their individualized education program (IEP) team members pushed themselves and me to understand the HOW of this work. Finally, an enormous debt of gratitude is owed to Terri Hamm, with whom I spent innumerable hours grappling with how administrators might lead this effort.

As noted by Cheryl, we are very grateful to our partners at the school project sites in further developing, refining, evaluating, and formalizing the Beyond Access Model. In collaboration with the New Hampshire Department of Education, we had an opportunity to use the Model as a process for helping IEP teams explore, select, and use accommodations for instruction and large-scale assessment. The ultimate vision of the Beyond Access for Assessment Accommodations project was to transition students from an alternate assessment based on alternate achievement standards to the general assessment with accommodations. We are very grateful to the New Hampshire Department of Education's staff and administrators for the opportunity and for their dedicated leadership. We appreciate the effort of our partners at these school project sites to explore this new application of the Model, which has further informed its development and expanded our learning. The unwavering commitment of all of our partners along the way to develop educational systems that presume competence of students and that promote membership, participation, and learning in the general education classroom is a model for others. Thank you for all that you gave of yourselves.

Michael McSheehan

My involvement with this book is the culmination of vision that began many years ago in a classroom in Buffalo. I began my career at a time when working in natural settings and pragmatic language intervention were considered to be progressive ideas in the field of speech-language pathology. Over the past 30 years, I have been fortunate to work with two exceptional mentors, Judy Duchan and Nan Lund. Early in my career I came to value the importance of typical environments and typical opportunities and strived to support children with disabilities to be where they could benefit from interactions with their peers who were typically developing. I worked in both segregated and inclusive settings and learned firsthand how much children benefit socially, communicatively, and academically when in typical settings. It was a natural next step to focus on providing communication supports, including augmentative communication, within the general education classroom so that students with disabilities could learn and demonstrate what they learned about the general education curriculum. I am grateful to my mentors for their ongoing support.

Rae M. Sonnenmeier

*To the students, families, educators, and administrators
who worked with us in developing and refining the
Beyond Access Model*

Introducing the Beyond Access Model

Beyond Access to General Education

When we met Jay, he was in a fourth-grade classroom after having been included in general education since first grade. When he was in the general education classroom, he was taught pre- and early academic skills by a paraprofessional who used discrete trial instructional methods, often in a separate area at the side or back of the classroom. Jay left the general education classroom several times a day to receive special education and related services focused on following one- and two-step commands, making requests, responding to yes/no questions, and learning functional life skills. He had positive relationships with his peers. He also had access to an augmentative and alternative communication (AAC) device limited to a nine-item display that did not allow him to communicate about age-appropriate academic or social topics. His educational team had only met once in the previous year, to write his individualized education program (IEP).

Members of Jay's team were concerned about the meaningfulness and relevance of Jay's placement in a general education classroom because of the modified curriculum the team was teaching Jay and because the curriculum was disconnected from the general education classroom instruction. As Jay grew older, his parents and his team wondered if the discrepancy between Jay's understanding and the general education curriculum suggested that Jay ought to spend more time outside of the general education class learning functional skills than in the general education classroom with his peers without disabilities.

Jay's educational program and his team's questions illustrate the key debates in the field regarding appropriate learning expectations, curriculum, communication, and educational placement. Prior to 1997, special education law did not specifically address general curriculum involvement of students with disabilities. The Individuals with Disabilities Education Act (IDEA) Amendments of 1997 (PL 105-17), however, stated that quality education for students with disabilities could be made more effective by "having high expectations for such children and ensuring their access in the general curriculum to the maximum extent possible" (p. 5). This language shifted the focus of IDEA from simply assuring that students with disabilities were provided with a free appropriate public education to improving teaching and learning by enhancing their involvement and progress in the general curriculum.

The Individuals with Disabilities Education Improvement Act (IDEA) of 2004 (PL 108-446) added a new emphasis to the access requirements of IDEA 1997.

> Since the enactment and implementation of the Education for All Handicapped Children Act of 1975 [PL 94-142], this title has been successful in ensuring children with disabilities and the families of such children access to a free appropriate public education and in improving educational results for children with disabilities. However, the implementation of this title has been impeded by low expectations, and an insufficient focus on applying replicable research on proven methods of teaching and learning for children with disabilities. Almost 30 years of research and experience has demonstrated that the education of children with disabilities can be made more effective by—(A) *having high expectations for such children and ensuring their access to the general education curriculum in the regular classroom,* to the maximum extent possible, in order to (i) meet developmental goals and, to the maximum extent possible, the challenging expectations that have been established for all children; and (ii) be prepared to lead productive and independent adult lives, to the maximum extent possible. (p. 3; emphasis added)

We[1] developed the Beyond Access (BA) Model, in part, to address the emphasis in IDEA on high expectations, access to the general curriculum, and general education classroom placement. The Model also promotes learning the general education curriculum content and communication commensurate with same-age peers for students with intellectual and/or other developmental disabilities (IDD).[2] This chapter describes how Jay's educational program and his educational teams changed over the 3-year period in which the BA Model was being developed and demonstrated. His story illustrates the possibilities as well as some of the challenges faced by teams in planning for and implementing supports for each student's *membership* in the general education classroom, *participation* in general education instruction, *communication* commensurate with same-age peers, and *learning* of general education curriculum content within the general education classroom. His story also illustrates the critical role of collaborative teaming and administrative leadership in achieving these goals.

---

[1]Faculty and staff from the Institute on Disability at the University of New Hampshire with more than 60 years of combined experience in inclusive education, augmentative communication, collaborative teaming, and systems change.

[2]Readers may refer to the Preface for a discussion of the students for whom the BA Model was developed and a discussion of terminology used in this book.

JAY

Jay was an engaging and friendly 10-year-old boy with autism (Sonnenmeier, McSheehan, & Jorgensen, 2005). He had been diagnosed by a developmental pediatrician when he was 2 years, 8 months of age. He had a charming smile, loved trains, and was an active participant in family activities. According to all members of his educational team, although Jay was 10 years old, he was perceived to be functioning at the 2-year-old level. When we probed to understand the source of that perception, we found a report in his school records from the school district's developmental disabilities specialist who assessed Jay's academic level to be between 18 and 24 months, based on an informal assessment of Jay's abilities when he was chronologically 8 years, 9 months of age.

Jay was noted to have a poor attention span and sensory issues, and he did not perform well in high-demand situations. Motor imitation skills were reported to be difficult. Jay did not use his voice for speech; he used some manual sign approximations (e.g., MORE, ME) and natural gestures including a "two-finger point" to indicate a variety of messages such as, "I want that," "What is that?" and "I don't like that." Matching skills were a relative strength, including matching pictures, letters, numbers, and words.

Jay had access to a nine-message GoTalk speech-generating device (SGD). Each button was overlaid with a single word/single icon (Boardmaker Picture Communication Symbols) and spoke recorded messages to make requests such as I NEED A BREAK, I WANT A DRINK, and MORE PLEASE. Although he would occasionally point to a message on the device in response to requests to do so, such as "Point to the __," Jay was reportedly inconsistent in his use of the device. He did not show a reliable yes/no response with his voice, head nods, or with the SGD. Jay did not have access to age-appropriate academic content or social vocabulary.

Jay spent about half his day in his fourth-grade classroom in his neighborhood school. His desk was in a row alongside his peers and a one-to-one paraprofessional sat next to him. He joined the class for morning meeting and storytime after lunch, and he attended art and music with his peers. Jay was considered a member of his classroom as evidenced by having a desk and a place for his belongings alongside his peers, socializing during snack and various noninstructional times in class, and participating in recess and lunch with his peers. In general, Jay was a passive participant in most class activities. During academic instruction, Jay was taught primarily by the paraprofessional in a multilevel or parallel curriculum. About half of the time he used materials related to the general education lesson. The paraprofessional used discrete trial methods to teach Jay skills such as counting, one-to-one correspondence, color recognition, and matching. Jay participated in adapted physical education and received 45-minute sessions of speech-language therapy, occupational therapy, and special education consultation one time each week.

Jay had generally positive relationships with his peers, who were eager to sit next to him and provide him with assistance. Jay did not use conventional language to greet his peers but rather would approach them with a smile and a light touch to their body or hair. The other students might laugh and do it back to Jay.

Jay had great difficulty with activity-to-activity and location-to-location transitions. In particular, he showed distress when taken to the restroom, and his behavior was becoming increasingly challenging several times a day prior to this routine. He was frequently taken out of the classroom to work on using the restroom, sometimes up to 40 minutes at a time. Jay showed a variety of emotions—happiness, confusion, frustration, uncertainty, anger, discomfort—in nonverbal ways, such as hitting himself or pushing materials away from him. He used vocalizations with varied intonation suggesting positive or negative affect.

JAY'S EDUCATIONAL TEAM

Jay's educational team comprised his parents (father and stepmother), a special education teacher whose job title was "inclusion facilitator" (Jorgensen, Schuh, & Nisbet, 2006), a child-specific paraprofessional, a district-level technology team coordinator (who was a speech-language pathologist [SLP]), a building-level SLP, a certified occupational therapist assistant (COTA), and an adapted physical education teacher. This team had met once during the previous year to develop Jay's IEP and had not engaged in any instructional planning meetings for a year prior to the beginning of their work with the BA Model.

ADMINISTRATIVE SUPPORT FOR PARTICIPATION IN THE BEYOND ACCESS PROJECT

Jay's school district had a long history of support for inclusive education, and one of the authors had known the special education coordinator and special education teacher for almost 20 years. We recruited the district to participate in the federally funded model demonstration project and worked with three students in two schools over the course of 3 years. During the first year of the BA project, the district provided Jay's educational team with release time (and substitutes for the classroom teacher and paraprofessional) to attend 5 full days of professional development related to their participation in the project. School and district administrators also agreed to meet with a project staff member periodically to check in regarding the project's progress and to problem-solve any difficulties that arose. The administrators were responsive to our recommendations about changes in service delivery (e.g., a shift from pull-out to push-in services, increasing service time for the SLP, supporting the SLP and COTA to work with Jay during the same block of time) and the need for a weekly planning meeting for the team.

FIRST STEPS

During the first 2 months of the project, one project staff member led the team in a comprehensive baseline assessment process that involved gathering information about:

- Jay's participation in general education instruction
- Jay's academic, communication, movement, behavior, social, emotional, and functional skills

- The current methods of instruction and provision of supports for academic learning and communication
- Knowledge and skills represented on the educational team
- Collaboration among team members, including the quality of current team functioning and their capacity to utilize their expertise to support Jay's learning
- Organizational issues such as the school's philosophy about inclusive education, their local professional development plan, the structure of the school day, and the roles of various administrators in educational leadership

A variety of activities were used to gather this information including 1) a review of Jay's educational records to gather historical and current information such as evaluations and other reports, past and current IEPs, and progress reports; 2) examples of Jay's work and his communication; 3) written questionnaires completed by school-based team members; 4) multiple observations at school; 5) interviews with team members; 6) a home visit and interviews with Jay's parents; and 7) follow-up interviews to clarify information gathered. All of the information gathered was analyzed and synthesized to identify themes and possible recommendations for enhancing Jay's membership, participation, and learning within the general education classroom and for enhancing team collaboration.

After that information was compiled, the project staff member synthesized major findings and themes and presented them back to the team, including Jay's parents, during a 90-minute meeting. The team had the opportunity to provide feedback, ask questions, and clarify any of the findings presented. Once the team agreed on the findings of the assessment, several recommendations were made related to enhancing Jay's membership, participation, communication, and learning within the general education classroom and improving team collaboration.

The team decided that they wanted to prioritize two recommendations. First, they wanted to try out new supports for Jay's bathroom routine, feeling that until that went more smoothly, they were unlikely to make progress on enhancing Jay's participation and learning during other parts of the day. They also wanted to try new methods and supports for enhancing the validity and reliability of Jay's yes/no response. Although project staff viewed the bathroom routine recommendation as quite far removed from the efforts to enhance Jay's participation and learning of general education curriculum content, it was decided that getting team member buy-in was essential, and so they agreed to focus on the goals that were prioritized by the team.

PROFESSIONAL DEVELOPMENT

Findings from the baseline assessment revealed variability in team members' commitment to, experience with, and proficiency related to inclusive education best practices. For example, Jay's general education teacher had never had a student with autism in her class, and she reported that she had not received any training to date for engaging Jay in her class (3 months into the school year). The district-level technology team coordinator and the building special education teacher had many years of experience with students with autism and other IDD, but supporting students to fully participate in and learn the age-appropriate general education curriculum represented a new skill set for them. The SLP and COTA were experienced professionals but were accustomed to a pull-out model of service delivery and were not confident about the rationale or the strategies for providing their services within the general education classroom. Each team member was used to providing his or her services in solitary and had little experience working together to develop, implement, and evaluate supports for Jay's participation in a general education lesson.

Thus, the BA project staff recommended that Jay's team attend a series of professional development workshops provided to all of the school sites participating in the BA Model demonstration project. Over the course of the next 2 years, Jay's team attended workshops on presumed competence, AAC, positive behavior supports, instructional planning, curriculum modification, literacy, and collaborative teaming.

EXPLORING AND DESCRIBING NEW SUPPORTS

For several weeks following the assessment findings and recommendations meeting, a project staff member made weekly visits to the school, modeling and coaching team members to try out new supports for the bathroom routine and Jay's communication. An analysis of the bathroom routine and the associated challenging behaviors revealed that Jay had had a positive experience at camp the previous summer when he had to use the bathroom prior to swimming, using only a verbal cue to get ready for swimming by going to the bathroom. The team decided to try three new supports to make the school bathroom routine more manageable. First, they changed his visual schedule (between-event daily schedule), deleting the visual reminder for the bathroom. This helped to decrease anxiety for Jay predicting this heretofore unsuccessful routine. Second, they decided to take Jay to a men's bathroom instead of to the women's faculty bathroom. And third, they used the following script to support Jay's use of the bathroom: *"Jay, on our way to gym class, we'll stop at the restroom. Remember last summer at camp when you used to go to the restroom to get ready for swimming? We'll do the same thing to get ready for gym."* Within a few days of consistent use of this routine, bathroom visits became less stressful for Jay and for his paraprofessional.

The second recommendation that the team prioritized was related to their desire to have confidence in Jay's yes/no communication response. A new routine for using YES and NO symbols on the GoTalk was introduced. The YES and NO symbols were positioned in new locations on the device. Members of the team, including the classroom teacher, paraprofessional, related services providers, and peers, provided many daily opportunities for Jay to respond to yes/no questions that asked for his preference or opinion (instead of questions with a right or wrong answer). In addition, Jay's communication partners modeled using the GoTalk for their own yes/no responses in casual conversation.

Following the 2-month trial of the new supports for Jay and his team, we encouraged the team to reflect on what was working, what needed to be revised, the strategies that they wanted to try next, and any new insights that they had experienced.

One of the more significant challenges for Jay's team was their belief in the assessment that Jay was functioning at a 2-year-old level. At team meetings at the beginning of the project, some team members expressed doubt that Jay would ever be able to learn grade-level academic curriculum content. Introducing a perspective of presuming competence and high expectations (based primarily on the work of Donnellan [1984] and Biklen [1999]), we asked the team, "Just for a few months, would you suspend your judgments about Jay's potential and, instead, assume for the meantime that he can learn?" The team agreed to apply the "least dangerous assumption of presumed competence" to Jay's abilities and to suspend evaluating his abilities and achievement *until* he had a reliable means of communication and they were assured that supports were provided to him accurately and consistently (Jorgensen, 2005; Jorgensen, McSheehan, & Sonnenmeier, 2007). The construct of the least dangerous assumption of presuming competence will be described more fully in Chapter 3.

IMPLEMENTING AND DOCUMENTING THE OUTCOMES OF SUPPORTS

The BA project work with Jay's educational team during the remainder of fourth grade and all of fifth grade focused on three major goals:

1. Supporting Jay to be an active participant in general education activities and instruction
2. Providing Jay with a communication system and related supports that would enable him to communicate in a way that was commensurate with his same-age peers and participate in and demonstrate learning of general education curriculum
3. Having effective and efficient weekly instructional planning meetings for the core members of Jay's team

Participation

Early in the process of implementing different instructional supports, Jay's classroom teacher tried a new way of supporting Jay's participation in classroom activities based on the least dangerous assumption of presumed competence. For example, one of the class activities was for other students to comment on "What I like about you" while the selected student sat in front of the class. During the week that it was Jay's turn, Jay initially took his place sitting in front of the class, then he relocated himself to the back of the class and generally appeared not to be attending to what the other students were saying they liked about him. Instead of assuming Jay was not attending, his teacher commented on some things she had recently learned about Jay and his interests (based on the project staff's home visit). She commented on things in Jay's bedroom and his favorite toys. Jay responded by returning to the front of the room, facing the teacher, smiling, and making "happy" vocalizations. It was the first time that this teacher felt as if she connected with Jay and was an important turning point for her in seeing Jay as a participating member of her classroom—a student with whom she could connect and teach.

Jay's membership and participation as a general education student was a primary focus of the work with him and his team, as evidenced by planning for Jay's involvement in a class play. Prior to participation in the BA project, Jay's team might have looked for a role for Jay such as standing with his peers while they said their lines or helping to make props. Instead, the team and peers engaged in some creative thinking about how Jay could use his GoTalk to participate in a meaningful way. Jay's participation began by engaging in decision making with his peers via yes/no responses, with Jay signaling agreement or disagreement with possible statements the master of ceremonies would say to introduce and guide the audience through the play. In a small-group discussion, with Jay in his active role, his peers suggested Jay might speak lines of the master of ceremonies. The team convened a meeting to explore ways he might do so. Because one of Jay's IEP goals was related to sequencing, nine messages were programmed into the GoTalk that corresponded to an order of numbers displayed on the device. Supported to learn the sequence during rehearsals with his peers, Jay had a valued role in the group. He was learning that pushing the buttons on his communication device had a function. And during the play, Jay's orderly presentation served as a successful guide for his peers and the audience.

A second major focus of supporting Jay's more active participation in general education instruction was creating modified materials that were linked to the general education curriculum. Because of the team's belief that Jay was functioning at a 2-year-old level, they were skeptical of Jay's ability to read, and they wondered how Jay would participate in reading instruction and activities. Presuming Jay's competence, they developed reading materials for him from the grade-level curriculum, adapting fifth-grade novels to a late first-grade/early second-grade reading level. Their first attempt was to create a modified version of *Maniac Magee* (Spinelli, 1990), rewritten and enhanced with symbols from the PixWriter software and hand drawings by Jay's peers of key story events. The text was rewritten to maintain the integrity of the story, including major parts of the story that would be included in the chapter quizzes and assessment of reading comprehension. Jay had access to the grade-level chapter book and to the modified book during self-selected and guided reading activities. His peers supported Jay during partnered reading activities. As the year progressed, Jay demonstrated emergent literacy behaviors such as holding the book right side up, turning pages one at a time, scanning the text with his eyes, and eventually independently using his index finger to point to words one at a time in a sentence and vocalizing each word with intonation.

Communication System and Supports

After considering which features of an AAC device would meet Jay's communication needs, a recommendation was made for Jay's team to engage in a trial of a DynaMyte (DynaVox Technologies), a dynamic display SGD with the capacity for a large vocabulary. We were able to loan Jay a DynaMyte for exploration during summer vacation between fourth and fifth grade. When Jay returned to school in the fall, Jay's mother told us that not only had he intently explored its layout and features, systematically selecting and listening to the messages on several pages, but he also seemed to make the connection that he could use the device to communicate. For example, Jay and his siblings enjoyed finding airplanes in the sky and would often look out a window and see who could locate one and point to it first. One day, Jay cued up the dictionary page in the DynaMyte and located the symbol for AIRPLANE, selected it, and ran to the window. Moments later his mother heard an airplane fly by their house.

The focus during fifth grade included identifying core (frequently occurring words) and content-specific vocabulary and seeking meaning in all of Jay's communication attempts. The team, with project staff support, also explored a new instructional approach to teach use of the core vocabulary on the SGD. This approach, a modified version of the System for Augmenting Language (SAL; Romski & Sevcik, 1996), promoted modeling the use of communication boards by the classroom teacher, other staff, and Jay's peers. Through this and various other direct instructional approaches, Jay was demonstrating functional use of the SGD and was constructing two- to four-word sentences with the new vocabulary.

One day Jay's fifth-grade teacher led a story recall activity in which students recalled various events that happened in the *Maniac Magee* book. The students called out story events such as, "Maniac ran away from home" and "Maniac met Amanda." We happened to be observing in the classroom this day and saw something surprising happen when Jay's team applied the least dangerous assumption that he was learning to read, though he communicated his understanding in unconventional ways.

After the students had generated about 10 events, the teacher started to bring the activity to a close, saying, "Okay, if you flip through your book, let's just do two more for now." Jay's paraprofessional was conscientiously trying to get Jay to pay attention to the various events the other students were recalling by pointing to them in Jay's picture-enhanced *Maniac McGee* book. Each time she would try to direct Jay to look at a particular page connected with what peers were brainstorming, he would turn back to a previous page. After he turned back to a previous page and tapped repeatedly in the same area of the page, the paraprofessional noticed that Jay was tapping on one particular event from the story. The paraprofessional raised her hand, was called on by the teacher, and said, "Jay keeps pointing to, 'He lived at the zoo in the deer pen and ate what the deer ate.'"

Without missing a beat, the classroom teacher laughed and said, "Oh, yeah, you guys forgot that. Good one, Jay. Thanks!" Jay clapped his hands, his nearest classmate gave him a high-five, and Jay grinned from ear to ear. These incidents proved to be significant for the team, and they redoubled their efforts to support Jay's participation in literacy activities.

Weekly Instructional Planning

Historically, the special education teacher and paraprofessional were primarily responsible for developing instructional materials for Jay. After participating for 2 months in the BA project, the team understood the value of a collaborative instructional planning process. The first challenge was to find time in all team members' schedules to participate in a 1-hour weekly planning meeting. The team discussed possibilities, and without administrative intervention, rearranged their schedules to accommodate the need.

For several months, a project staff member led the team meetings to model effective facilitation, discussion, and decision-making processes. Written minutes were generated at each team meeting and shared with members not in attendance. The roles of facilitator, timekeeper, and recorder were assumed by the team members as they became comfortable with the meeting agenda and process.

Team members shared responsibility for creating instructional materials such as the modified reading texts and communication boards. This increased each team member's understanding of the types of supports that were being used and distributed the work load among team members with specific areas of expertise. The SLP and the paraprofessional began meeting to design communication supports for specific lessons. Likewise, the SLP and COTA began meeting to plan for joint therapy sessions and provision of services within the classroom.

REVIEWING AND SUSTAINING RESULTS

We discussed the following reflection questions periodically during our involvement with Jay's team.

- How accurately and consistently is the team providing supports?
- Do team members have the knowledge and skills needed to plan for and implement these supports?
- How is the team functioning?
- What does the team need to change in order to be more effective in teaching and supporting Jay?
- What kind of administrative support do team members need to do their jobs more effectively?

The responses to the previous questions were addressed in an effort to ensure the supports were being implemented as planned, with all team members providing a particular support. If there was not consensus among the team members about the accuracy and consistency of the provision of the supports, then more work was done to ensure this. It was not until there was strong evidence that supports were being provided accurately and consistently that the following questions were asked.

- What evidence do we have of Jay's learning?
- What does the evidence show?
- How confident are we that this evidence is a valid reflection of his abilities?

Evidence examined by the team included videotaped examples of Jay in class, checklists related to the provision of specific supports, work samples, lesson plans, and so forth. The team discussed any potential changes that needed to be made. Organizational issues were shared with administrators as needed.

BEFORE AND AFTER BEYOND ACCESS

There were many changes in how Jay's team supported him to be a member of the general education classroom, to actively participate in instruction and activities, and to learn the general education curriculum content. These changes allowed Jay to move beyond simply having *access* to the general education curriculum to actually *participating* in general education instruction and demonstrating his *learning* of that curriculum content through general education instruction in the general education classroom (with support from special education and related services).

Prior to his team's use of the BA Model, Jay

- Had no way to communicate age-appropriate academic or social vocabulary
- Was not a full participant in his general education classroom
- Experienced significant behavioral challenges at bathroom time
- Often experienced frustration at not understanding what was expected of him, the steps in a task, and the schedule of the day
- Was not interacting much with the general education classroom teacher or with his peers during instruction

After his team began using the BA Model, Jay

- Used the bathroom with fewer behavior incidents
- Hit himself less out of frustration
- Had access to more than 100 messages related to the curriculum (by the end of fourth grade and much more by the end of fifth grade)
- Used communication displays that had 9–49 items per display
- Demonstrated increased ability to spell and recognize words in print
- Participated in much of the instruction in the general education classroom
- Used an SGD to request, ask questions, answer questions, make comments, and demonstrate knowledge (creating two- to four-word sentences)

Prior to their using the BA Model, Jay's team

- Met once or twice a year to write Jay's IEP
- Provided related services primarily outside of the general education classroom
- Wrote IEP goals and objectives that were discipline specific, not related to the general education curriculum
- Did not share in the responsibility for designing and using adapted materials
- Judged Jay to be functioning at a 2-year-old level

After they began using the BA Model, Jay's team

- Met weekly to plan instruction and modifications
- Generated minutes from their instructional planning meetings
- Wrote IEP goals and objectives that were more closely aligned with the general education curriculum
- Shared responsibility for making adapted materials
- Believed that Jay's learning was dependent on the quality of the collaborative teaming and the supports provided to him

LESSONS LEARNED AND BEYOND ACCESS OUTCOMES

The following outcomes were found from three research studies conducted with teams that used the BA Model (Jorgensen et al., 2007; McSheehan, Sonnenmeier, Jorgensen, & Turner, 2006; Sonnenmeier et al., 2005).

- The BA Model holds promise for supporting membership, participation, communication, and learning by students with IDD who are thought to be unable to learn general education curriculum content from general education instruction in a general education classroom.

- Presuming students' competence may be central to a team's willingness to persist in trying new strategies, even in the face of ambiguous or contested data.

- For many students with IDD, difficulties with communication are often interpreted as lack of intelligence and ability to learn general education curriculum content. Providing effective AAC and assistive technology (AT) are essential supports for learning.

- Clearly defined roles, collaborative skills, and use of a variety of team meeting processes and teaming structures support a team's ability to support students' membership, participation, communication, and learning.

CONCLUSION

The remainder of this book provides additional detail about the conceptual and research foundations of the BA Model, along with instructions for putting it to use in your school. These chapters address

- A detailed description of the four phases of the Model
- Instructions for using each phase of the Model with students and teams
- Research- and values-based rationale for using the Model
- Explication of the Model's best practices related to presumed competence, membership, participation, communication, learning, and collaborative teaming
- The role of the BA facilitator and administrative leadership team (ALT) in implementing and evaluating the Model
- Examples of students and their teams using the Model
- Suggestions regarding systems and organizational changes that support using the Model

Chapter 2 will 1) provide a context for why and how the BA Model was developed, 2) provide research-based support for its various components and features, and 3) introduce the Model's four iterative phases.

REFERENCES

Biklen, D. (1999). The metaphor of mental retardation: Rethinking ability and disability. In H. Bersani Jr. (Ed.), *Responding to the challenge: Current trends and international issues in developmental disabilities: Essays in honor of Gynnar Dybwad* (pp. 35–52). Brookline, MA: Brookline Books.

Donnellan, A. (1984). The criterion of the least dangerous assumption. *Behavioral Disorders, 9,* 141–150.

Education for All Handicapped Children Act of 1975, PL 94-142, 20 U.S.C. §§ 1400 *et seq.*

Individuals with Disabilities Education Act (IDEA) Amendments of 1997, PL 105-17, 20 U.S.C. §§ 1400 *et seq.*

Individuals with Disabilities Education Improvement Act (IDEA) of 2004, PL 108-446, 20 U.S.C. §§ 1400 *et seq.*

Jorgensen, C.M. (2005). The least dangerous assumption: A challenge to create a new paradigm. *Disability Solutions, 6*(3), 1, 5–9, 13.

Jorgensen, C.M., McSheehan, M., & Sonnenmeier, R. (2007). Presumed competence reflected in the educational programs of students with IDD before and after the Beyond Access professional development intervention. *Journal of Intellectual and Developmental Disabilities, 32*(4), 248–262.

Jorgensen, C.M., Schuh, M.C., & Nisbet, J. (2006). *The inclusion facilitator's guide.* Baltimore: Paul H. Brookes Publishing Co.

McSheehan, M., Sonnenmeier, R., Jorgensen, C.M., & Turner, K. (2006). Beyond communication access: Promoting learning of the general education curriculum by students with significant disabilities. *Topics in Language Disorders, 26*(3), 266–290.

Romski, M.A., & Sevcik, R. (1996). *Breaking the speech barrier: Language development through augmented means.* Baltimore: Paul H. Brookes Publishing Co.

Sonnenmeier, R.M., McSheehan, M., & Jorgensen, C.M. (2005). A case study of team supports for a student with autism's communication and engagement within the general education curriculum: Preliminary report of the Beyond Access Model. *Augmentative and Alternative Communication, 21*(2), 101–115.

Spinelli, J. (1990). *Maniac Magee.* New York: Little, Brown.

History, Rationale, and Framework of the Beyond Access Model

The field of special education has seen many changes regarding expectations for what students can learn and communicate and what are considered appropriate curricula, optimal learning environments, and suitable supports for communication. This chapter opens with a historical review of the field of special education with respect to these educational issues and then describes the current state of policy and practice. The BA Model is then described, including its core beliefs and assumptions about student learning and an outline of a systematic process for closing the gap between those core beliefs and current practices to promote positive educational outcomes for students with IDD.

HISTORY: CURRICULUM AND EDUCATIONAL ENVIRONMENTS

When the Education for All Handicapped Children Act of 1975 (PL 94-142) was passed, students with IDD were typically educated in special schools or self-contained classrooms, and their educational programs were tailored to the perceived developmental level of the student (Calculator & Jorgensen, 1994). So a 16-year-old with an assumed developmental age of 2 would be taught to stack blocks, imitate, match objects to pictures, and so forth. By the early 1980s, best practices dictated that students with IDD should have a functional, life-skills curriculum grounded in the domains of domestic, leisure, work, and community living (Brown et al., 1983). During this era, elementary-age students with IDD were taught to make beds, shop in a simulated store set up in the school, and set the table for lunch. High school students were taken into the community to learn how to cross streets, pay for purchases at a store, ride public transportation, and work in a supervised employment setting.

By the mid- to late-1980s, the concept of integrating students with IDD into general education classes was promoted, though not widely adopted, as a way to increase students' social skills and social relationships (Stainback & Stainback, 1985). Students' IEP objectives were implemented by finding opportunities within general education instruction for them to learn functional or access skills. During this era, a student with IDD might build a pyramid out of sugar cubes during a unit on early civilizations (to work on fine motor skills), construct a piñata during a unit on Central America (to work on identifying colors), or activate a switch to advance slides during a class presentation (to work on cause and effect skills). As students moved into middle and high school, their participation in general education decreased, and they spent more time learning in the community.

By the early 1990s, best practices for students with IDD reflected at least part-time placement in an age-appropriate general education classroom, modification of curriculum and instruction, augmentative communication that enabled students to communicate about social and academic topics, and a focus on typical social relationships (Calculator & Jorgensen, 1994). Assumptions about *what* a child with IDD could learn began to shift instruction toward the same curriculum priorities as students without disabilities (both academic and social)— although with considerable modification and a continued emphasis on functional skills and activities of daily living. Practices of *where* a child would learn reflected small increases in the amount of time students spent in general education classrooms, though this practice was still not widely adopted. An examination of trends from 1989 to 1995 in the national averages of placement data show that less than 20% of students with labels of "mental retardation" (the label in federal special education law for students that this book refers to as students with IDD) were spending 80% of their day in a general education classroom, and less than 35% of students with mental retardation were spending between 40%–79% of their day in a general education classroom (Handler, 2003).

The trend to place students in general education settings raised questions regarding student outcomes based on placement in inclusive versus separate education programs. Studies of outcomes for students with IDD educated in inclusive settings compared with those receiving separate education (pull-out academic instruction or self-contained special education classrooms) consistently demonstrated benefits of inclusive settings over separate settings. Specifically, students with IDD in inclusive settings showed higher rates of contact with peers without disabilities and higher likelihood to be identified as a member of a social network by peers without disabilities (Fryxell & Kennedy, 1995), better performance in reading and math (Cole, Waldron, & Majd, 2004), significantly higher gains in adaptive behavior, and no significant differences in gains in social competence (Fisher & Meyer, 2002) when compared with students with IDD educated in separate settings.

In the late 1990s and into early 2000s, IDEA 1997, the No Child Left Behind (NCLB) Act of 2001 (PL 107-110), and a growing body of research showing that students with IDD were capable of learning general education curriculum content promoted the inclusion of students with disabilities in local and state accountability systems through their participation in large-scale assessments (McGregor & Vogelsberg, 1998; Ryndak, Morrison, & Sommerstein, 1999). Accountability for gaining access to and progressing in the general education curriculum by students with IDD had become codified in educational policy.

HISTORY: COMMUNICATION

The 1970s saw the emergence of AAC as a field, with the 1980s representing a time of immense growth and refinement (Zangari, Lloyd, & Vicker, 1994). During this time there was a shift in practice regarding the delivery of AAC services to individuals with severe IDD. Throughout the 1970s, people thought to have severe intellectual disabilities were excluded from AAC services because they were considered to be "nonsymbolic communicators" and therefore presumed unable to benefit from AAC. Decision-making guidelines regarding who would benefit from AAC services were based on a readiness or prerequisite model. For example, it was thought that an individual needed to demonstrate "at least Stage V sensorimotor intelligence" (including understanding of using a means to obtain an end and cause-effect relationships) and "at least 18 months mental age; or ability to recognize at least at photograph level" before AAC services could be initiated (Shane & Bashir, 1980, p. 409). This practice was challenged by AAC researchers, such as Romski and Sevcik, who noted "neglect for the unique needs of persons with severe intellectual disabilities appears to have stemmed from the assumption that some prerequisite skills must be in place before an individual can be considered a candidate for an AAC system" (1988, p. 83).

Since the mid-1980s, "'candidacy' guidelines for AAC intervention [were] gradually replaced by guidelines based on communication needs" (Beukelman & Mirenda, 1992, p. 100). The Communication Needs Model was developed with an emphasis on documenting the communication needs of an individual, determining how many of these needs were met through current communication techniques, and reducing the number of unmet communication needs through systematic AAC interventions (Beukelman & Mirenda, 1992). The daily communication needs of a child, determined through observations, interviews, and ecological inventories within age-appropriate settings such as the general education classroom, began to define best practices in AAC (Beukelman & Mirenda, 1992; Calculator & Jorgensen, 1991; Mirenda & Calculator, 1993). In practice, AAC systems and supports focused on providing students with a means to communicate about activities of daily living and personal assistance (e.g., EAT, DRINK, BATHROOM, I NEED A BREAK). Beukelman and Mirenda acknowledged that the Communication Needs Model "has limitations because it is not sufficiently comprehensive and does not facilitate planning for the future" (1998, p. 147).

Beukelman and Mirenda (1992, 1998, 2005) articulated the Participation Model to advance comprehensive AAC decision making and planning beyond the present to include planning for the future. The Participation Model, revised over the years and endorsed by the American Speech-Language-Hearing Association (2004) as a framework for carrying out AAC assessment and interventions, "provides a systematic process for conducting AAC assessments and designing interventions based on the functional participation requirements of peers without disabilities of the same chronological age as the person who may communicate through AAC" (Beukelman & Mirenda, 2005, p. 136). This shift—using the communication patterns of age-appropriate peers as the benchmark for identifying the communication needs of students with IDD—resulted in viewing communication as the means by which students could engage socially and academically at school, at home, and in the community.

STATE OF THE FIELD IN 2009

As we head toward the end of another decade in this field, many policies have been clarified and much knowledge has been gained regarding the education of students with IDD. The reauthorization of IDEA in 2004 preserved the requirement that all students with disabilities make progress within the general education curriculum. Best practices in AAC support its use for students with IDD who do not meet their academic and social communication needs by speech alone, and syntheses of 30 years of research looking at academic learning by individuals with IDD in the areas of reading (Browder, Wakeman, Spooner, Ahlgrim-Delzell, & Algozzine, 2006), math (Browder, Spooner, Ahlgrim-Delzell, Harris, & Wakeman, 2008), and science (Courtade, Spooner, & Browder, 2007) demonstrate the growing evidence base that students with IDD are capable of learning academics. Unfortunately, the overwhelming majority of this research has been conducted in either clinical or specialized settings; very few of the studies have been conducted in general education settings. In addition, these syntheses reveal content areas in which core components (as defined by the corresponding general education content area organizations, such as the National Reading Council) have been minimally examined (e.g., five studies examining phonemic awareness) or content areas in which there have been no studies at all (e.g., algebra, physical science, life science). Meanwhile, evidence continues to emerge correlating placement in the general education classroom with improved learning outcomes (Blackorby, Chorost, Garza, & Guzman, 2003; Quenemoen, 2008). Researchers have come to challenge their colleagues to conduct research on learning for students with IDD within inclusive classrooms and other educational settings where students with disabilities are present in natural proportions (Jorgensen & McSheehan, 2008).

Nevertheless, differences in perspectives regarding the acquisition and application of this knowledge to the educational programs of students with IDD persist among self-advocates, researchers, policy makers, administrators, educators, and families. Tensions and gaps in research to practice exist in many areas including: beliefs regarding students' potential for learning academics, the relative importance of teaching academics compared with teaching functional skills, the provision of AAC supports, and the relative value of inclusive versus separate educational placement.

Beliefs About Students' Potential to Learn Academics

Many people believe that it is possible to determine an individual student's capacity for learning academics by conducting an evaluation of his or her intelligence, using a test such as the Wechsler Intelligence Scale for Children–Fourth Edition (WISC-IV; Wechsler, 2003). When students are labeled as having an intellectual disability because they score below a predetermined cutoff point on a test such as the WISC-IV, a series of educational program decisions are set into motion that usually include a reduced focus on academics and an increased focus on functional skills (Jorgensen, 2005b). This is different from the student whose learning problems are associated with a sensory difference, an emotional challenge, or a specific learning disability, in which those students' educational programs focus on searching for the instructional methods and materials that will *uncover the student's potential to learn academics*. The learning potential of students labeled with

IDD often continues to be presumed to be by definition, less than that of other students, and, in some cases, finite.

Academics and Functional Skills

It is common for instruction and assessment for students with IDD to be weakly aligned with general education curriculum standards, even with the research on learning academics and the policy mandates for accountability through large-scale assessment of all students' progress in the general education curriculum (Browder et al., 2004; Kleinert & Kearns, 2001). Notions from the 1980s and 1990s persist, perpetuating the belief that "many academic classes enrolling typical students are simply not relevant to the educational needs of students with severe disabilities" (Giangreco & Putnam, 1991, p. 257) because 1) the content is not seen as necessary for the future lifestyles of people with IDD (e.g., they will never need biology or physics); 2) the content is too advanced for their cognitive abilities; and 3) the "modifications necessary for meaningful participation would be so extreme that the academic development of non-disabled students might be jeopardized" (Brown et al., 1989, p. 11).

The debate about the relative importance of academics and functional skills in students' educational programs (Tashie, Jorgensen, Shapiro-Barnard, Martin, & Schuh, 1996) has been heightened with the movement toward holding local schools accountable for academic learning by students with IDD. We consider this movement toward academic learning as indicative of the next *transformation* in special education (following an earlier transformation from the developmental to the functional curriculum model); others argue for what they term an additive approach to change, exemplified in the following excerpt from Browder and Spooner.

> In our view, there is a continued and ongoing importance in teaching functional skills to students with severe disabilities and having students apply those skills in community environments. Extending the curriculum for students with severe disabilities to include academic tasks is not like the transformation that occurred when educators began to forgo skills that were not age appropriate to focus on functional ones. Instead, using an additive approach, it is possible to focus on both academics and functional skill needs. Students with severe disabilities continue to need instruction that prepares them for life after high school, including such tasks as grocery shopping, preparing a meal, cleaning a house or apartment, negotiating forms of public transportation (e.g., bus, subway, taxi), getting along with co-workers, and paying bills. Preparation for making the transition to work also is critically important for the continued success of students with severe disabilities. These real-life activities can also provide a meaningful context for academic learning. The acquisition of sight words will be more meaningful when paired with functional activities such as learning to recognize warnings on product labels (Collins & Stinson, 1995), shop for groceries (Lalli & Browder, 1993), or keep track of a job list (Browder & Minarovic, 2000). Counting and discriminating between types of money will be more useful when paired with learning to make purchases (Westling, Floyd, & Carr, 1990) or buy a snack (Gardill & Browder, 1995; McDonnell, 1987). (2006, p. 6–7)

Augmentative and Alternative Communication Supports

Even with the evidence that students with severe IDD can benefit from AAC, the practice guidance that students with severe IDD should be provided AAC, and emphasis on core and academic vocabulary for AAC, practices in the field are not reflecting these advances. Snell and her colleagues (2003) reported that many practitioners continue to make decisions regarding AAC practices based on assumptions such as

1. Language age equals mental age.

2. Lack of prerequisite skills means that students should not be engaged in higher-level instruction.

3. The severity of students' diagnosed disability reflects their potential to learn.

4. Students' lack of past progress does not justify expending resources for AAC.

Analyses from at least 10 states where students participate in alternate assessments based on alternate achievement standards (i.e., the assessment for students with significant cognitive disabilities) suggests that the majority of those students would qualify for AAC but are not presently using it—at least not as documented for the purposes of assessment (Kearns, 2008; McSheehan, Sundar, & Fedorchak, in preparation). For many students with IDD, the design of their AAC systems often focuses on vocabulary related to basic needs (e.g., HUNGRY, BATHROOM, NEED A BREAK) and a lack of commitment to teaching literacy with communication (Erickson, Koppenhaver, Yoder, & Nance, 1997).

Augmentative Communication and Instructional Planning Models

Decisions about AAC supports and services for many students with IDD continue to be based on decision-making and planning models that restrict students' learning of general education curriculum content based on assumptions about students' cognitive and communication abilities. Such assumptions of students' abilities may reflect a level of confidence in previous assessment findings that is unwarranted if those assessments were conducted prior to adequate AAC interventions or if there was not an effective and efficient communication system in place for the student.

Soto (2009) suggested a process for adapting curriculum and participation in instruction that requires confidence on the part of educators to identify any mismatch between student's needs and abilities and the cognitive, linguistic, sensory, and motor demands of the lesson. Beukelman and Mirenda's (2005) Participation Model provides for four levels of educational participation:

1. Competitive (expected to meet the same educational/academic standards)

2. Active (expected learning outcomes are not the same as those of peers and progress is evaluated according to the IEP)

3. Involved (expected to learn content in cross-curricular areas such as communication, social, and motor skills, rather than in academic subjects)

4. None (in which students are passive, uninvolved with peers, or participate in substantially different activities and instruction)

They were clear to qualify this last level of educational participation as a "highly undesirable option" that "requires prompt remediation" (2005, p. 401). As stated in her Foreword to this book, Mirenda has shifted her thinking since the 2005 book was published.

> I believed that, for some students with significant intellectual disabilities, the goals of instruction in general education classrooms should be primarily in areas such as communication, social, and motor skill development rather than in "academic" areas such as reading, math, or science. I *was* being conservative in my assumption that academics were not on the radar screen for some students.

Such an emphasis on functional skills or functional academics over general academic knowledge and skills for some students continues to be represented in special education instructional planning models. Many of these instructional models recommend the completion of a discrepancy analysis between the student's abilities and the demands of the lesson (Downing, 2008; Janney & Snell, 2004; Wehmeyer, Lance, & Bashinski, 2002). Such practices are based on the assumption that a valid assessment of a student's abilities (e.g., cognitive abilities) is able to be measured prior to the exploration and implementation of adequate AAC supports.

These practices contrast with models of response to intervention (RTI; National Association of State Directors of Special Education [NASDSE], 2008) that recommend that all students receive high-quality general education instruction from a general education teacher in the general education setting (known as a *universal intervention*). If further intervention is necessary, then it is done in addition to the universal intervention as targeted and/or intensive interventions. That is, a student might receive 90 minutes of the universal instruction and, in addition, receive 30 minutes of targeted intervention and 30 minutes of intensive instruction daily.

Educational Placement

Although no studies conducted since the late 1970s have shown an academic advantage for students with IDD educated in separate settings (Falvey, 2004), the place where students learn continues to vary from state to state in the United States. Trends in placement data show an overall increase in the percent of time spent in general education classrooms, but students with IDD are still less likely to spend the majority of the day in a general education classroom compared with students with many other disabilities. In the 2008 Global Summit on Education focusing on inclusive education, Thomas Parrish of the American Institutes for Research shared data showing that since the early 1990s, the national average of students placed in separate facilities has remained unchanged. In addition, when demonstrating variation of the least restrictive environment (LRE) among states, he showed that 78% of students with disabilities in North Dakota are spending 80% or more of their day in the LRE (general education classroom), whereas this holds true for only 10% of students with disabilities in Virginia. He asked, "Can the most appropriate placement in North Dakota be so different from what is suitable in Virginia?" (Parrish, 2008).

These national placement data contrast with our research and that of other leaders in the field (e.g., Wehmeyer & Agran, 2006) that identify the general education classroom as the optimal place where access to the general education curriculum occurs and do not reflect application of the research showing the benefits of placement in a general education classroom (including that students with IDD placed in general education classes score higher on standardized assessments of reading and math; Blackorby et al., 2003; Wagner & Blackorby, 2004).

The differences in perspectives regarding students' potential for learning academics, balancing academic learning and functional skills instruction, appropriate AAC supports, and the location of students' educational programs function as barriers to students' access to and learning of general education curriculum content within heterogeneous general education classrooms and deny the opportunity to learn from general education instruction. Additional barriers to the widespread implementation of inclusive education best practices include the following.

- Lack of adequate preservice personnel preparation and ongoing professional development and technical assistance regarding effective inclusive education practices (e.g., Jorgensen, Fisher, Sax, & Skoglund, 1998; Jorgensen, Schuh, & Nisbet, 2006)

- Inconsistent implementation or absence of effective structures, processes, and skills for team collaboration (e.g., Hunt, Soto, Maier, Muller, & Goetz, 2002; Jackson, Ryndak, & Billingsley, 2000; Rainforth, York, & Macdonald, 1992)

- Ineffective strategies for implementing and monitoring the provision of instruction and supports with accuracy and consistency to foster student learning (e.g., Jorgensen et al., 2006; Snell & Janney, 2005)

- Weak administrative leadership to provide the resources necessary for quality instruction, AAC, and team collaboration for sustainable inclusive education practices (e.g., Ainscow, 2005; Villa & Thousand, 2000)

THE BEYOND ACCESS MODEL

The Beyond Access (BA) Model for Promoting the Learning of General Education Curriculum Content for Students with the Most Significant Disabilities (Jorgensen, Sonnenmeier, & McSheehan, 2001; McSheehan, Sonnenmeier, & Jorgensen, 2002; see Figure 2.1) was designed to close the gap between promising research findings and current practices to achieve the following vision: *When students with IDD are provided with appropriate instruction and supports, they can learn grade-level academic skills and communicate in ways that are commensurate with their same-age peers without disabilities.*

The BA Model provides a framework for working toward this vision by

- Redefining the standards for access to the general education classroom, the general education curriculum, general education instruction, and

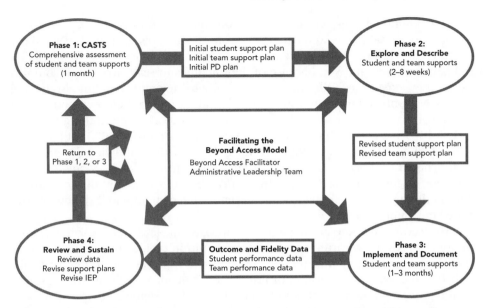

Figure 2.1. The Beyond Access Model: A four-phase professional development model for school leadership and team collaboration to promote the membership, participation, and learning of general education curriculum by students with intellectual and/or other developmental disabilities in the general education classroom. (From McSheehan, M., Sonnenmeier, R.M., & Jorgensen, C.M. [2009]. Membership, participation, and learning in general education classrooms for students with autism spectrum disorders who use AAC. In D.R. Beukelman & J. Reichle [Series Eds.] & P. Mirenda & T. Iacono [Vol. Eds.], *Augmentative and alternative communication series: Autism spectrum disorders and AAC* [p. 427]. Baltimore: Paul H. Brookes Publishing Co.; adapted by permission.) (*Key:* CASTS, Comprehensive Assessment of Student and Team Supports; IEP, individualized education program; PD, professional development.)

communication supports based on the least dangerous assumption of presuming students' competence (Biklen, 1999; Donnellan, 1984; Jorgensen, McSheehan, & Sonnenmeier, 2007)

- Facilitating full membership in the general education classroom and active participation in the general education instruction as the primary context for learning
- Implementing a student and team planning process grounded in high-quality professional development
- Organizing the implementation and monitoring of inclusive education best practices for students and their teams into a coherent, reiterative, and manageable process of assessment, implementation, evaluation, reflection, and revision, promoting continuous program improvement

A significant difference between the BA Model and other instructional planning models is the likelihood that more time and effort are given to supporting students' academic learning than to activities of daily living. So, although we acknowledge the need for and actively promote practices that facilitate functional skill development within typical routines (e.g., working on buttoning your coat when getting ready to go out to the playground, communicating lunch choices directly with the lunch staff in a school cafeteria, learning a job alongside a peer during the summer), our *ultimate* priorities lie with academic learning.

Two additional considerations inform our ultimate priorities. The first is supported by personal stories and exemplars from the lives of adults with IDD. Many self-advocates report not being at all independent in their activities of daily living and personal care, and yet, because of their abilities to read, write, and communicate, they experience fulfilling lives. Not only being employed, but also having careers. Not only living in the community, but also owning their own homes. Not only having a say about what they eat and wear, but also determining the path of their lives and controlling their own supports (Kochmeister, 2003; Rubin et al., 2001; Williams, M.B., 2000; Williams, R., 1992). For these individuals, emphasis on functional skills was not the key to independent living. Independence, freedom, employment, and self-determination came with the nature of the relationships in these people's lives as well as academic engagement and learning to read, write, and communicate.

The second consideration for our emphasis on academic learning (again, without disregard for learning functional skills within typical routines) is reflected in an honest examination of the employment and other life outcomes for adults with IDD following two decades of prioritizing functional skills on IEPs through community-based instruction. Smith and Clark (2007) reported that people with disabilities have a significantly lower rate of employment than people without disabilities (36% versus 74% according to the 2006 American Community Survey [ACS]). Winsor and Butterworth (2007) found that of the individuals with IDD receiving supports from state agencies, less than a quarter (22%) of those individuals participated in integrated employment, whereas more than half (56.5%) were served in facility-based settings. Their analysis showed a decrease in the percentage of people served in facility-based segregated settings (from 60% in 1999 to 57% in 2004) and also a slight decrease in the percentage served in integrated employment (from 25.5% in 1999 to 22% in 2004; Winsor & Butterworth, 2007). With these conditions, we are hard pressed to say that prioritizing functional skills over academics is sufficiently accomplishing the desired independence, freedom, employment, and self-determination in the lives of people with IDD.

In summary, the BA Model was designed in an effort to promote application of current research findings and progressive thinking regarding students with IDD learning general education curriculum content within general education settings. The next section begins with some questions that might help a particular IEP team determine whether using the BA Model is appropriate for their team. Then, we describe the critical role of an in-school or outside facilitator who leads a team in using the Model. And, finally, the four major components of the Model are described, including: 1) foundational best practices in educating students with IDD; 2) a four-phase IEP team process for assessing, exploring, implementing, and evaluating student and team supports; 3) ongoing professional development for team members; and 4) support and monitoring by an ALT.

Who Should Use the Beyond Access Model?

It is important to note what the BA Model is *not* before considering whether it may be appropriate for a particular IEP team's use. The BA Model is *not*

- A cookbook approach to planning
- Doable without strong administrative support
- Used solely by special education teachers

- For planning curriculum in a self-contained classroom
- A quick fix to resolve differences of perspective between educators and families
- A way to prove whether students should be included in general education
- A substitute for individual team members having training and experience educating students with IDD

The BA Model *can* help teams address some of the challenges to providing a quality education to students with IDD. The following outcomes have been reported in one or more of the three evaluation studies conducted with teams using the BA Model (Jorgensen et al., 2007; McSheehan, Sonnenmeier, Jorgensen, & Turner, 2006; Sonnenmeier, McSheehan, & Jorgensen, 2005).

- More efficient and effective team meetings
- Improved team collaboration
- Improved school–family relationships
- Identification of five categories of presumed competence evidenced in IEPs
- Greater presumed competence of students to learn general education curriculum
- Enhanced student membership, participation, and opportunities for learning in the general education classroom and curriculum
- Improvements in students' communication skills and AAC outcomes
- Improvements in students' demonstration of learning
- A shift in the location of service delivery from outside to within the general education classroom
- An increase in the percentage of the day students were reported to be in the general education classroom

Although not yet documented in published research, based on our experiences and initial data collected during the development of the BA Model, we believe that the BA Model *may* also help teams address the following issues:

- Improving the knowledge and skills of team members who do not have training or experience in educating students with IDD
- Resolving team member differences with respect to the rationale for students' inclusion in general education
- Building shared responsibility between general and special education
- Coordinating special education and related services to better support the educational priorities of the general education classroom
- Guiding the planning of students' participation in general education instruction
- Writing IEPs that are aligned with the general education curriculum
- Making data-based judgments about the effectiveness of instruction and supports
- Documenting student learning

Although there are no hard and fast rules that will determine which teams are good candidates for using the BA Model, we have outlined a series of "start-up" activities that will assist with ensuring sufficient understanding and support among the IEP team and administration, which should be in place prior to beginning to use the Model (see Chapter 10). These activities include ensuring that all members of a student's IEP team, including the parents/guardians and school administrators, have an understanding of the BA Model and have expressed their support for using the Model for a specific period of time, ideally for at least 1 year.

Who Guides a Team in Using the Model?

Similar to other schoolwide initiatives to implement best practices such as Positive Behavior Interventions and Supports (PBIS; Warren et al., 2004) and RTI (NASDSE, 2008), teams need the support and guidance of a skilled professional to successfully implement the BA Model. To date, the BA Model has been used effectively in schools that have had consultation and ongoing support from an outside consultant—either a university-based faculty member who worked as part of a federally funded model demonstration project or a consultant in private practice with extensive experience in inclusive education and experience in or access to experts in augmentative communication—who works in close partnership with an in-house team leader or administrator.

Schools that have an ongoing relationship with an outside consultant tend to be more successful in implementing innovative practices than schools that do not have this resource (Olson, 1994). That said, we do believe that there are many professionals working in schools today who have the skills and dispositions necessary to support teams to use the BA Model. The skills and dispositions of a BA facilitator are described in Chapters 6–10 and can serve as a guide for deciding whether a team has the in-house capacity for using the BA Model or whether they need to seek outside consultation from experts in the fields of inclusive education and/or augmentative communication. Laurie Lambert, a BA facilitator in a New Hampshire elementary school, reflects on her use of the BA Model in this book's Afterword.

Beyond Access Model Best Practices

The four phases of the BA Model help to increase implementation of a number of values- and evidence-based practices, including high expectations for student learning, with a focus on practices for quality inclusive education, quality AAC supports, collaborative teaming, and mentoring (Jorgensen, McSheehan, & Sonnenmeier, 2002a, 2002b, 2002c). Each of these practices is explicated through a number of specific indicators. Appendix A contains a Best Practices Rating Scale that may be used by teams to identify their strengths and weaknesses for the purposes of planning professional development or for adding new people to the team who have needed knowledge and skills. The following are brief descriptions of these categories of practices.

High Expectations and Least Dangerous Assumption of Presumed Competence
The inherent value and dignity of students with IDD is respected. Students with IDD pursue the same learner outcomes as students without disabilities. When

students do not demonstrate content knowledge or skills, the principle of the least dangerous assumption of presumed competence applies, and all aspects of their educational programs continue to reflect high expectations (Biklen, 1999; Donnellan, 1984; Jorgensen, 2005b; Jorgensen et al., 2007).

General Education Class Membership and Full Participation
Students with IDD are members of age-appropriate general education classes in their neighborhood schools. These students have access to the full range of learning and social experiences and environments offered to students without disabilities. Students with IDD actively participate in the general education instruction in the general education classroom as provided by the general education teacher, with supports from special education and related services, in the form of specially designed instruction and supplementary aids and services provided as needed (e.g., Fisher & Ryndak, 2001; Jackson et al., 2000; Jorgensen, 1998; McGregor & Vogelsberg, 1998; Stainback & Stainback, 1996; Villa & Thousand, 1995).

Quality Augmentative and Alternative Communication
Students with IDD are provided with accurate and reliable AAC supports and services that enable them to communicate about the content of the academic curriculum and in social situations with adults and age-appropriate classmates. Discrepancies in communication performance with age-appropriate classmates are used to inform the design and provision of AAC supports and services (e.g., Beukelman & Mirenda, 2005; National Joint Committee on the Communication Needs of Persons with Severe Disabilities, 1992, 2002; Romski & Sevcik, 1996; Snell et al., 2003).

Curriculum, Instruction, and Supports
Students with IDD can learn the general education curriculum and can learn (some of) it via general education instruction. Consistent with RTI, curriculum and instruction are designed to accommodate the full range of student diversity. Accommodations supplement universally designed instruction and are provided to facilitate engagement in general education instruction for all students. Instructional groupings include students with IDD. Additional (more intensive) supports and modifications are provided to facilitate engagement in the general education curriculum via general education instruction as needed. Individualized or pull-aside instruction is provided to students with IDD only as a last resort to enable them to make progress within the general education curriculum. Students learn functional or life skills within typical routines in the general education classroom or other inclusive activities and environments (e.g., Calculator & Jorgensen, 1994; Giangreco, Cloninger, & Iverson, 1998; Jorgensen, 1998).

Team Collaboration
General and special education teachers, related services providers, and parents/guardians demonstrate shared responsibility by collaborating in the design, implementation, and evaluation of students' educational programs. Teams develop discipline-specific skills, enhance communication skills, and utilize meeting structures and team processes for effective collaboration (e.g., Garmston & Wellman, 1999; Hunt et al., 2002; Kaner, 1996; Rainforth et al., 1992).

Professional Development

Professional development is job embedded, including workshops, onsite coaching, mentoring, and reflective practice. It is provided for general and special education staff together, with team members learning alongside one another, and is linked to improved educational outcomes for students with IDD (e.g., Danielson, 1996; Senge et al., 2000).

Ongoing Authentic Assessment

Authentic, performance-based assessments are conducted within typical activities in inclusive environments for the purpose of identifying students' learning and communication styles, preferences and interests, academic strengths and weaknesses, and need for support (e.g., Goossens', 1989).

Family–School Partnerships

Families and schools are partners in creating quality inclusive educational experiences for students with IDD. Families are connected to resources for developing their own leadership and advocacy skills (e.g., Giangreco et al., 1998).

Special and General Education Reform

Administrators provide leadership to align general and special education reform and improvement with respect to the creation of a community of learners that is inclusive of students with IDD (e.g., Lipsky & Gartner, 1997; Olson, 1994; Senge et al., 2000).

Although all of the best practices are important, five form the core of the BA Model.

1. Presume that students are competent to learn and communicate about age-appropriate social and academic topics

2. Value students as full, equal members of age-appropriate, heterogeneous general education classrooms

3. Plan for and support students' full participation in the general education classroom with evidence-based general education instruction and individualized materials, communication, technology, physical, and emotional supports (including continuous improvement in the design and use of AAC)

4. Prioritize students' learning of the general education curriculum content with evidence-based general education instruction and individualized material, communication, technology, physical, and emotional supports

5. Engage in effective collaborative teaming to implement best practices through the BA Model phases

Beyond Access Model Outcomes

Outcomes of using the BA Model (see Figure 2.1) fall into two main categories: ultimate and intermediate outcomes. *Ultimate outcomes* are represented by students' membership, participation, and learning of general education curriculum content in the general education classroom. *Intermediate outcomes,* by contrast, facilitate or create the conditions for realizing ultimate outcomes. Intermediate outcomes include 1) presuming competence, 2) collaborative teaming, 3) the provision of other student-level supports (e.g., academic vocabulary available in the AAC system, opportunities for communicating during instruction), and 4) other student or team outcomes that, in and of themselves, are not representative of changes in membership and participation in the general education classroom or learning of the general education curriculum via general education classroom activities.

By distinguishing ultimate and intermediate outcomes in this way, teams are more likely to collect the right data for the right purposes and avoid the trap of misinterpreting improved team effort (e.g., number of hours spent programming a device, number of lessons planned, quantity of supports provided in class) as improvements in students' membership, participation, and learning. Clearly articulating ultimate outcomes also helps teams avoid the trap of overvaluing increased student performance *outside the context of typical general education settings* (e.g., increasing conversational turns and increasing length of message constructed using the SGD during pull-out instruction in the speech therapy room, demonstrating learning of specialized vocabulary lists via pull-out instruction in the special education teacher's office).

Data on intermediate and ultimate outcome measures are gathered during Phase 1: Comprehensive Assessment of Student and Team Supports (CASTS) and serve as a baseline against which we measure the effect of the BA Model.

Four Phases of Assessment, Instructional Planning, Implementation, and Evaluation

Four iterative phases comprise the BA Model, including 1) comprehensive assessment of student and team supports; 2) exploration and description of promising instructional, communication, and collaborative teaming supports; 3) implementation and documentation of the use of the most promising supports; and 4) review of data collected to determine which supports are sustainable. Each of the four phases is briefly described here; Chapters 6–9 describe the phases in detail, including examples.

Phase 1: Comprehensive Assessment of Student and Team Supports
Implementing the BA Model begins with completing a CASTS (McSheehan et al., 2006; see Chapter 6 for a detailed how-to description of the CASTS with sample forms, processes, and products from experienced BA teams). Two essential questions frame the CASTS:

1. What supports are currently in place that promote the student's full membership, participation, communication, and learning of general education core academics within the general education classroom?

2. How does the team currently work together to support these outcomes?

The process for conducting a CASTS is different from other types of assessments with which educators may be familiar. It is completed over the course of several weeks and involves gathering information from multiple sources. Information is synthesized and presented back to team members to confirm accuracy. Information gathered is compared and contrasted with current best practices in the field.

Discrepancies in the information gathered are probed to understand the differences in team members' perspectives.

A CASTS involves gathering information about

- The student's participation in general education instruction within the general education classroom
- The student's perceived proficiency in reading, writing, math, science, and other academic areas as appropriate
- The student's learning style, social/behavioral skills, and communication abilities
- The current use of tiered interventions, accommodations, modifications, and other supports for instruction and assessment
- The current use of AAC and AT
- The knowledge and skills represented in the team
- The collaboration among team members, including the quality of current team functioning and their capacity to utilize their expertise to support the student's learning
- Administrative policies and procedures

The process of completing a CASTS involves the following steps.

- Review reports and relevant records to gather historical and current information
- Review the current IEP
- Review written questionnaires completed by all team members (including parents/guardians)
- Conduct multiple observations of the student and team at school
- Observe the student at home
- Interview team members, including parents/guardians
- Conduct follow-up interviews to clarify information gathered
- Analyze the findings and generate possible recommendations for enhanced membership, participation, and learning by the student and improved team collaboration

The findings are presented to the team after all of the information is compiled and themes are identified. As categories of findings from the CASTS activities are reported (e.g., school context, the student, the team), team members engage in a consensus-building process in which they 1) add any missing and highly relevant information, 2) seek clarification or propose revisions to any inaccurate information, and 3) state their level of agreement with the accuracy of each category of information. Using these recommended processes results in a high level of shared understanding and high agreement for action among the team members. This same process is used for recommending and prioritizing action steps related to student instructional and communication supports, team supports, and professional development.

Phase 2: Explore and Describe

Two questions focus the team's work during the explore and describe phase of the BA Model.

1. What supports are needed for the student's full engagement in and learning of general education curriculum content (e.g., unit/lesson planning, adapting materials, designing an AAC system)?

2. How does the team need to work together to support the student's full engagement and learning (e.g., redefining their roles, increasing planning time, gaining new knowledge and skills, preparing adapted materials)?

The team explores and describes 1) specific AAC features that will provide the student access to vocabulary and foster language (and literacy) development that is related to the academic learning standards; 2) instructional accommodations and supports for the student to engage in the classroom activities; 3) effective meeting structures, decision-making processes, and teaming skills to support team collaboration; and 4) the professional development that is needed to enhance the team members' knowledge and skills to achieve the desired student outcomes (see Chapter 7 for a comprehensive how-to description of this phase and samples of forms, processes, and products from experienced BA teams).

During this phase of the Model, team members are encouraged to embrace a "Let's try it and see how it works" approach (adapted from Goossens', 1989). This approach supports the team to be creative and open minded, particularly if a team member is unsure about how a given strategy might work. The team refines the strategies over time. Promising student and team supports are identified for implementation in Phase 3 of the Model.

Phase 3: Implement and Document

The team systematically implements and gathers performance data on the promising student and team supports during Phase 3 of the Model (see Chapter 8 for a comprehensive how-to description of this phase and samples of forms, processes, and products from experienced BA teams). The team engages in professional development activities related to the desired student outcomes. The BA facilitator coaches the team to focus on improving the consistency and quality of the communication and instructional supports provided and checking to see that the team is achieving the desired outcomes (presumed competence, membership, participation, learning, and collaborative teaming). By reviewing documentation of the student's performance, including student work samples, observation notes regarding the student's engagement in the classroom, and videotaped samples of the student's participation in lessons, the team examines the accuracy and consistency of the supports provided and the student's performance in communicating and engaging the classroom activities over time. Concurrently, by reviewing documentation of the team's performance based on observation notes of team meetings and meeting evaluations, the team is able to describe their accuracy and consistency in using collaborative teaming practices.

Phase 4: Review and Sustain

The fourth phase of the BA Model consists of a systematic review of and reflection on the student and team performance data (see Chapter 9 for a how-to description of this phase with sample forms, processes, and products from experienced BA teams). During team meetings, the BA facilitator guides the team to use reflective practice methods (Montie et al., n.d; Weir, Jorgensen, & Dowd, 2002) to evaluate the delivery of the student and team supports and reflect on the patterns of student and team performance. The team identifies areas that need further exploration for possible addition to the student or team supports (revisit Phase 2). This leads to further data collection and analysis of student and team performance (revisit Phase 3), review and reflection of the performance summaries (revisit Phase 4), and further revisions. This iterative process leads to increased confidence in the student's work as evidence of learning of the general education curriculum and the quality of team performance in providing specific supports.

Professional Development

A schedule of professional development is tailored to the specific needs of each student's team based on the findings of the CASTS baseline assessment. This professional development can consist of in- and out-of-school workshops, team work sessions, modeling and coaching, and reflective practice. Professional development mirrors the Model's best practices and may include topics such as presuming students' competence (Jorgensen, 2005b); effective teaming practices such as collaborative teaming, problem solving, conflict resolution, and evaluating student and team progress (e.g., Jorgensen et al., 2002c); instructional planning, accommodations, and curriculum modifications (Jorgensen, 2005a); AAC and AT; positive behavior supports; literacy instruction; and writing standards-based IEPs.

Administrative Leadership Team

Every team that uses the BA Model is supported and monitored by an ALT consisting of the building principal, a special education administrator (building- or district-level or both), the team's special education case manager/team leader, and the BA facilitator who guides use of the Model with the IEP team. The ALT meets on a regularly scheduled basis—usually once a month—to 1) ensure that the IEP team has the supports necessary to implement the Model, 2) plan and facilitate the professional development plan, 3) link the IEP team's work to broader school improvement initiatives, 4) provide mediation in the case of unresolvable team conflict, and 5) ensure the Model's fidelity of implementation. Chapter 10 provides a comprehensive description of the ALT's membership, roles, and activities.

CONCLUSION

This chapter has provided the historical backdrop to the development of the BA Model, its research foundations, and a description of the Model's four phases. Chapter 3 elaborates on one of the core best practices of the Model—presuming students' competence to communicate about and learn general education curriculum content.

REFERENCES

Ainscow, M. (2005). Developing inclusive education systems: What are the levers for change? *Journal of Educational Change, 6*(2), 109–124.

American Speech-Language-Hearing Association. (2004). *Roles and responsibilities of speech-language pathologists with respect to augmentative and alternative communication: Technical report.* Rockville, MD: Author.

Beukelman, D., & Mirenda, P. (1992). *Augmentative and alternative communication: Management of communication disorders in children and adults.* Baltimore: Paul H. Brookes Publishing Co.

Beukelman, D., & Mirenda, P. (1998). *Augmentative and alternative communication: Management of severe communication disorders in children and adults* (2nd ed.). Baltimore: Paul H. Brookes Publishing Co.

Beukelman, D., & Mirenda, P. (2005). *Augmentative and alternative communication: Supporting children and adults with complex communication needs* (3rd ed.). Baltimore: Paul H. Brookes Publishing Co.

Biklen, D. (1999). The metaphor of mental retardation: Rethinking ability and disability. In H. Bersani, Jr. (Ed.), *Responding to the challenge: Current trends and international issues in developmental disabilities: Essays in honor of Gunnar Dybwad* (pp. 35–52). Cambridge, MA: Brookline Books.

Blackorby, J., Chorost, M., Garza, N., & Guzman, A. (2003). The academic performance of secondary students with disabilities. In M. Wagner, C. Marder, J. Blackorby, R. Cameto, L. Newman, P. Levine, et al. (Eds.), *The achievements of youth with disabilities during secondary school. A report from the National Longitudinal Transition Study–2* (NLTS2; pp. 4–14). Menlo Park, CA: SRI International.

Browder, D., Flowers, C., Ahlgrim-Delzell, L., Karvonen, M., Spooner, F., & Algozzine, R. (2004). The alignment of alternate assessment content to academic and functional curricula. *Journal of Special Education, 37,* 211–224.

Browder, D.M., & Minarovic, T. (2000). Using sight words in self-instruction training for employees with moderate mental retardation in competitive jobs. *Education and Training in Mental Retardation and Developmental Disabilities, 35,* 78–89.

Browder, D.M., & Spooner, F. (2006). Why teach the general curriculum? In D.M. Browder & F. Spooner (Eds.), *Teaching language arts, math, and science to students with significant cognitive disabilities* (pp. 6–7). Baltimore: Paul H. Brookes Publishing Co.

Browder, D., Spooner, F., Ahlgrim-Delzell, L., Harris, A., & Wakeman, S. (2008). A meta-analysis on teaching mathematics to students with significant cognitive disabilities. *Exceptional Children, 74,* 407–432.

Browder, D., Wakeman, S., Spooner, F., Ahlgrim-Delzell, L., & Algozzine, R.F. (2006). A comprehensive review of reading for students with significant cognitive disabilities. *Exceptional Children, 72,* 392–410.

Brown, L., Long, E., Udvari-Solner, A., Schwarz, P., VanDeventer, P., Ahlgren, C., et al. (1989). Should students with severe intellectual disabilities be based in regular or in special education classrooms in home schools? *Journal of The Association for Persons with Severe Handicaps, 14*(1), 8–12.

Brown, L., Nisbet, J., Ford, A., Sweet, M., Shiraga, B., York, J., et al. (1983). The critical need for nonschool instruction in educational programs for severely handicapped students. *Journal of The Association for People with Severe Handicaps, 8*(3), 71–77.

Calculator, S.N., & Jorgensen, C.M. (1991). Integrating AAC instruction into regular education settings: Expounding on best practices. *Augmentative and Alternative Communication, 7,* 204–214.

Calculator, S.N., & Jorgensen, C.M. (1994). *Including students with severe disabilities in schools: Fostering communication, interaction, and participation.* San Diego: Singular Press.

Cole, C.M., Waldron, N., & Majd, M. (2004). Academic progress of students across inclusive and traditional settings. *Mental Retardations, 42*(2), 136–144.

Collins, B.C., & Stinson, D.M. (1995). Teaching generalized reading of product warning labels to adolescents with mental disabilities through the use of key words. *Exceptionality, 5,* 163–181.

Courtade, G., Spooner, F., & Browder, D.M. (2007). A review of studies with students with significant cognitive disabilities that link to science standards. *Research and Practice in Severe Disabilities, 32,* 43–49.

Danielson, C. (1996). *Enhancing professional practice: A framework for teaching.* Alexandria, VA: Association for Supervision and Curriculum Development.

Donnellan, A. (1984). The criterion of the least dangerous assumption. *Behavioral Disorders, 9,* 141–150.

Downing, J.E. (2008). *Including students with severe and multiple disabilities in typical classrooms: Practical strategies for teachers* (3rd ed.). Baltimore: Paul H. Brookes Publishing Co.

Education for All Handicapped Children Act of 1975, PL 94-142, 20 U.S.C. §§ 1400 *et seq.*

Erickson, K., Koppenhaver, D., Yoder, D., & Nance, J. (1997). Integrated communication and literacy instruction for a child with multiple disabilities. *Focus on Autism and Other Developmental Disabilities, 12,* 142–150.

Falvey, M. (2004). Toward realizing the influence of "Toward realization of the least restrictive educational environments for severely handicapped students." *Research and Practice for Persons with Severe Disabilities, 29*(1), 9–10.

Fisher, D., & Ryndak, D.L. (2001). *The foundations of inclusive education: A compendium of articles on effective strategies to achieve inclusive education.* Baltimore: TASH.

Fisher, M., & Meyer, L. (2002). Development and social competence after two years for students enrolled in inclusive and self-contained educational programs. *Research and Practice for Persons with Severe Disabilities, 27*(3), 165–174.

Fryxell, D., & Kennedy, C.H. (1995). Placement along the continuum of services and its impact on students' social relationships. *Journal of The Association for Persons with Severe Handicaps, 20*(4), 259–269.

Gardill, M.C., & Browder, D.M. (1995). Teaching stimulus classes to encourage independent purchasing by students with severe behavior disorders. *Education and Training in Mental Retardation and Developmental Disabilities, 30,* 254–264.

Garmston, R., & Wellman, B. (1999). *The adaptive school: A sourcebook for developing collaborative groups.* Norwood, MA: Christopher-Gordon Publishers.

Giangreco, M., Cloninger, C., & Iverson, V. (1998). *Choosing outcomes and accommodations for children (COACH): A guide to educational planning for students with disabilities* (2nd ed.). Baltimore: Paul H. Brookes Publishing Co.

Giangreco, M., & Putnam, J. (1991). Supporting the education of students with severe disabilities in regular education environments. In L. Meyer, C. Peck, & L. Brown (Eds.), *Critical issues in the lives of people with severe disabilities* (pp. 245–270). Baltimore: Paul H. Brookes Publishing Co.

Goossens, C. (1989). Aided communication intervention before assessment: A case study of a child with cerebral palsy. *Augmentative and Alternative Communication, 5,* 14–26.

Handler, B. (2003). *Special education practices: An evaluation of educational environmental placement trends since the regular education initiative.* Paper presented at the Annual Meeting of the American Educational Research Association, Chicago.

Hunt, P., Soto, G., Maier, J., Muller, E., & Goetz, L. (2002). Collaborative teaming to support students with augmentative and alternative communication needs in GE classrooms. *Augmentative and Alternative Communication, 18,* 20–35.

Individuals with Disabilities Education Act (IDEA) Amendments of 1997, PL 105-17, 20 U.S.C. §§ 1400 *et seq.*

Individuals with Disabilities Education Improvement Act (IDEA) of 2004, PL 108-446, 20 U.S.C. §§ 1400 *et seq.*

Jackson, L., Ryndak, D., & Billingsley, F. (2000). Useful practices in inclusive education: A preliminary view of what experts in moderate to severe disabilities are saying. *Journal of The Association for Persons with Severe Handicaps, 25*(3), 129–141.

Janney, R., & Snell, M. (2004). *Teachers' guides to inclusive practices: Modifying schoolwork* (2nd ed.). Baltimore: Paul H. Brookes Publishing Co.

Jorgensen, C. (1998). *Restructuring high school for all students: Taking inclusion to the next level.* Baltimore: Paul H. Brookes Publishing Co.

Jorgensen, C. (2005a). An inquiry based instructional planning model that accommodates student diversity. *International Journal of Whole Schooling, 1*(2), 5–14, 46.

Jorgensen, C. (2005b). The least dangerous assumption: A challenge to create a new paradigm. *Disability Solutions, 6*(3), 1, 5–9, 15.

Jorgensen, C., Fisher, D., Sax, C., & Skoglund, K. (1998). Innovative scheduling, new roles for teachers, and heterogeneous grouping: The organizational factors related to student success in inclusive, restructuring schools. In C. Jorgensen (Ed.), *Restructuring high schools for all students: Taking inclusion to the next level* (pp. 29–48). Baltimore: Paul H. Brookes Publishing Co.

Jorgensen, C.M., & McSheehan, M. (2008, January/February). How applied research informs assessment policy for students with intellectual and other developmental disabilities: Lessons from New Hampshire. *TASH Connections, 32*(1), 14–16.

Jorgensen, C., McSheehan, M., & Sonnenmeier, R. (2002a). *Best practices that promote the learning of the GE curriculum content by students with significant disabilities.* Unpublished manuscript, University of New Hampshire, Institute on Disability, Durham.

Jorgensen, C., McSheehan, M., & Sonnenmeier, R. (2002b). *Mentor skills that promote the learning of the GE curriculum content by students with significant disabilities.* Unpublished manuscript, University of New Hampshire, Institute on Disability, Durham.

Jorgensen, C., McSheehan, M., & Sonnenmeier, R. (2002c). *Structures, processes, and skills in teaming that promote the learning of the GE curriculum content by students with significant disabilities.* Unpublished manuscript, University of New Hampshire, Institute on Disability, Durham.

Jorgensen, C.M., McSheehan, M., & Sonnenmeier, R. (2007). Presumed competence reflected in the educational programs of students with IDD before and after the Beyond Access professional development intervention. *Journal of Intellectual and Developmental Disabilities, 32*(4), 248–262.

Jorgensen, C.M., Schuh, M.C., & Nisbet, J. (2006). *The inclusion facilitator's guide.* Baltimore: Paul H. Brookes Publishing Co.

Jorgensen, C.M., Sonnenmeier, R., & McSheehan, M. (2001). *Beyond Access: A model that promotes learning of general education curriculum content for students with the most significant disabilities.* Durham: University of New Hampshire, Institute on Disability.

Kaner, S. (1996). *Facilitator's guide to participatory decision-making.* Gabriola Island, British Columbia, Canada: New Society Publishers.

Kearns, J. (2008). *Preliminary analysis of the Learner Characteristics Inventory in eight states.* Paper presented at the Project Director's Conference, Office of Special Education Programs, U.S. Department of Education, Washington, DC.

Kleinert, H.L., & Kearns, J.F. (2001). *Alternate assessment: Measuring outcomes and supports for students with disabilities.* Baltimore: Paul H. Brookes Publishing Co.

Kochmeister, S. (2003, February). *To have a voice is to have a choice.* Retrieved October 12, 2008, from http://www.users.dircon.co.uk/~cns/sharisa.html

Lalli, J.S., & Browder, D.M. (1993). Comparison of sight word training procedures with validation of the most practical procedure in teaching reading for daily living. *Research in Developmental Disabilities, 14*, 107–127.

Lipsky, D.K., & Gartner, A. (1997). *Inclusion and school reform: Transforming America's classrooms.* Baltimore: Paul H. Brookes Publishing Co.

McDonnell, J. (1987). The effects of time delay and increasing prompt hierarchy strategies on the acquisition of purchasing skills by students with severe handicaps. *Journal of The Association for the Severely Handicapped, 1*(2), 227–236.

McGregor, G., & Vogelsberg, R. (1998). *Inclusive schooling practices: Pedagogical and research foundations. A synthesis of the literature that informs best practices about inclusive schooling.* Baltimore: Paul H. Brookes Publishing Co.

McSheehan, M., Sonnenmeier, R., & Jorgensen, C. (2002). Communication and learning: Creating systems of support for students with significant disabilities. *TASH Connections, 28*(2), 9–13.

McSheehan, M., Sonnenmeier, R., Jorgensen, C.M., & Turner, K. (2006). Beyond communication access: Promoting learning of the GE curriculum by students with significant disabilities. *Topics in Language Disorders, 26*(3), 266–290.

McSheehan, M., Sundar, V., & Fedorchak, G. (in preparation). *Preliminary analysis of the characteristics of students participating in New Hampshire's alternate assessment.* Durham: University of New Hampshire.

Mirenda, P., & Calculator, S.N. (1993). Enhancing curricular design. *Clinics in Communication Disorders, 3*(2), 43–58.

Montie, J., York-Barr, J., Kronberg, R., Stevenson, J., Vallejo, B., & Lunders, C. (n.d.). *Reflective practice: Creating capacities for school improvement.* Minneapolis: University of Minnesota, Institute on Community Integration.

National Association of State Directors of Special Education. (2008). *NASDSE explains Response to Intervention.* Retrieved October 12, 2008, from http://dev.cenmi.org/focus/downloads/August06/GATA06-04.pdf

National Joint Committee on the Communication Needs of Persons with Severe Disabilities. (1992). Guidelines for meeting the communication needs of persons with severe disabilities. *ASHA, 34*(Suppl. 7), 2–3.

National Joint Committee on the Communication Needs of Persons with Severe Disabilities. (2002). Access to communication services and supports: Concerns regarding the application of restrictive "eligibility" policies (Technical report). *Communication Disorders Quarterly, 23*, 145–153.

No Child Left Behind (NCLB) Act of 2001, PL 107-110, 115 Stat. 1425, 20 U.S.C. §§ 6301 *et seq.*

Olson, L. (1994, May 4). Critical friends. *Education Week*, 20–27.

Parrish, T. (2008). *Measuring progress towards inclusion.* Paper presented at the Global Summit on Education 2008: Inclusive Practices for Students with Disabilities, Washington, DC.

Quenemoen, R. (2008). *Measuring progress towards inclusion.* Paper presented at the Global Education Summit 2008: Inclusive Practices for Students with Disabilities, Washington, DC.

Rainforth, B., York, J., & Macdonald, C. (1992). *Collaborative teams for students with severe disabilities: Integrating therapy and educational services.* Baltimore: Paul H. Brookes Publishing Co.

Romski, M.A., & Sevcik, R. (1988). Augmentative and alternative communication systems: Considerations for individuals with severe intellectual disabilities. *Augmentative and Alternative Communication, 4*(2), 83–93.

Romski, M.A., & Sevcik, R. (1996). *Breaking the speech barrier: Language development through augmented means.* Baltimore: Paul H. Brookes Publishing Co.

Rubin, S., Biklen, D., Kasa-Hendrickson, C., Kluth, P., Cardinal, D., & Broderick, A. (2001). Independence, participation, and the meaning of intellectual ability. *Disability and Society, 16*, 415–429.

Ryndak, D., Morrison, A., & Sommerstein, L. (1999). Literacy before and after inclusion in GE settings: A case study. *Journal of The Association for Persons with Severe Handicaps, 24*, 5–22.

Senge, P., Cambron-McCabe, N., Lucas, T., Smith, B., Dutton, J., & Kleiner, A. (2000). *Schools that learn: A fifth discipline fieldbook for educators, parents, and everyone who cares about education.* New York: Doubleday Dell Publishing Group.

Shane, H., & Bashir, A. (1980). Election criteria for the adoption of an augmentative communication system: Preliminary considerations. *Journal of Speech and Hearing Disorders, 45,* 408–414.

Smith, F.A., & Clark, D.M. (2007). *Disability and occupation.* Boston: Institute for Community Inclusion.

Snell, M.E., Caves, K., McLean, L., Mollica, B.M., Mirenda, P., Paul-Brown, D., et al. (2003). Concerns regarding the application of restrictive "eligibility" policies to individuals who need communication services and supports: A response by the National Joint Committee for the Communication Needs of Persons with Severe Disabilities. *Research and Practice for Persons with Severe Disabilities, 28,* 70–78.

Snell, M.E., & Janney, R. (2005). *Teachers' guides to inclusive practices: Collaborative teaming* (2nd ed.). Baltimore: Paul H. Brookes Publishing Co.

Sonnenmeier, R.M., McSheehan, M., & Jorgensen, C.M. (2005). A case study of team supports for a student with autism's communication and engagement within the GE curriculum: Preliminary report of the Beyond Access Model. *Augmentative and Alternative Communication, 21*(2), 101–115.

Soto, G. (2009). Academic adaptations for students with AAC needs. In D.R. Beukelman & J. Reichle (Series Eds.) & G. Soto & C. Zangari (Vol. Eds.), *Augmentative and alternative communication series: Practically speaking: Language, literacy, and academic development for students with AAC needs* (pp. 131–142). Baltimore: Paul H. Brookes Publishing Co.

Stainback, S., & Stainback, W. (1985). *Integration of students with severe handicaps into regular schools.* Reston, VA: Council for Exceptional Children.

Stainback, S., & Stainback, W. (1996). *Inclusion: A guide for educators.* Baltimore: Paul H. Brookes Publishing Co.

Tashie, C., Jorgensen, C., Shapiro-Barnard, S., Martin, J., & Schuh, M. (1996). High school inclusion: Strategies/barriers. *TASH Connections, 22,* 19–22.

Villa, R., & Thousand, J. (Eds.). (1995). *Creating an inclusive school.* Alexandria, VA: Association for Supervision and Curriculum Development.

Villa, R.A., & Thousand, J.S. (Eds.). (2000). *Restructuring for caring and effective education: Piecing the puzzle together* (2nd ed.). Baltimore: Paul H. Brookes Publishing Co.

Wagner, M., & Blackorby, J. (2004). *Overview of findings from wave 1 of the special education elementary longitudinal study (SEELS).* Menlo Park, CA: SRI International.

Warren, J.S., Edmonsen, H.M., Griggs, P., Lassen, S.R., McCart, A., Turnbull, A.P., et al. (2004). Urban applications of schoolwide positive behavior support: Critical issues and lessons learned. In L. Bambara, G. Dunlap, & E. Schwartz (Eds.), *Positive behavior support: Critical articles on improving practice for individuals with severe disabilities* (pp. 376–87). Austin, TX: PRO-ED.

Wechsler, D. (2003). *Wechsler Intelligence Scale for Children* (4th ed.). San Antonio, TX: Harcourt Assessment.

Wehmeyer, M.L., & Agran, M. (2006). Promoting access to the general curriculum for students with significant cognitive disabilities. In D.M. Browder & F. Spooner (Eds.), *Teaching language arts, math, and science to students with significant cognitive disabilities* (pp. 15–37). Baltimore: Paul H. Brookes Publishing Co.

Wehmeyer, M.L., Lance, G.D., & Bashinski, S. (2002). Promoting access to the general curriculum for students with mental retardation: A multi-level mode. *Education and Training in Mental Retardation and Developmental Disabilities, 37*(3), 223–234.

Weir, C., Jorgensen, C., & Dowd, J. (Eds.). (2002). *Promoting excellence in college teaching: A "reflective practice" toolkit for coaches.* Durham: University of New Hampshire, Institute on Disability.

Westling, D.L., Floyd, J., & Carr, D. (1990). Effects of single setting versus multiple setting training on learning to shop in a department store. *American Journal on Mental Retardation, 94,* 616–624.

Williams, M.B. (2000). Just an independent guy who leads a busy life. In M. Fried-Oken & H.A. Bersani (Eds.), *Speaking up and spelling it out: Personal essays on augmentative and alternative communication* (pp. 231–236). Baltimore: Paul H. Brookes Publishing Co.

Williams, R. (1992). Natural supports on the fly: Between flights in Chicago. In J. Nisbet (Ed.), *Natural supports in school, at work, and in the community for people with severe disabilities* (pp. 11–16). Baltimore: Paul H. Brookes Publishing Co.

Winsor, J., & Butterworth, J. (2007). *National day and employment service trends in MR/DD agencies.* Boston: Institute for Community Inclusion.

Zangari, C., Lloyd, L.L., & Vicker, B. (1994). Augmentative and alternative communication: An historic perspective. *Augmentative and Alternative Communication, 10*(1), 27–59.

Foundations of the Beyond Access Model

Presuming Competence

For Jay, the student introduced in Chapter 1, team members' judgments about his intelligence influenced every aspect of his educational program. Several years before we began working with Jay's team, a report by the school district's developmental disabilities specialist of an informal assessment of his academic abilities described him as "functioning at a 2-year-old level." That pronouncement underscored most of the decisions about Jay's education. His communication system was designed with vocabulary and messages appropriate for a younger child, and he was being taught academic prerequisite skills such as sorting by categories (e.g., animals, colors, shapes), counting, and one-to-one correspondence. As Jay grew older and the general education curriculum became more demanding, his team members began to question whether he should be included in a general education class. They wondered if it might be more appropriate for Jay to be taught in a self-contained class or for his educational program to have an emphasis on learning functional life skills instead of learning academics. It seemed as if Jay's team did not expect him to change much as a result of his educational program. There was no talk within the team of "when Jay functions like a 5-year-old, we think his program should look like. . . ."

In our experience, the decisions made by Jay's team are not unique but rather exemplify the importance that judgments about competence hold in the life of a person with IDD. This chapter elaborates on this issue and suggests that presuming an individual student's competence to participate in, communicate about, and learn the general education curriculum may be an essential best

---

With permission from the publishers, this chapter is largely based on an article by Jorgensen, C. (2005). The least dangerous assumption: The challenge to create a new paradigm. *Disability Solutions*, 6(3), 1, 5–9, 13.

practice for developing high-quality educational programs that result in optimal learning and quality of life.

WHAT IF?

Imagine that the following description applies to Kelly, an 11-year-old student who has a label of IDD. Intelligence tests and adaptive behavior evaluations have assigned her an intelligence quotient (IQ) score of 40 and a developmental age of 36 months. She experiences seizures and sensory impairments. Her fine and gross motor movements are jerky and uncoordinated. She is sensitive to certain environmental stimuli such as bright lights, loud noises, and rough textures in her clothing. She has no conventional way of communicating; she uses facial expressions and seemingly random vocalizations to express a variety of emotions. She expresses frustration by running away from a task or sometimes by hitting herself or others. She does not appear to be able to read.

How does this information affect her parents' and educators' decisions about her educational program? Should it be assumed that these test results, labels, and observations are accurate representations of her current abilities and future learning potential? Does her educational program reflect content learning from the general education curriculum or is it based primarily on teaching functional life skills? Is she educated alongside other students with IDD or is she included in a general education class? Let's "walk through" two hypothetical scenarios that represent different decisions about Kelly's educational program to help us decide which path would be in her best interests now and in the future.

In the first scenario, let's assume that Kelly is not smart—that she does, in fact, have an intellectual disability, which is defined by significant limitations both in intellectual functioning and in adaptive behavior as expressed in conceptual, social, and practical adaptive skills that significantly affect an individual's ability to learn, according to the American Association on Intellectual and Developmental Disabilities (AAIDD; Luckasson et al., 2002). How might Kelly be treated? First, we might not try to teach her to read or, if we did, it would be functional sight words. Second, we might speak to her in language more appropriate to a younger child. Third, Kelly would probably spend her educational career being taught functional skills such as dressing, eating, shopping, cooking, and cleaning. In most states in the United States, she would be educated in a separate classroom alongside other students who also have IDD. If she did join the rest of the student body, it might be during lunch or perhaps in a class such as music or art.

The communication vocabulary and supports that we would make available to Kelly would likely correspond to our assessment of her subaverage intelligence and relate to the functional skills being taught. The messages might include HI, BYE, MORE, BATHROOM, HUNGRY, BREAK, I FEEL _____, YES, and NO, instead of age-appropriate social vocabulary and messages that would enable her to communicate about the general education curriculum.

We probably would discourage her from participating in the typical social life of her same-age classmates because we would assume that her disabilities were too significant for her to enjoy those same activities. Interactions between her and students without disabilities likely would be limited to their volunteering to be her peer buddy or helper. As she approached the end of her school career, the possibility of her attending college likely would not even be considered. Instead, we probably would begin planning for her to move into a group home, attend a day habilitation program or work in a sheltered environment, and pursue specialized leisure and recreational opportunities with other adults who have similar disabilities. We probably would not expect her to have opinions about world events, her future, love, or anything else considered to be above her cognitive level.

Now imagine that it is several years in the future. Advancements in brain scanning technology have made it possible to determine a person's intelligence. The brain scan results show, surprisingly, that Kelly has an average IQ of 100. She does not have an intellectual disability (IQ of below 70). What have been the consequences of our original assumption of intellectual disability being *wrong?* Has any harm been done?

Many people would say that we lost an opportunity to teach Kelly things she could have learned. We did not include her in the mainstream of general education as much as we could have, and she did not develop a wide network of social relationships. She missed out on the typical high school experience. We might have even negatively influenced her self-esteem by treating her as if she were not smart. We might have narrowed the possibilities for her future career or postsecondary education. And, certainly, we wasted a lot of money pursuing the wrong educational program.

Next, consider a different scenario regarding Kelly's educational program. We are not sure about what she knows or might be able to learn in the future, and we do not have conclusive data to guide our decision making. But in this scenario, we operate from a different set of assumptions. We treat Kelly as if she is smart, even though she cannot tell us what she knows. We question the validity of previous test results in light of her communication and movement difficulties. We enroll her in general academic classes, try to teach her to read, and support her with adapted materials and instructional supports. We take advantage of natural opportunities to teach her the functional skills that are essential for membership, full participation, and learning within typical school routines. We talk with her about current events. We make sure that her communication system includes words and concepts that are commensurate with someone her age who can think about current events, relationships, and the future. We offer postsecondary education as an option following graduation from high school in addition to planning for her to move into an apartment and possibly to own her own home in the future; work at a meaningful job of her choosing; travel; and participate in other typical leisure time activities. We also assume that she is capable of, and interested in, making friends and having long-term relationships with other people—both with and without disabilities.

Once again, many years in the future, a new and more accurate brain scan is invented. This time, however, it shows that Kelly actually does have an IQ score of 40. What have been the consequences of our original assumption of intelligence having been *wrong?* Has any harm been done?

Many people say nothing has been lost. Even though Kelly might not have learned much of the general education curriculum, her educational program offered her opportunities to develop lifelong interests, to make friends with students with and without disabilities, to be a part of the social life of the school, and to truly be part of the community after graduation. Because we took advantage of natural opportunities to teach her functional skills, she learned and generalized them better than if they had been taught in an isolated or specialized setting.

THE PREVAILING PARADIGM

In order to understand these two hypothetical scenarios, we first need to understand the prevailing paradigm that governs the way that most of us think about intelligence and intelligence testing, about the label of intellectual disability, and about the vision that we have for students with this label. Kuhn (1962) defined *paradigms* as shared world views that are so strong and institutionalized that only a sudden and dramatic break from these conventional perspectives can bring on a positive revolution in thinking. What is the prevailing paradigm about disability and competence? It is defined by four assumptions:

1. Intelligence is something that can be reliably measured.

2. *Intellectual disability* is defined as low levels of intelligence, and it, too, can be quantified—we can figure out who has an intellectual disability and who does not.

3. Students who experience intellectual disability cannot learn much general education content and, therefore, the benefits to their being in general education classes are limited.

4. When we are not sure that students know, understand, can learn, or have something to say, we presume that they do not and probably never will.

The influence of this paradigm is evident in both our beliefs about students' abilities and in the decisions that we make about their educational programs. Educational programs often have the following characteristics when people do *not* assume that students with IDD are competent and able to learn general education curriculum.

- Students may not be included in general education classrooms, or if they are, they may participate in functional portions of instructional routines but not in the discussion of ideas or content knowledge. In many instances, students will be given different materials and resources than those given to the rest of the class.

- People converse with students as if they are talking with a much younger child, and social and academic vocabularies and communication supports are geared to students' perceived developmental levels or IQ scores as measured by traditional assessments.

- Students are not supported to engage in social activities with same-age peers because those activities are deemed inappropriate or too advanced.

- Planning for students' futures does not typically include the choice of a postsecondary education; instead, career options are geared to lower skill jobs rather than to ones that require higher-order thinking or literacy skills.

FLAWS IN THE CONSTRUCT AND ASSESSMENT OF INTELLIGENCE AND INTELLECTUAL DISABILITY

An important step in challenging this prevailing paradigm is to understand the flaws in the constructs and assessment of both intelligence and intellectual disability. Berger and Luckmann's (1966) theory of the production and institutionalization of knowledge, for example, posited that "a society builds widespread agreement about what is real through social negotiations that produce truths that then become crystallized into the fabric of everyday life and thought" (Gabel, 2005, p. 299). Their theory suggests that the concept of intellectual disability is firmly instituted within society and is continually reinforced each time it is assumed to be real and true. In the United States, for example, the idea of intellectual disability is firmly rooted in law, human service policy and practice, educational systems, professional organizations, teacher education, teacher certification, and popular culture.

Biklen and Duchan stated that "the meanings of mental retardation are created from a particular cultural backdrop and from various points of view within that cultural context" and furthermore, that "mental retardation does not exist as fact separate from interpretation, but that it is a concept constructed to account for selected events, behaviors, or phenomena" (1994, p. 173).

Gould (1981) criticized some of the earliest attempts at assessing intelligence as being fraught with bad science, politics, and racism that resulted in the erroneous conclusion that people of northern European descent were more intelligent than non-Caucasians. Gardner (1983) has also criticized intelligence testing because the kinds of so-called intelligence measured by traditional IQ tests (verbal-linguistic and logical-mathematical) represent just two aspects of a complex, multidimensional construct (see also Smith, 1999). When we think about people with significant disabilities, skepticism about testing is particularly justified because they often have difficulties with expressive language, their bodies often move erratically, and they often have not been taught the language or skills assessed by intelligence and adaptive behavior tests. How would any of us score on an intelligence test if we could not talk, write, or type accurately? If we had not been exposed to or taught receptive or expressive language skills? If the sensory environment of the testing situation was stressful? If the people around us treated us as if we were "retarded"?

CHALLENGES TO TRADITIONAL CONSTRUCTS OF COMPETENCE AND INTELLECTUAL DISABILITY

Many people view intelligence as a fixed characteristic of an individual that does not change over time. In fact, IQ tests are by their very nature designed to measure aptitude, not achievement (which can certainly change over time). The tests designed to evaluate intelligence (e.g., WISC-IV [Wechsler, 2003], Wechsler Adult Intelligence Scale–Third Edition [WAIS-III; Wechsler, 1997]) have been criticized because they are unable to account for the challenges that may characterize the person's disability such as difficulty communicating, ability to deal with sensory stimuli, difficulties with attention, and a history of poor instruction and other educational opportunities (Donnellan & Leary, 1995; Gould, 1981; Smith, 1985).

Similarly, the use of adaptive behavior measures such as the Vineland Adaptive Behavior Scales–Second Edition (VABS-II; Sparrow, Balla, & Cicchetti, 2005) as a part of an assessment of competence often fail to recognize that some people with IDD have poor functional skills, yet are highly intelligent (Rubin et al., 2001). Donna Williams (2007), a self-advocate with autism, describes how she cannot bathe herself but is a published author and effective public speaker.

In recognition of changes in the paradigm of intellectual disability, the American Association on Mental Retardation changed its name to the American Association on Intellectual and Developmental Disabilities (AAIDD; 2007). Several states, including New Hampshire, have changed the terminology used in their developmental service system from *mental retardation* to *intellectual disability*.

AAIDD's definition of *intellectual disability* has also been changed to reflect the idea that individuals' competence is inextricably entwined with their environment. The new definition recognizes that

> An understanding of intellectual disability requires a multidimensional and ecological approach that reflects the interaction of the individual with the environment, and the outcomes of that interaction with respect to independence, relationships, societal contributions, participation in school and community, and personal well being. (AAIDD, 2002)

IDEA 2004 requires that all students with disabilities have access to, participate in, and make progress in the general education curriculum and that they pursue that curriculum, to the maximum extent appropriate, in (and with a clear preference for) the general education classroom (Wehmeyer, 2003). One reason that the LRE provisions of IDEA were strengthened between 1997 and 2004 may be the growing body of research that shows that students with IDD are more engaged, develop better communication and social skills, demonstrate literacy skills, and perform better on standardized measures of reading and math skills when they are included in general education classes (Baker, Wang, & Wahlberg, 1994/1995; Downing, Morrison, & Berecin-Rascon, 1996; Erickson, Koppenhaver, Yoder, & Nance, 1997; McGregor & Vogelsberg, 1998; Ryndak, Morrison, & Sommerstein, 1999; Wagner et al., 2003; Wehmeyer, Lattin, Lapp-Rincker, & Agran, 2003). Wehmeyer and Agran proposed, "The place where students with significant intellectual disabilities have access to the general curriculum is the general education classroom" (2006, p. 20).

Despite the research and policy supports for general education curriculum and classroom access, the majority of students with IDD in most states experience the lowest percentages of time in general education classes, with both special education and related services often being provided in separate environments (U.S. Department of Education, 2006). Perhaps the most compelling reason for questioning the paradigm of intellectual disability is the body of research that shows that, with the right instruction bolstered by high expectations, children with IDD can learn to read and acquire other academic skills (Biklen & Cardinal, 1997; Broderick & Kasa-Hendrickson, 2001; Browder & Spooner, 2006; Ryndak et al., 1999).

PROPOSITION FOR A PARADIGM SHIFT

Kuhn (1962) said it is only when we question a prevailing paradigm that we can open ourselves to changing not only our beliefs but our actions. We agree with many self-advocates, parents, and other researchers that subscribing to the paradigm of intellectual disability leads to low expectations for students with IDD. These low expectations result in segregated educational programs, poor or absent instruction in literacy and content learning, and narrow visions for students' futures. Thus, changing our paradigm about intelligence and intellectual disability is central to promoting students' learning, inclusion, achievement, and quality of life.

A framework for resolving lingering uncertainties about students' abilities and educational program designs can be found in the criterion of the least dangerous assumption. Donnellan described this criterion in the following way.

> Given that the long-term goal of education is to ensure that students acquire the skills necessary to be able to live, work, and recreate as independently as possible as adults; and given that there are a variety of educational means or strategies currently available for instruction; and given that, through lack of conclusive data, we are currently forced to make assumptions about the relative impact of various strategies on the long-term goals, which assumptions will have the least dangerous effect on the likelihood that the goal will be attained? (1984, p. 148)

Donnellan answered the question by suggesting that the least dangerous assumption is to assume competence and provide opportunities consistent with high expectations because to assume incompetence and not provide such opportunities could be more harmful, if one's assumptions were ever proved to be wrong. Think back to the two scenarios about Kelly for evidence of this principle.

Biklen offered a "guiding principle for creating contexts for communication and participation" and stressed "that difficulties with demonstrating ability not be taken as evidence of intellectual incompetence" (1999, p. 50). Furthermore, he argued, "as a matter of basic sensitivity and good educational practice, educators must presume that the person is intelligent" (p. 50).

Jorgensen (2006) integrated Donnellan's least dangerous assumption principle with Biklen's recommendation to presume competence (i.e., intelligence) and proposed that the least dangerous assumption is to presume a student is competent to learn and communicate about the general education curriculum and to design educational programs and supports based on that assumption.

If we are seeing more and more examples of people whose experiences do not align with the prevailing paradigm, then a new paradigm must be developed that accounts for these new phenomena. This paradigm would be characterized by the following precepts.

- All people have different talents and skills.
- Intelligence is not a one-dimensional construct.
- Intelligence (or its absence) cannot be measured accurately and reliably enough to base students' educational programs and future goals on intelligence test results.

- Students learn best when they feel valued, when people hold high expectations for them, and when they are taught and supported well.

- When we are not sure what students can learn, presume competence and the ability to learn.

If schools adopt the new paradigm of a least dangerous assumption and the presumption of competence, then the following would be evident.

- Person-first language is used, keeping the focus on the person rather than on his or her disability label (so that people say "students with autism," not "autistic students").

- Language that classifies students based on their functioning or developmental levels is not used; rather, descriptions of students focus on their abilities and needs.

- All students are provided with a means to communicate about the same academic and social topics as their peers without disabilities.

- Annual goals on IEPs reflect content standards from the general education curriculum and the functional skills necessary for students to fully participate in the mainstream of school and community life.

- Students are seen as capable of learning the general education curriculum; educators do not predict that certain students will never acquire certain knowledge or skills.

- People speak directly to students rather than speaking to students through a buffer supplied by paraprofessionals or other people who are considered to be assisting the students.

- People use age-appropriate vocabulary, topics, and inflection when talking to students.

- In order to respect privacy, staff members discuss the students' personal care, medical needs, and other sensitive issues out of earshot from others and only with those people who genuinely need the information.

There are at least five reasons why we believe that the least dangerous assumption is to presume competence.

1. Human intelligence is a multifaceted construct rather than a unidimensional characteristic and measuring it with a test is invalid and leads to mistaken conclusions about a person's capacity to learn.

2. Assessments of students' IQ scores are seriously flawed when those students have complex communication needs and movement challenges.

3. Research shows that a growing number of children and adults labeled with an IDD show they are more capable when they have a means to communicate and are provided with high-quality instruction.

4. To presume incompetence could result in harm to our students if we are wrong.

5. Even if we are wrong about students' capacities to learn general education curriculum content, the consequences to the student of that incorrect presumption are not as dangerous as the alternative.

Those of us involved in the educational lives of students—parents, teachers, psychologists, SLPs, policy makers, and researchers—must decide what our least dangerous assumption will be and whether we can live with the possibility of being wrong. If we are not sure, then we might ask ourselves the following questions.

- How would I want to be treated if someday I were unable to communicate or demonstrate my competence?
- How would I want others to treat my child if he or she were in the same situation?
- What do adults with disabilities tell us about their educational experiences and how they want to be treated?
- What does research tell us?
- What does history tell us?

PRESUMING COMPETENCE AND THE BEYOND ACCESS MODEL

The BA Model is grounded in the presumption that all students are competent to learn the general education curriculum and communicate about both social and academic topics commensurate with their same-age peers without disabilities. Presuming that students are competent, however, *is not a prerequisite* to using the Model. We acknowledge that members of educational teams have a varied set of professional and personal experiences that have informed their beliefs about intelligence, disability, learning, and communication. Thus, we are not asking people to change their *beliefs* before using the BA Model; we are asking people to adopt *behaviors* that have been shown to promote the highest levels of learning by students. These behaviors—1) providing students with appropriate supports and a means to communicate about age-appropriate social and academic topics until they are communicating in a way that is commensurate with same-age peers, 2) supporting students to be fully participating members of general education instruction within the general education classroom, and 3) considering the quality of instruction and supports when evaluating students' performance—are described more fully in the next chapter.

CONCLUSION

The idea of presuming competence to communicate about and learn general education curriculum in the general education classroom is the lens through which the other BA practices operate. Chapter 4 describes how this particular view of presuming competence is evidenced in thinking about and supporting students' membership, participation, communication, and learning.

REFERENCES

American Association on Intellectual and Developmental Disabilities. (2002). *Definition of mental retardation.* Retrieved March 1, 2007, from http://www.aaidd.org/Policies/faq_mental_retardation.shtml

American Association on Intellectual and Developmental Disabilities. (2007). *Mental retardation is no more: New name is intellectual and developmental disabilities.* Retrieved March 1, 2007, from http://www.aaidd.org/About_AAIDD/MR_name_change.htm

Baker, E., Wang, M., & Wahlberg, H. (1994/1995). The effects of inclusion on learning. *Educational Leadership, 52,* 33–35.

Berger, P., & Luckmann, T. (1966). *The social construction of reality: A treatise in the sociology of knowledge.* Garden City, NY: Anchor Books.

Biklen, D. (1999). The metaphor of mental retardation: Rethinking ability and disability. In H. Bersani, Jr. (Ed.). *Responding to the challenge: Current trends and international issues in developmental disabilities: Essays in honor of Gunnar Dybwad* (pp. 35–52). Cambridge, MA: Brookline Books.

Biklen, D., & Cardinal, D. (1997). *Contested words, contested science.* New York: Teachers College Press.

Biklen, D., & Duchan, J. (1994). "I am intelligent": The social construction of mental retardation. *Journal of The Association for Persons with Severe Handicaps, 19*(3), 173–184.

Broderick, A., & Kasa-Hendrickson, C. (2001). "Say just one word at first": The emergence of reliable speech in a student labeled with autism. *Journal of The Association for Persons with Severe Handicaps, 26*(1), 13–24.

Browder, D.M., & Spooner, F. (Eds.). (2006). *Teaching language arts, math, and science to students with significant cognitive disabilities.* Baltimore: Paul H. Brookes Publishing Co.

Donnellan, A. (1984). The criterion of the least dangerous assumption. *Behavioral Disorders, 9,* 141–150.

Donnellan, A.M., & Leary, M.R. (1995). *Movement differences and diversity in autism/mental retardation: Appreciating and accommodating people with communication and behavior challenges.* Madison, WI: DRI Press.

Downing, J.E., Morrison, A.P., & Berecin-Rascon, M.A. (1996). Including elementary school students with autism and intellectual impairments in their typical classrooms: Process and outcomes. *Developmental Disabilities Bulletin, 24,* 20–45.

Erickson, K., Koppenhaver, D., Yoder, D., & Nance, J. (1997). Integrated communication and literacy instruction for a child with multiple disabilities. *Focus on Autism and Other Developmental Disabilities, 12*(3), 142–150.

Gabel, S. (2005). Social construction, mental retardation, and the stories people tell: An essay and review of the social construction of intellectual disability. *Mental Retardation, 43*(4), 199–306.

Gardner, H. (1983). *Frames of mind: The theory of multiple intelligences.* New York: Basic Books.

Gould, S.J. (1981). *The mismeasure of man.* New York: W.W. Norton.

Individuals with Disabilities Education Act (IDEA) Amendments of 1997, PL 105-17, 20 U.S.C. §§ 1400 *et seq.*

Individuals with Disabilities Education Improvement Act (IDEA) of 2004, PL 108-446, 20 U.S.C. §§ 1400 *et seq.*

Jorgensen, C. (2005). The least dangerous assumption: The challenge to create a new paradigm. *Disability Solutions, 6*(3), 1, 5–9, 13.

Jorgensen, C. (2006, August). *The least dangerous assumption: A challenge to create a new paradigm.* Keynote presentation at the 8th Annual Autism Summer Institute, University of New Hampshire, Durham.

Kuhn, T. (1962). *The structure of scientific revolutions.* Chicago: University of Chicago Press.

Luckasson, R., Borthwick-Duffy, S., Buntinx, W., Coulter, D., Craig, E., Reeve, A., et al. (2002). *Intellectual disability: Definition, classification, and systems of supports* (10th ed.). Washington, DC: American Association on Intellectual Disability.

McGregor, G., & Vogelsberg, R.T. (1998). *Inclusive schooling practices: Pedagogical and research foundations. A synthesis of the literature that informs best practices about inclusive schooling.* Baltimore: Paul H. Brookes Publishing Co.

Rubin, S., Biklen, D., Kasa-Hendrickson, C., Kluth, P., Cardinal, D., & Broderick, A. (2001). Independence, participation, and the meaning of intellectual ability. *Disability and Society, 16,* 415–429.

Ryndak, D., Morrison, A., & Sommerstein, L. (1999). Literacy before and after inclusion in general education settings: A case study. *Journal of The Association for Persons with Severe Handicaps, 24*(1), 5–22.

Smith, D.J. (1985). *Minds made feeble.* Rockville, MD: Aspen.

Smith, P. (1999). Drawing new maps: A radical cartography of developmental disabilities. *Review of Educational Research, 69*(2), 117–144.

Sparrow, S.S., Balla, D., & Cicchetti, D. (2005). *Vineland Adaptive Behavior Scales* (2nd ed.). Circle Pines, MN: American Guidance Service.

U.S. Department of Education. (2006). *Twenty-sixth annual report to Congress on the implementation of the Individuals with Disabilities Education Act of 2004.* Washington, DC: Author.

Wagner, M., Marder, C., Blackorby, J., Cameto, R., Newman, L., Levine, P., et al. (2003). *The achievements of youth with disabilities during secondary school. A report from the National Longitudinal Transition Study-2 (NLTS2).* Menlo Park, CA: SRI International. Available at http://www.nlts2.org/reports/2003_11/nlts2_report_2003_11_complete.pdf

Wechsler, D. (1997). *Wechsler Adult Intelligence Scale–III.* San Antonio, TX: Harcourt Assessment.

Wechsler, D. (2003). *Wechsler Intelligence Scale for Children* (4th ed.). San Antonio, TX: Harcourt Assessment.

Wehmeyer, M. (2003). Defining mental retardation and ensuring access to the general curriculum. *Education and Training in Developmental Disabilities, 38*(3), 271–282.

Wehmeyer, M.L., & Agran, M. (2006). Promoting access to the general curriculum for students with significant cognitive disabilities. In D.M. Browder & F. Spooner (Eds.), *Teaching language arts, math, and science to students with significant cognitive disabilities* (pp. 15–37). Baltimore: Paul H. Brookes Publishing Co.

Wehmeyer, M., Lattin, D., Lapp-Rincker, G., & Agran, M. (2003). Access to the general curriculum of middle school students with mental retardation: An observational study. *Remedial and Special Education, 24*(5), 262–272.

Williams, D. (2007, August). *Beyond appearances.* Keynote presentation at the 9th Annual Autism Summer Institute, University of New Hampshire, Durham.

Membership, Participation, and Learning

This chapter describes and provides numerous examples of three of the core best practices and ultimate outcomes of the BA Model—membership, participation, and learning. First, we provide an overview of how membership and participation provide the context for enhancing learning. We then describe the importance of, strategies for enhancing, and indicators for membership, participation, and learning.

In our experience, many educators begin their planning for instruction by asking questions about how to modify the curriculum content and materials based on unwarranted lack of confidence in student abilities. These perceptions of student abilities are inaccurate, in part, because of insufficient AAC supports. In doing so, there is a risk of the trap presented in Jay's story in Chapter 1. "How do I modify a lesson on computing addition problems for a student functioning at the 2-year-old level?" or "How do I modify a fourth-grade novel to make sense for a student with low-functioning autism?" These questions lead a teacher to create a version of the curriculum that is different from the one taught to students without disabilities and then to design ways to teach it that also may be different from the instructional plan for students without disabilities.

It is understandable that educators want to prioritize their attention to support student learning. In the instructional planning process, however, prioritizing the content to be learned over the context and the instructional processes through which it will be taught may mislead educators to make changes in educational programming that are not aligned with their vision of inclusive education. For example, follow this teacher's line of thinking: "This book would have to be significantly modified to work for him. The book will be so different from that of his classmates that we will have to pull him aside to provide individualized instruction. Being in the general education classroom appears unnecessary with so much pull-aside instruction. I could teach him this modified book better

55

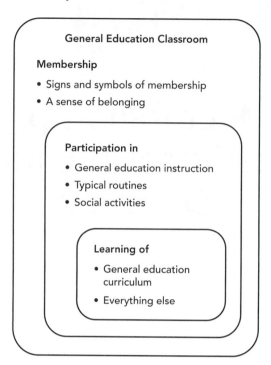

Figure 4.1. Conceptual framework for embedding learning of general education curriculum in the context of membership and participation within the general education classroom for students with intellectual and/or other developmental disabilities.

if he came to my resource room and I pulled in the other two students in the building who are functioning at his level."

Figure 4.1 depicts the BA approach to learning in the context of membership and participation. It is apparent in this figure that learning is situated in general education classroom membership and participation is situated in general education instruction. In this model, intensive support planning for students' learning must ensure that membership and participation are in place in order to maximize the social opportunities in the general education classroom and the academic instruction offered there.

MEMBERSHIP

Educators and psychologists have reported that students' presence in the classroom as members of the learning community—a member of both social and academic activities—is a requirement for optimal student learning.

In his award-winning film, *Including Samuel*, filmmaker Dan Habib (2007) tells the story of his 8-year-old son Samuel's full inclusion in a second-grade general education classroom in his neighborhood school. Habib recalls the angst that he and his wife Betsy felt when they first learned of the severity of Samuel's disabilities. After a long day of therapy and doctor's appointments when Samuel was a toddler, they would compare notes about how he was doing with various motor skills and development. Over time, they realized that their focus on Samuel's disabilities—fixing his body and making him conform to a standard of normality—was not only inhibiting their relationship with Samuel but also was frustrating Samuel. As their journey with Samuel continued, Dan and Betsy met and heard the stories of parents of older children with disabilities, as well as adults with disabilities. They realized that accepting Samuel just as he was and fully including him in all aspects of family, school, and community life would be more likely to result in Samuel having a good life than a narrow focus on what Samuel could not do. "More than anything, his mother and I want Samuel to have a deep sense of belonging" (Habib, 2007).

Kunc (1992) asked us to consider how the basic premises of Maslow's (1970) hierarchy of needs leading to self-actualization have been distorted for people with disabilities. Maslow posited that individuals do not seek the satisfaction of a need at one level until the previous level of need is met. In Maslow's original hierarchy, physiological needs—food, water, shelter, and warmth—form the base of a five-level pyramid. The second level of Maslow's pyramid is safety, and the third level is love and belonging. Maslow stressed that only when we are "anchored in community do we develop self-esteem, the need to assure ourselves of our own worth as individuals" (Kunc, 1992, p. 28). The fourth level represents elements of self-esteem—achievement, mastery, recognition, and respect. And the fifth, or highest level, is self-actualization, characterized by the pursuit of inner talent, creativity, and fulfillment.

When applied to people with disabilities, the order of the third and fourth levels is often switched. That is, people with disabilities are required to demonstrate skill and accomplishment as a prerequisite to belonging. For example, students with disabilities are often required to be able to perform certain academic skills *before* they are included in a general education classroom, even though this requirement violates both the spirit and the letter of special education law (Kluth, Villa, & Thousand, 2001/2002). Or, they are required to demonstrate a certain level of cognitive development before being exposed to general education curricula. Adults with disabilities are told that they must pass vocational evaluations showing that they have mastered particular skills before they can move from a sheltered workshop to a typical work setting.

Researchers have investigated the meaning and interpretation of membership on students with disabilities. Schnorr (1990) found that part-time inclusion had a significant effect on the membership and belonging of a student named Peter. Schnorr used participant observation and in-depth interviews over a 7-month period to study a first-grade class in which Peter, who had a moderate intellectual disability, participated on a part-time basis. Peter spent most of his school day in a self-contained classroom. He joined a first-grade class for a period each morning as well as for classes such as music, art, library, and physical education. Using inductive and ongoing data analysis techniques, Schnorr's observations and interviews revealed three themes that characterized classroom membership: where students belong, what they do, and with whom they play. With respect to Peter's membership in the class, several conclusions were drawn. First, "part-time is different, not just less. Peter's experience differed in kind as well as amount. He did not share in the first grade experience as defined by the students" (Schnorr, 1990, p. 238). A second conclusion was that Peter was not viewed by the other students as a member of the class because he engaged in different activities inside the classroom, often with different materials and instructional methods. A third element that seemed to define Peter as an outsider rather than a member of this classroom was that other students only nominated classmates as friends if they were members of the same class. Peter's membership in the self-contained classroom and his visitor status in the first-grade classroom almost guaranteed that he would not be considered among the pool of potential friends by his classmates (Tashie, Shapiro-Barnard, & Rossetti, 2006).

Williams and Downing (1998) found that middle school students' perceptions of membership incorporated feeling welcomed, wanted, and respected by classmates and teachers; being familiar with classmates and having friends who understand them; feeling as if they belong to a group and/or class as a whole; having fun; and feeling comfortable.

Strully and Strully (1985) described how their daughter Shawntell was one of the first students with IDD to be included in a general education classroom in her neighborhood school. They focused on Shawntell's membership within the classroom and school because they believed that belonging and friendships were essential to Shawntell's quality of life while she was in school and when she became an adult. Many years later, after Shawntell had grown to adulthood, Strully mused:

> Now that I am getting older, I sometimes awaken in the middle of the night worrying about what will happen to Shawntell when her mother and I are no longer around to advocate for her. It is at these times when I am sure that it will be more important for Shawntell to have real friends who care about her and want to spend time with her than it will be for her to be able to tie her shoes, or set the table, or make a sandwich. When we have been faced with important decisions about Shawntell's education or adult life, returning to that basic human need for belonging has helped us make decisions that we think will most likely lead to Shawntell's happiness and quality of life. (2006)

Membership in the general education class represents students having access to valued social roles and the symbols of belonging, such as having a desk, being given class jobs, going on field trips, and having one's name called during attendance. In addition, through the lens of presumed competence, the symbols of the student's membership, sense of belonging, and social roles within the classroom would reflect a vision of equity and reciprocity with classmates who do not have disabilities. Working toward this vision would include exploring ways to enhance a student's communication system until he or she has an effective and efficient means through which to communicate socially about the same topics and in a way that is commensurate with same-age peers.

Enhancing Membership to Enhance Learning

During the orientation to the BA Model and in ongoing professional development provided to school teams (including administrators and parents), journal articles, book chapters, videos, and guest presentations from other parents or adults with disabilities are shared to emphasize the importance of membership in general education.

Although a student does not need to be included in general education all day, every day in order for a team to begin using the Model, we suggest that students be included in a general education classroom for at least two core academic subjects (i.e., math, language arts, social studies, science). The team then uses the BA Model to focus on improving instruction and supports (including AAC) to the student during these two periods of the day, prior to expanding the student's inclusion within other classroom lessons and activities. We want to make it clear that we are not advocating for students to be "included part time," but rather suggesting that focusing on two core academic periods a day can provide a place for the team to begin the process of learning to use the BA Model.

McSheehan, Sonnenmeier, Jorgensen, and Turner (2006) investigated perceptions of five students' IEP team members regarding the effect of the first phase of the BA Model (the CASTS, a baseline assessment) on several variables, including students' classroom membership within the general education classroom. Prior to teams' engagement in the CASTS process, we asked them to estimate the student's level of membership (and participation) in the general education classroom at 0%–20%, 20%–40%, 40%–60%, 60%–80%, or 80%–100%. Across the five students, average team ratings were 0%–20% for two students, 20%–40% for two other students, and 40%–60% for the fifth student. Six months following the CASTS assessment, the amount of time spent in the general education classroom increased for all of the students. Ratings for one student increased from 0%–20% to 20%–40%, and ratings for the remaining four students increased to 60%–80%. A follow-up inquiry at 9 months revealed that all five students were in the general education classroom for 80% or more of the day. These findings show how using the BA Model can increase the amount of time a student spends within the general education classroom, and thus increase the likelihood that he or she will be perceived by others as a member of that classroom. This is a necessary, though not sufficient, step in fostering the student's learning within the general education classroom.

Membership indicators can be used by teams to plan action steps if certain indicators are absent or partially present (see Table 4.1). Outcome measures of membership are also used to monitor the effect of using the BA Model (see Chapter 7 for a description and sample of the Student and Team Outcomes Survey). A couple of examples that illustrate changes made by teams to improve a student's membership within the classroom are presented next.

Previously, Julie's desk had been placed at the back of class, not alongside other students who sat in groups of four. Her desk was moved up to be alongside her classmates, and the paraprofessional's materials were stored on a table at the back of the classroom.

Jamie consistently arrived 15 minutes late for homeroom, missing calendar time, during which important reading and math skills were learned. It was determined that the cause of his tardiness were special education transportation schedules and his need to do sensory-motor activities to help organize him and increase attention prior to going to classes. Jamie started riding the regular school bus, and his sensory motor activities were integrated into a whole-class warm-up activity done just prior to sitting down for the calendar activity.

Table 4.1.　Sample indicators of student membership in the general education classroom

---

The student attends the school he or she would attend if he or she did not have a disability.

The student is a member of an age-appropriate general education class.

The student's name is on all class lists, lists of groups put on the board, job lists, and so forth.

Related services are delivered primarily through consultation in the classroom.

The student receives the same materials as students without disabilities, with supports (i.e., accommodations, adaptations) provided as necessary.

The student passes classes with other students, arriving and leaving at the same time.

The student has a locker/cubby alongside students without disabilities.

The student rides the same school bus as his or her peers without disabilities.

From McSheehan, M., Sonnenmeier, R.M., & Jorgensen, C.M. (2009). Membership, participation, and learning in the general education classroom for students with autism spectrum disorders who use AAC. In D.R. Beukelman & J. Reichle (Series Eds.) & P. Mirenda & T. Iacono (Vol. Eds.), *Augmentative and alternative communication series: Autism spectrum disorders and AAC* (p. 418). Baltimore: Paul H. Brookes Publishing Co; adapted by permission.

Jimmy's educational team felt that he needed to learn vocational skills in order to prepare him for the world of work after high school. Instead of delivering the attendance sheets during first period when other students were engaged in core academics, Jimmy's team agreed to enroll him in a biology class where all students took turns being responsible for organizing the lab equipment storage cabinet and keeping a terrarium clean.

PARTICIPATION

Research, practice guidelines, and disability policy have identified engagement and participation as positively correlated to educational achievement and to quality-of-life outcomes of children and adults with disabilities (Brophy & Good, 1986; Greenwood, 1991; Hemmingsson & Jonsson, 2005; National Joint Committee on the Communication Needs of Persons with Severe Disabilities, 2002; World Health Organization, 2001). Although students with IDD may exhibit characteristics that seem to inhibit their full engagement and participation in classroom activities (e.g., movement, sensory, communication, learning, and behavior difficulties), research has shown that engagement can be positively influenced by 1) the choice of instructional method; 2) the characteristics of the learning environment; 3) the interactions between the student and his or her teachers, other support providers, and peers; 4) accommodations and supports for dealing with sensory stimuli; and 5) interventions that help the student manage his or her emotional and behavioral needs.

The choice of the learning environment itself—whether students are placed in self-contained or general education classrooms—can also influence engagement and participation. Hunt, Farron-Davis, Beckstead, Curtis, and Goetz (1994) studied the effects of placing students with severe disabilities in general education versus special education classes. They found that in addition to higher overall quality of their IEPs, students with disabilities who were full-time members of general education classes were significantly more actively engaged and initiated more to others than students in special education classes.

Helmstetter, Curry, Brennan, and Sampson-Saul (1998) studied nine students with severe disabilities who spent part of their day in both general and special education classrooms. In comparison to special education classrooms, general education classrooms provided more instruction, utilized more whole-class instruction, provided a comparable amount of one-to-one instruction, addressed academic content more, and utilized peers without disabilities more and special education staff less. Also in comparison with special education classrooms, however, students in general education classrooms were less actively engaged and more passively engaged in instruction, engaged in a comparable amount of time during independent work, and were less actively engaged and more passively engaged with teachers and paraprofessionals. These results emphasize the importance of providing adequate supports for meaningful engagement to realize students' full potential for learning in a general education classroom.

Goodman and Williams (2007) reviewed a variety of academic interventions for students with autism spectrum disorders in inclusive classrooms and found that several interventions increased students' academic engagement, including auditory focus cues (including songs), visual aids (e.g., visual schedules, highlighting important text, note-taking templates), concrete and hands-on models (e.g., base-10 blocks, tactile alphabet letters, models of molecules, mini-calendars), clear expectations for responses to questions, offering choices, and incorporating movement activities.

Peer support interventions have also been found to contribute to higher levels of active engagement for students with and without disabilities (Shukla, Kennedy, & Cushing, 1999), increased social interactions (Kennedy, Cushing, & Itkonen, 1997), decreased levels of problem behavior (McDonnell, Mathot-Buckner, Thorson, & Fister, 2001), improved academic performance (Dugan et al., 1995), and the acquisition of functional skills (Werts, Caldwell, & Wolery, 1996). Moreover, the effectiveness of peer support interventions has been documented across grade levels (i.e., elementary, middle, and high school) and disability categories (e.g., intellectual disabilities, autism, multiple disabilities).

Although there is a need for continued research on the interventions and supports that make the most positive effect on both engagement and learning for any particular student, the BA Model is based on the notion that higher levels of meaningful participation will benefit all students with disabilities. In addition, the BA Model's emphasis on participation reflects the current state of the field in which AAC supports and services are not routinely provided to all students with IDD who need these supports and services. Given this, the validity of measures of student abilities are questionable. Thus, planning for participation must include a focus on AAC supports prior to judgments about student performance.

Participation in the general education class represents students' active engagement in the social and academic life of the classroom. Given the focus of this book, we emphasize participation in general education instructional routines. Through the lens of presumed competence, participation in general education instruction would reflect a vision of the student with IDD engaging in the same variety and frequency of instructional routines (e.g., large-group lecture, small-group cooperative activities, labs, seat work) in the same academic areas as students without disabilities. Working toward this vision would include exploring ways to enhance a student's communication system until he or she had an effective and efficient means through which to communicate academically (speaking, reading, writing, listening) about the same topics and in a way that was commensurate with same-age peers.

Enhancing Participation to Enhance Learning

During the orientation to the BA Model and in ongoing professional development provided to school teams (including administrators and parents), journal articles, book chapters, videos, and guest presentations from other educators, parents, or adults with disabilities are shared to emphasize the importance of participation in general education academic instruction.

As mentioned previously, although a student does not need to participate in general education academics all day, every day in order for a team to begin using the Model to enhance participation, we suggest that students are included in a general education classroom for at least two core academic subjects (i.e., math, language arts, social studies, science). The team then uses the BA Model to focus on improving instruction and supports (including AAC) to the student during these two periods of the day, prior to expanding the student's academic participation within other classroom lessons and activities.

Classroom instruction occurs through a variety of arrangements, such as writing on a black- or whiteboard; one-to-one instruction by an adult; partnering with a classmate in a learning activity; small-group teacher-directed instruction; student-managed cooperative learning groups; large-group lecture; large-group discussions; and a variety of individual learning activities such as seat work, library research, lab experiments, and so forth. Similar to tracking percentage time in class as a membership indicator, educators can also track the occurrence and distribution of engagement in instructional routines. The goal should be to move toward students' involvement in the same routines, in the same proportion, at the same times as classmates without disabilities, acknowledging, of course, individualization of supports.

The BA Model promotes instructional planning based on the notion that all students can participate and learn the general education curriculum when they are presumed competent, valued as true classroom members, and supported to fully participate. Consistent with this belief, the BA Model encourages teams to ask, "What supports are needed for this student to engage in the same lesson as his or her classmates?" As described at the beginning of this chapter, this question is crafted to move teams away from questions that presume high confidence in past measures of the student's present level of performance. To answer this question, a five-step planning process is used. Specific examples of implementing this planning process based on the work of BA teams are presented in Chapter 8.

The five-step framework for instructional planning for full participation is presented next.

1. Identify the subject and skill being taught (e.g., math: computation; reading: fluency).

2. Identify what classmates do to show that they are engaged in the instruction (e.g., listen to teacher, turn pages of a book, answer questions, fill in a worksheet).

3. Identify how the target student can demonstrate those same or similar behaviors through the same or alternate means of communicating or demonstrating engagement (e.g., depress switch to turn page of a book, select messages on SGD to answer questions, select messages on SGD and peer scribes answer onto worksheet).

4. Identify what supports the target student needs in order to participate and what supports would help elicit or teach the behaviors in Step 3 (e.g., switch connected to computer to read electronic book, modeling by peers using switches or SGD).

5. Identify what planning must be done by team members to ensure that the supports are available and delivered at the time they are needed (e.g., download electronic book and connect switch to computer, program the SGD with necessary messages or vocabulary).

Through the lens of participation (contrasted with the lens of learning), the first goal is for students to be engaged with the instruction delivered by the general education classroom teacher alongside and with their classmates. Even though they may not yet be demonstrating learning of the same curriculum content as their classmates, the target student is engaged in the learning process that is similar to their classmates.

Participation indicators can be used by teams to plan action steps if certain indicators are absent or partially present (see Table 4.2). Outcome measures of student participation within the general education classroom activities and routines are also used to monitor the effect of using the BA Model (see Chapter 7 for

Table 4.2. Sample indicators of student participation in general education classroom routines, activities, and lessons

The student participates in classroom and school routines (e.g., Pledge of Allegiance, lunch count, jobs, errands, eating lunch) in typical locations.

The student participates in school plays, field trips, and community service activities.

The student passes classes with other students, arriving and leaving at the same time.

The student participates in classroom instruction in similar routines as students without disabilities. For example, the student participates in whole-class discussions, at the board, in small groups, and when called on by the teacher.

The student has a way to communicate the same academic messages that are expected of other students in the instructional routines.

- *Whole-class discussions:* brainstorming, calling out answers, taking notes, engaging in social side talk
- *At the board:* writing answers, drawing figures
- *In small groups:* commenting to classmates, sharing information, taking notes, socializing
- *When called on by the teacher:* sharing information

The student completes assignments and other work products (with adaptations and modifications) as students without disabilities do.

A high school student engages in outside-of-school, age-appropriate, and inclusive environments (e.g., service learning) similar to classmates without disabilities.

a description and sample of the Student and Team Outcomes Survey). Examples that illustrate changes teams made to increase a student's participation in classroom instruction are presented next.

Tyler's teacher had not called on him to provide answers when checking class homework because he was not given homework. To remedy this, the teacher began assigning a few homework problems for Tyler. He completed the homework with his parents and practiced giving the answer when requested. In class, the teacher now calls on him to share an answer.

Theresa had been pulled out of class for sensory-motor activities to help organize her body. Sometimes she was pulled from group read-aloud activities because it was difficult to assist her to sit with the group on the floor during reading. To address this, the occupational therapist (OT) conducted an observation of how Theresa was supported to participate in the reading group. She generated a list of sensory-motor accommodations (e.g., bean bag chair, weighted blanket, fidget tools) and then provided occupational therapy services in class to model how to provide these accommodations to facilitate Theresa's participation in the reading group.

LEARNING

Researchers have called for instruction in academics to be an educational priority if students are to achieve desired outcomes and make progress (Browder, Wakeman, Spooner, Ahlgrim-Delzell, & Algozzine, 2006; Erickson & Koppenhaver, 1995). As discussed in both Chapters 1 and 2 of this book, there is research supporting the idea that students with IDD can learn academic content. Comprehensive reviews of the literature related to reading (Browder et al., 2006), mathematics (Browder, Spooner, Ahlgrim-Delzell, Wakeman, & Harris, 2008), and science (Courtade, Spooner, & Browder, 2007) provide additional examples of students with IDD acquiring academic skills. These syntheses, along with other qualitative studies and anecdotal reports, suggest that learning general education academics is not only relevant but also a priority for this population (see, for example, Erickson, Koppenhaver, Yoder, & Nance, 1997).

In addition, many researchers are beginning to rethink the notion that students with IDD may progress through the curriculum in a way that is quite different from students without disabilities. Mirenda noted

> Research supports that learners with and without disabilities may be more similar than previously thought. Most—if not all—students with autism can benefit from literacy instruction that incorporates the use of multiple instructional strategies that are carefully matched to the stages or phases of development through which all readers pass on their way from emergent reading to skilled reading. (2003, p. 275)

Learning as a Result of Membership and Participation

Promoting full membership and pursuing the five-step instructional planning process for a student's participation in the general education classroom described previously sets the stage for a student's demonstration of both anticipated and unanticipated learning. In a survey of 38 educators who had been using the BA Model for 6 months to promote membership and participation for five students (McSheehan et al., 2006), 56 examples of previously unexpected learning were reported in the areas of reading, writing, and math. Jay (the student from Chapter 1) had never been exposed to grade-level novels. Beginning in fifth grade, books were rewritten for him from a fifth-grade reading level to a second-grade reading level, while preserving the essential content. The text was enhanced with symbols and drawings of events from the book. Initially, these supports were put into place to foster Jay's participation with age-appropriate materials on the same topics as his classmates. Toward the end of the school year, however, after repeated engagement with the adapted novels, Jay began vocalizing as he independently turned pages in his books and tracked text with his index finger. He varied his intonation and began to pause on words and at the ends of sentences—similar to his classmates reading aloud. In addition, he participated in quizzes, tests, and an end-of-year review of all of the novels by selecting from multiple-choice formats programmed into his SGD. By selecting some of the right answers, Jay demonstrated that he had not only participated in the various instructional routines, but he also had learned some of the academic content expected of his classmates—which previously had not been expected of him.

Students with disabilities placed in a general education classroom for the majority of their day score higher on standardized measures of reading and math than students in other placements (Wagner et al., 2003). Large-scale, statewide assessment or standardized measures of achievement can provide an IEP team with academic learning outcome information about their student's educational program. Classroom-based measures of learning, however, are the most frequent and user-friendly measures for ongoing assessment and instructional improvement. These measures include grades on homework, quizzes, chapter tests, or projects. Such measures for students with IDD are essential to documenting and evaluating the efficacy of supports (see Chapter 7). In order to have this rich information at hand, teams must ensure that opportunities for students to complete relevant graded products are provided. Tracking these opportunities and monitoring for the number of products available for review will help IEP teams take advantage of this form of ongoing, authentic assessment. Tracking these opportunities and monitoring for the number of products relative to classmates may also be a helpful indicator of progress.

When using curriculum-based measures and other similar or standardized measures, it can be helpful to poll the IEP team for the collective impression regarding student achievement relative to grade-level expectations or general achievement standards. We have found wide discrepancies in team member perceptions of student proficiencies in academic content areas using an approach adapted from Ketterlin-Geller, Alonzo, Braun-Monegan, and Tindal (2007). Team members were asked to rate the student's performance relative to grade-level expectations on a scale from 1 (very low proficiency) to 5 (very high proficiency). The discrepancies provided an opportunity for the team to dialogue about what they consider evidence of learning and then to provide their individual rationales for why they perceive a student's present level of performance (proficiency) to be different from that of their teammates' perceptions.

CONCLUSION

This chapter described and provided a rationale for why membership, participation, and learning, anchored in the first best practice of presuming competence, are important best practices of the BA Model. In addition to the priorities chosen to enhance students' learning of general education curriculum content, teams must maintain a vigilant focus on membership and participation. Chapter 5 discusses the fifth core BA Best Practice—collaborative teaming.

REFERENCES

Brophy, J.E., & Good, T.L. (1986). Teacher behavior and student achievement. In M.C. Wittrock (Ed.), *Handbook of research on teaching* (3rd ed., pp. 328–375). New York: Macmillan.

Browder, D.M., Spooner, F., Ahlgrim-Delzell, L., Wakeman, S.Y., & Harris, A. (2008). A meta-analysis on teaching mathematics to students with significant cognitive disabilities. *Exceptional Children, 74,* 407–432.

Browder, D.M., Wakeman, S.Y., Spooner, F., Ahlgrim-Delzell, L., & Algozzine, B. (2006). Research on reading for individuals with significant cognitive disabilities. *Exceptional Children, 27*(4), 392–408.

Courtade, G., Spooner, F., & Browder, D.M. (2007). A review of studies with students with significant cognitive disabilities that link to science standards. *Research and Practice in Severe Disabilities, 32,* 43–49.

Dugan, E., Kamps, D., Leonard, B., Watkins, N., Rheinberger, A., & Stackhaus, J. (1995). Effects of cooperative learning groups during social studies for students with autism and fourth-grade peers. *Journal of Applied Behavior Analysis, 28,* 175–188.

Erickson, K., & Koppenhaver, D. (1995). Developing a literacy program for children with severe disabilities. *Reading Teacher, 48*(8), 676–684.

Erickson, K., Koppenhaver, D., Yoder, D., & Nance, J. (1997). Integrated communication and literacy instruction for a child with multiple disabilities. *Focus on Autism and Other Developmental Disabilities, 12*(3), 142–150.

Goodman, G., & Williams, C. (2007, July/August). Interventions for increasing the academic engagement of students with autism spectrum disorders in inclusive classrooms. *Teaching Exceptional Children,* 53–61.

Greenwood, C.R. (1991). Longitudinal analysis of time engagement, and achievement in at-risk versus no-risk students. *Exceptional Children, 57,* 521–534.

Habib, D. (Producer). (2007). *Including Samuel* [DVD]. Concord, NH: Author.

Helmstetter, E., Curry, C.A., Brennan, M., & Sampson-Saul, M. (1998). Comparison of general and special education classrooms of students with severe disabilities. *Education and Training in Mental Retardation and Developmental Disabilities, 33*(3), 216–227.

Hemmingsson, H., & Jonsson, H. (2005). An occupational perspective on the concept of participation in the International Classification of Functioning, Disability and Health: Some critical remarks. *American Journal of Occupational Therapy, 59,* 569–576.

Hunt, P., Farron-Davis, F., Beckstead, S., Curtis, D., & Goetz, L. (1994). Evaluating the effects of placement of students with severe disabilities in general education versus special classes. *Journal of The Association for Persons with Severe Handicaps, 19*(3), 200–214.

Kennedy, C.H., Cushing, L.S., & Itkonen, T. (1997). General education participation improves the social contacts and friendship networks of students with severe disabilities. *Journal of Behavioral Education, 7,* 167–189.

Ketterlin-Geller, L.R., Alonzo, J., Braun-Monegan, J., & Tindal, G. (2007). Recommendations for accommodations: Implications of (in) consistency. *Remedial and Special Education 28*(4), 194–206.

Kluth, P., Villa, R., & Thousand, J. (December 2001/January 2002). "Our school doesn't offer inclusion" and other legal blunders. *Educational Leadership, 59*(4), 24–27.

Kunc, N. (1992). The need to belong: Rediscovering Maslow's hierarchy of needs. In R. Villa, J. Thousand, W. Stainback, & S. Stainback (Eds.), *Restructuring for caring and effective education: An administrative guide to creating heterogeneous schools* (pp. 25–40). Baltimore: Paul H. Brookes Publishing Co.

Maslow, A. (1970). *Motivation and personality.* New York: Harper & Row.

McDonnell, J., Mathot-Buckner, C., Thorson, N., & Fister, S. (2001). Supporting the inclusion of students with moderate and severe disabilities in junior high school general education classes: The effects of classwide peer tutoring, multi-element curriculum, and accommodations. *Education and Treatment of Children, 24,* 141–160.

McSheehan, M., Sonnenmeier, R.M., & Jorgensen, C.M. (2009). Membership, participation, and learning in the general education classroom for students with autism spectrum disorders who use AAC. In D.R. Beukelman & J. Reichle (Series Eds.) & P. Mirenda & T. Iacono (Vol. Eds.), *Augmentative and alternative communication series: Autism spectrum disorders and AAC* (pp. 413–442). Baltimore: Paul H. Brookes Publishing Co.

McSheehan, M., Sonnenmeier, R.M., Jorgensen, C.M., & Turner, K. (2006). Beyond communication access: Promoting learning of the general education curriculum by students with significant disabilities. *Topics in Language Disorders, 26*(3), 266–290.

Mirenda, P. (2003). "He's not really a reader...": Perspectives on supporting literacy development in individuals with autism. *Topics in Language Disorders, 23*(4), 271–282.

National Joint Committee on the Communication Needs of Persons with Severe Disabilities (2002). Access to communication services and supports: Concerns regarding the application of restrictive "eligibility" policies (Technical report). *Communication Disorders Quarterly, 23,* 145–153.

Schnorr, R. (1990). "Peter? He comes and goes...": First graders' perspectives on a part-time mainstream student. *Journal of The Association for Persons with Severe Handicaps, 15*(4), 231–240.

Shukla, S., Kennedy, C.H., & Cushing, L.S. (1999). Intermediate school students with severe disabilities: Supporting their social participation in general education classrooms. *Journal of Positive Behavior Interventions, 1,* 130–140.

Strully, J. (2006, October). *Friendship and our children.* Symposium conducted at the New Hampshire Family and Consumer Leadership Series, Hampton Beach.

Strully, J., & Strully, C. (1985). Friendship and our children. *Journal of The Association for Persons with Severe Handicaps, 10*(4), 224–237.

Tashie, C., Shapiro-Barnard, S., & Rossetti, Z. (2006). *Seeing the charade: What we need to do and undo to make friendships happen.* Nottingham, United Kingdom: Inclusive Solutions.

Wagner, M., Marder, C., Blackorby, J., Cameto, R., Newman, L., Levine, P., et al. (2003). *The achievements of youth with disabilities during secondary school. A report from the National Longitudinal Transition Study-2 (NLTS2).* Menlo Park, CA: SRI International. Available at http://www.nlts2.org/reports/2003_11/nlts2_report_2003_11_complete.pdf

Werts, M.G., Caldwell, N.K., & Wolery, M. (1996). Peer modeling of response chains: Observational learning by students with disabilities. *Journal of Applied Behavior Analysis, 29,* 53–66.

Williams, L.J., & Downing, J.E. (1998). Membership and belonging in inclusive classrooms: What do middle school students have to say? *Journal of The Association for Persons with Severe Handicaps, 23*(2), 98–110.

World Health Organization. (2001). *The international classification of functioning, disability, and health.* Geneva, Switzerland: Author.

Collaborative Teaming

The desired student outcomes of membership, participation, communication, and learning are more likely to be achieved if a strong collaborative team is supportive of and actively engaged in using the BA Model. The importance of collaborative teaming as a BA Model strategy is consistent with the findings of more than 30 years of research on inclusive education. For example, Thousand and Villa noted that "in schools that have successfully restructured to meet the needs of all students, personnel consistently identify collaborative teams and the 'collaborative teaming' group decision-making process that they employ as keystones to their success" (1992, p. 73).

Team members are engaged from the first moment that the decision to use the BA Model is explored. Once team members agree to use the BA Model, they are active participants in each of the four phases of the Model. The team participates in the initial description of the student and reaches agreement on his or her strengths and educational needs. Team members also examine evidence of and then agree on *their own* strengths and needs. They work together to explore new supports for the student's membership, participation, and learning, and they work together on improving their own team collaboration. The team strives for fidelity in implementing supports that show promise for improving student and team outcomes. Team members agree on the indicators of effectiveness for evaluating both student and team supports, and they work with school administrators to ensure sustainability of new practices that are found to be effective.

Kaner's (1996) description of participatory groups aligns well with the description of a BA team. A participatory group is characterized by 1) participation by all, not just a few members; 2) the coexistence of opposing viewpoints; 3) shared understanding of all points of view; and 4) members supporting one another to express their points of view. By contrast, in a conventional group 1) "the fastest thinkers and most articulate speakers get more air time" (Kaner, 1996,

p. xiv); 2) differences of opinion are treated as conflict; 3) members do not know where one another stands; 4) minority views are rarely expressed; and 5) decisions are made by the loudest members or those with more positional power.

Although much is known about effective collaborative teaming, research and experience reveal that many teams struggle with how to implement effective collaborative teaming practices. Teams frequently face numerous systemic and organizational barriers to their members working together effectively, such as role confusion, lack of planning time, lack of access to professional development specific to students with IDD, and related service delivery models that are ineffective (Garmston & Wellman, 1999; Jorgensen, Fisher, Sax, & Skoglund, 1998; McCarthy et al., 1998; Rainforth, York, & Macdonald, 1992; Villa & Thousand, 1995). The BA Model actively engages teams (and administrators) in examining their existing collaborative teaming practices, identifying their strengths and areas of need, developing a plan for addressing those areas of need, and reviewing the effectiveness of the strategies implemented based on that plan.

Without duplicating here the existing work on collaborative teaming by others in the field, this chapter describes 1) the members of the IEP team, 2) team member dispositions and skills, 3) the role of the BA facilitator, and 4) the structures and processes through which the BA Model is implemented.

TEAM MEMBERSHIP

All members of a student's IEP team and someone who serves as the BA facilitator are integral to the activities and processes of the BA Model. Thus, the student's parents/guardians, a general education teacher or teachers, a special education teacher[1], and the many other professionals who are likely to be on the IEP team, such as an SLP, OT, physical therapist (PT), adaptive physical education teacher, paraprofessional, and, by law, a representative of the student's Local Education Agency (LEA), will all be involved in implementing the BA Model. Other team members may include a reading specialist, transition coordinator, AT specialist, hearing and vision specialists, behavior consultant, or other professionals from within or outside the school. The student him- or herself participates in the IEP team beginning in middle or early high school and may participate in some activities of the BA Model.

The BA facilitator can be one of the regular IEP team members, someone from the student's school district who is not a member of the student's team, or someone from outside the school district such as an educational consultant or university faculty member. The role of the BA facilitator is described in a subsequent section of this chapter.

---

[1]Special education teachers have different job titles, including case manager, case coordinator, learning specialist, or inclusion facilitator. This person may be a member of a student's building-based IEP team or may serve in an itinerant role across several schools in a district. In this book, we use the generic term *special education teacher*.

TEAM MEMBER DISPOSITIONS AND SKILLS

Chapters 6–9 describe the four phases of the BA Model. For each phase, particular dispositions are needed by team members in order to engage that phase's activities most effectively. Presuming positive intentions is the one overarching team member disposition that must be present in every aspect of team members' work (Garmston & Wellman, 1999).

When team members presume one another's positive intentions—toward the student, the student's family, and other team members—honest and open conversation about important matters is possible. Team members are effective when they take others' comments at face value. Presuming positive intentions reduces the possibility of one team member perceiving threats or challenges from another. Team members who presume one another's positive intentions act as if others mean well by validating their concerns, acknowledging their questions, and maintaining a nondefensive posture. When team members presume one another's positive intentions, they are more likely to restrain impulsive responses that can be triggered by their own emotions.

Two types of skills are needed by the various team members: 1) disciplinary skills related to their professional role on the team and 2) communication skills for engaging in productive conversations during and outside of team meetings. A description of disciplinary skills is beyond the scope of this chapter. Table 5.1 depicts a chart that one BA team developed to clarify each member's role in support of the student. Other BA teams may choose to create a similar chart to clarify their roles. Many authors have identified communication skills that promote effective collaborative teaming, and the skills in Table 5.2 are particularly relevant to engaging in the BA Model activities.

BEYOND ACCESS FACILITATOR DISPOSITIONS AND SKILLS

There are many professionals working in schools today who have the skills and dispositions necessary to serve as a BA facilitator to support teams using the BA Model. The BA facilitator might be a special education teacher who has experience in inclusive education and who has a number of students with intensive support needs on her caseload. The BA facilitator might be a related services provider (e.g., SLP, OT) who not only has disciplinary experience and skills but also credibility among his or her colleagues with respect to students' overall educational needs (not just those related to communication, movement, or sensory challenges, for example). The BA facilitator likely has many years of experience working with students with diverse needs; has additional training beyond his or her initial degree, certification, or license; and has taken a leadership role in promoting inclusive education in the school. It is likely that the BA facilitator will not only serve in the role of facilitator of the BA Model but will also provide input as a disciplinary expert. Balancing these two roles will require the BA facilitator to be clear about which role he or she is in at any one particular time.

The BA facilitator's role is defined as much by what he or she does not do as by what he or she does. The BA facilitator is *not* a parent advocate. He or she is

Table 5.1. Sample team member roles and responsibilities chart

Team member	Roles and responsibilities
General education teacher	Consider the learning styles and needs of all students when planning lessons and units
	Identify supports needed to successfully include students in all classroom activities and instruction
	Communicate the need for student and classroom supports to appropriate team members and administrators
	Participate in planning for and implementing accommodations and modifications
	Facilitate student interactions
	Work with the special education teacher to write progress reports and report cards
Paraprofessional	Facilitate interactions among students
	Support the student's use of augmentative and alternative communication (AAC)
	Provide instructional and other supports under the direction and supervision of professional staff
	Support the successful use of technology throughout the student's day
	Create modified instructional materials under the direction and supervision of professional staff
Special education teacher	Facilitate team meetings, communicate with parents, and monitor the provision of supports to the student
	Coordinate the input from consultants
	Ensure that the paraprofessional gets the support needed to fulfill his or her role
	Know, monitor, and troubleshoot what is coming up with the general educational program
	Facilitate the educational and social applications of AAC and other technology
	Model strategies and techniques for the paraprofessional
	Instruct substitute educators on the needs of the student
	Collect data for the purpose of determining the accuracy of support and monitoring student performance
	Work with the classroom teacher to write progress reports and report cards
Speech-language pathologist	Ensure that the paraprofessional gets the support needed to fulfill his or her role
	Meet with consultants after school visits
	Develop and supervise the accomplishment of communication goals within school activities/routines
Occupational therapist/certified occupational therapist assistant	Support the paraprofessional to learn occupational therapy strategies and fulfill his or her role
	Demonstrate, model, and train the paraprofessional and other team members in appropriate areas
	Plan and work with consultants to ensure the student's success

Role	Responsibilities
Physical therapist	Support the paraprofessional to learn physical therapy strategies and fulfill his or her role Demonstrate, model, and train the paraprofessional and other team members in appropriate areas Plan and work with the team to ensure the student's participation and learning
Reading specialist	Provide literacy supports and services to students Demonstrate, model, and train the paraprofessional and other team members in literacy supports and strategies Plan and work with the team and consultants to ensure the student's successful literacy learning
Consultants	Collaborate with the family and other members of the student's team to ensure the student's successful membership, participation, and learning in an age-appropriate general education classroom Work with administrators to shift policies and practices to better support inclusive education Demonstrate, model, and train appropriate team members in instructional strategies, inclusive lesson planning/design, augmentative communication strategies and technologies, curriculum modifications, positive behavior supports, and facilitation of peer relationships, based on identified student and team needs Provide updates to the team and school administrators on a regular basis, particularly after visits Monitor the efficacy of consultation services through meetings with the team, building-level special education administrator, principal, and district-level special education director
Principal	Provide support and resources in order to ensure the successful education of students Communicate and collaborate regularly with building-level special education administrators and district-level special education directors Ensure the fidelity of implementation of the Beyond Access (BA) Model Demonstrate inclusive values through leadership and administrative activities Allocate resources as necessary Support inclusive practices through professional development and staff supervision
Special education director	Provide support and resources in order to ensure the successful inclusion of students in age-appropriate general education classrooms in their neighborhood schools Communicate and collaborate regularly with building-level special education administrators and principals Ensure the fidelity of implementation of the BA Model Allocate resources as necessary Ensure that relevant special education laws and regulations are being followed

Table 5.2. Descriptions and indicators of team member communication skills

Pausing

Effective team members pause during conversation and discussion for a variety of purposes. Pausing encourages active listening by team members. When a group monitors for the use of pausing, their productivity and satisfaction increases.

Indicators

Team members listen attentively to others' ideas.

Team members allow time for others to think after asking a question or making a response.

Team members paraphrase silently what others are saying to further understand their communications.

Team members wait until others have finished before entering a conversation.

Paraphrasing

Effective team members paraphrase to promote mutual understanding and valuing of others' contributions. Paraphrasing validates what another has said, fosters active listening, and accommodates different team members' learning styles. When a group monitors for paraphrasing, their work becomes clearer and more cohesive.

Indicators

Team members use paraphrases that acknowledge and clarify content and emotions.

Team members use paraphrases that summarize and organize.

Team members use paraphrases that relate a topic of conversation from specific examples to broader themes and vice versa.

Probing for specificity

Effective team members seek to clarify information before engaging in decision making. Problem definition, problem solving, and solution generation all rely on specificity for success.

Indicators

Team members seek agreement on the meaning of words.

Team members ask questions to clarify facts, ideas, and stories.

Team members ask questions to clarify explanations, implications, and consequences.

Team members ask questions to uncover assumptions, points of view, beliefs, and values.

Putting ideas on the table and taking them off

Effective team members share their ideas. Knowing when and how to pull ideas off the table is equally important. Ideas can be both facts (e.g., data about student learning, school events, teacher demographics) and impressions (e.g., opinions about what student outcomes tell us about their learning style, support needs, or motivation).

Indicators

Team members state the intention of their communication ("I'd like to offer a comment that may add some information to this discussion." Or, "I'd like to make a suggestion that may help us get unstuck.").

Team members reveal all relevant information related to the idea.

Team members consider the intended communication for relevance and appropriateness before speaking.

Team members state facts, inferences, ideas, opinions, and suggestions.

Team members explain reasons behind statements, questions, and actions.

Team members withdraw or announce the modification of their own ideas, opinions, and points of view.

Team members maintain focus on one agenda topic at a time.

Paying attention to self and others

Effective team members are attentive to themselves and to others. Meaningful dialogue and discussion are fostered when team members show awareness of what they are saying, how they are saying it, and how others are receiving and responding to their ideas.

Indicators

Team members maintain awareness of their own thoughts and feelings while having them.

Team members maintain awareness of their own voice patterns, including tone of voice and rate of speech.

Team members maintain awareness of their own nonverbal communication, including the use of eye contact, gestures, and facial expressions.

Team members maintain awareness of their own use of physical space.

Team members maintain awareness of others' voice patterns, including tone of voice and rate of speech.

Team members maintain awareness of others' nonverbal communication, including the use of eye contact, gestures, and facial expressions.

Team members maintain awareness of others' use of physical space.

Team members maintain awareness of the group's task, mood, and relevance of own and others' contributions.

Pursuing a balance between advocacy and inquiry

Team members increase their effectiveness when they create a balance between advocating for their point of view and inquiring about others' points of view. To balance means to spend equal amounts of time and energy advocating for one's own ideas and inquiring into the ideas of others.

Indicators

Team members advocate for their own ideas.

Team members inquire into the ideas of others.

Team members act to provide equitable opportunities for participation by encouraging all team members to contribute to the conversation.

Team members present rationale for positions, including underlying assumptions, facts, and personal feelings.

Team members disagree respectfully and openly with ideas and offer a rationale for disagreement.

Team members ask others about their reasons for reaching and occupying a position.

From Garmston, R.J., & Wellman, B.M. (1999). *The adaptive school: A sourcebook for developing collaborative groups* (pp. 37–47). Norwood, MA: Christopher-Gordon Publishers; adapted by permission.

an advocate for the student's membership, participation, and learning and sees his or her role as helping the team to do its best work by using the BA Model. The BA facilitator does *not* supplant the role of the special education teacher or any other team member. He or she may supplement the roles of other team members and share his or her expertise with them. The BA facilitator does *not* make decisions about what the team will or will not do to support the student. He or she does help the team consider many options and make sustainable decisions for the benefit of the student. And the BA facilitator does *not* serve in a supervisory or evaluative role. Whether he or she is an in-district employee or an outside consultant, his or her role is to support the team with the ultimate goal of increasing their capacity to implement the BA Model's Best Practices.

Three broad sets of skills are needed by the BA facilitator to successfully implement the BA Model: 1) management and administration skills; 2) data collection, analysis, and synthesis skills; and 3) facilitation skills.

Management and Administration Skills

A critical role of the BA facilitator is managing information and data related to a team's use of the BA Model (taking care not to unnecessarily duplicate information kept in the student's cumulative folder). The BA facilitator is responsible for coordinating the collection and organization of students records (including the student's IEP and previous evaluations); local and state curriculum frameworks, standards, and/or grade-level expectations; and correspondence with the team, including the student's parent/guardian, related to the BA Model. As the team works through each phase of the Model, additional documents need to be organized and managed, including 1) the CASTS findings and recommendations (Phase 1); 2) data collected regarding potential supports and strategies (Phase 2); 3) student and team support plans, team members' professional development plans, and performance data related to the implementation of student and team supports (Phase 3); and 4) materials related to referrals and input from the ALT (Phase 4). In addition, the BA facilitator assumes responsibility for scheduling meetings, maintaining meeting minutes, arranging for professional development activities, and managing resource materials related to BA Best Practices (e.g., journal articles, book chapters, AT).

It is particularly helpful for all of the documents and data to be archived in digital form. It is also helpful for the BA facilitator to keep paper copies in a collection of three-ring binders stored in a secure location. Rather than prescribe an organizational framework for managing and administrating, we encourage each BA facilitator to use a system that works best for his or her style and the team's needs.

Data Collection, Analysis, and Synthesis Skills

The BA Model involves an iterative process of collection, analysis, and synthesis of data that are considered by the team in making decisions about student and team supports. During the CASTS (Phase 1), the BA facilitator is responsible for 1) creating and administering team member questionnaires and interviews; 2) reviewing and synthesizing information from student, team, and school records and artifacts; 3) conducting and documenting observations; and 4) summarizing and synthesizing all of the data collected for themes. It is essential that the BA facilitator be skilled in probing for a deeper understanding and synthesizing what has been learned. For example, the BA facilitator is responsible for developing a CASTS summary that integrates often disparate bits of information into a cohesive story about the student and team's current performance within a current context that then forms the foundation for making decisions for how to proceed with the next phase of the Model. These data collection, analysis, and synthesis skills are necessary as the team moves through each phase of the Model and makes decisions about which student and team supports to explore and describe (Phase 2), implement and document (Phase 3), and review and sustain (Phase 4). The quality of the decisions made rests, in part, on the quality of the data collected and the analysis and synthesis of those data.

Facilitation Skills

A third set of skills relates to facilitating team meetings, team member skills, data review, and sustainable decision making. A *facilitator* is

> An individual who enables groups and organizations to work more effectively; to collaborate and achieve synergy. She or he is a "content neutral" party who by not taking sides or expressing or advocating a point of view during the meeting, can advocate for fair, open, and inclusive procedures to accomplish the group's work. A facilitator can also be a learning or a dialogue guide to assist a group in thinking deeply about its assumptions, beliefs and values, and about its systematic processes and context. (Kaner, 1996, p. xi)

A facilitator encourages the full participation of everyone in the group, promotes mutual or shared understanding, fosters inclusive and sustainable solutions, and teaches team members new thinking skills (Kaner, 1996).

An effective BA facilitator works with the team to implement the BA Model through specific skills (or role dimensions) including coaching, mentoring, presenting, and mediating (Garmston & Wellman, 1999; Jorgensen, Schuh, & Nisbet, 2006). These skills are used in a variety of contexts such as during team meetings, classroom observations, and professional development workshops. Descriptions of these skills and corresponding indicators are depicted in Table 5.3. Examples of

Table 5.3. Descriptions and indicators of Beyond Access facilitator skills

Managing

Managing information and data related to using the Beyond Access (BA) Model is an essential skill. Documents need to be organized; correspondence with team members, including family members, needs to be documented; professional development plans need to be monitored; and schedules need to be managed throughout each phase of implementing the BA Model.

Indicators

The BA facilitator coordinates collecting and organizing the student's records (including the student's individualized education program [IEP] and previous evaluations).

(continued)

Table 5.3. *(continued)*

The BA facilitator coordinates collecting and organizing local and state curriculum frameworks, standards, and/or grade-level expectations.

The BA facilitator manages correspondence with the team, including the student's parent/guardian, related to the BA Model.

The BA facilitator organizes and manages an archive of BA Model documents including:

- The Comprehensive Assessment of Student and Team Supports (CASTS) findings and recommendations (Phase 1)
- Data collected regarding potential supports and strategies (Phase 2)
- Student and team support plans, team members' professional development plans, and performance data related to the implementation of student and team supports (Phase 3)
- Materials related to referrals and input from the administrative leadership team (ALT) (Phase 4)

The BA facilitator schedules meetings and maintains meeting minutes.

The BA facilitator arranges for professional development activities and manages resource materials related to BA Best Practices (e.g., journal articles, book chapters, assistive technology [AT]).

Collecting, analyzing, and synthesizing data

The BA Model involves an iterative process of collection, analysis, and synthesis of data that are considered by the team in making decisions about student and team supports. It is essential that the BA facilitator be skilled in collecting, analyzing, and synthesizing data. These skills are necessary as the team moves through each phase of the Model for making decisions about which student and team supports are needed to complete a CASTS (Phase 1), explore and describe (Phase 2), implement and document (Phase 3), and review and sustain (Phase 4). The quality of the decisions made rests, in part, on the quality of the data collected and the analysis and synthesis of those data.

Indicators

The BA facilitator creates and administers team member questionnaires and interviews.

The BA facilitator reviews and synthesizes information from student, team, and school records; student work samples; and other artifacts.

The BA facilitator conducts and documents observations of student and team performance.

The BA facilitator summarizes and synthesizes often disparate bits of information into a cohesive story about the student and team's performance.

The BA facilitator collects and synthesizes team reflections on student and team performance.

Promoting best practices within the system

BA facilitators are uniquely positioned with their teams and within their school systems to see evidence of best practices. They are also positioned to educate others about best practices and assist team members, administrators, and others in the school community about the need for improvement.

Indicators

The BA facilitator develops and maintains close working relationships with schoolwide committees, including the school board, PTA, or community council.

The BA facilitator uses leadership skills to promote quality inclusive education, students' access to AAC and AT, and general school reform and systems change.

The BA facilitator provides sustained support to teams as they make decisions regarding students' educational programs.

The BA facilitator coordinates and provides professional development for professionals, administrators, paraprofessionals, family members, and the general community regarding best practices in inclusive education and communication supports for students with disabilities.

The BA facilitator promotes the development of students' self-determination and the leadership skills of their families by connecting them with self-advocacy and community resources.

Facilitating

BA facilitators lead meetings in which the purpose is increasing shared understanding of an issue and shared decision making, planning, or problem solving. The BA facilitator directs the processes used in the meeting, manages the energy within the group, and maintains a focus on one topic and one process at a time. BA facilitators must balance their role as facilitator of a meeting with their role within the school system and their role based on their professional expertise.

Indicators

The BA facilitator has knowledge of his or her cognitive style, beliefs, emotional states, intentions, strengths, and limitations.

The BA facilitator ensures facilitation decisions are based on group needs rather than on personal preferences.

The BA facilitator understands the team's culture, developmental level, group dynamics and history, relationship with the BA facilitator, external environment, and conflicting demands.

The BA facilitator applies this understanding of him- or herself and the team to ensure facilitation decisions are individualized to the group.

The BA facilitator utilizes a variety of models and tools to understand team dynamics, including tools to understand individual personalities, learning styles, and varying levels of concern across different topics.

The BA facilitator focuses the team on clear outcomes and supports them to achieve those outcomes.

In meetings, the BA facilitator ensures that the team maintains their focus on one topic and uses one process at a time.

The BA facilitator encourages shared facilitation of meetings.

The BA facilitator evaluates his or her success as a leader relative to team outcomes, including the degree of shared understanding of issues, shared decision making, efficient and effective planning, and problem solving.

When leading meetings, the BA facilitator monitors for and addresses any effects due to his or her role within the system and his or her knowledge from professional expertise.

The BA facilitator varies the ways that team members participate in meetings by using techniques such as open dialogue and discussion, structured dialogue and discussion, formal presentations and reports, case study analysis, and small-group work.

Presenting

BA facilitators present information to team members to increase knowledge and skills and to affect attitudes. When BA facilitators act as presenters, they adopt many stances—expert, colleague, novice, or friend—and use many strategies of presentation, such as lectures, cooperative learning, study groups, and simulations.

Indicators

The BA facilitator presents information in a manner that is clear and organized.

The BA facilitator uses technology for presenting (e.g., PowerPoint) as appropriate.

The BA facilitator uses a variety of strategies for presenting including lectures, cooperative learning, study groups, and simulations to accommodate different learning styles.

The BA facilitator varies presentation strategies and activities relative to the desired outcome (i.e., increasing knowledge, improving skills, changing attitudes).

Consulting

BA facilitators provide technical information and advocate for best practices by consulting with team members and others within the school and community.

Indicators

The BA facilitator is knowledgeable about best practices in curriculum supports for students with intellectual and/or other developmental disabilities (IDD).

(continued)

Table 5.3. *(continued)*

The BA facilitator is knowledgeable about best practices in communication supports for students with IDD.

The BA facilitator is knowledgeable about team dynamics and team collaboration.

The BA facilitator is responsive to individual team member's requests for consultation and assists them to develop priorities for consultation relative to the entire team's needs.

The BA facilitator provides technical information to team members regarding best practices in educating students with IDD.

The BA facilitator provides technical information to team members regarding best practices in team collaboration to support students with IDD.

Modeling

BA facilitators model when they provide exemplars of specific skills or complexes of skills. Modeling can involve talking aloud about one's rationale and underlying thoughts related to the particular behavior modeled.

Indicators

The BA facilitator models best practices to promote the development of team members' professional expertise.

The BA facilitator models best practices to build organizational capacity (e.g., facilitating effective meetings, pausing and paraphrasing in meeting interactions).

As a teaching strategy, the BA facilitator talks aloud about the rationale and underlying thoughts related to a particular behavior modeled.

The BA facilitator practices skills in front of individual team members and the entire team.

The BA facilitator utilizes information about him- or herself, individual team members, and the team as a whole to prioritize which skills he or she will model.

The BA facilitator self-evaluates his or her performance of a skill in front of individual team members and the team as a whole.

The BA facilitator solicits feedback from individual team members and the team as a whole on his or her use of that skill.

Coaching

BA facilitators coach team members to take action toward their own goals. They coach by observing and providing feedback from a nonjudgmental stance. When coaching, BA facilitators support team members to reflect on their practices and evaluate their own performance.

Indicators

The BA facilitator educates team members on the dynamics and benefits of coaching.

The BA facilitator conducts observations of team members working with each other and with the student.

The BA facilitator observes at times when skills from the student and team support plans and the professional development plans may be demonstrated.

The BA facilitator elicits the team member's impressions of observed events and perceptions of that team member's own performance.

The BA facilitator provides feedback to team members in a timely fashion based on information gathered through direct observation.

The BA facilitator gives feedback from a nonjudgmental stance, using previously agreed-on criteria to assess performance.

The BA facilitator balances praise and critical feedback.

The BA facilitator directs team members to relevant professional development resources as appropriate.

Mediating

Effective teams keep their attention focused on increasing their professional and organizational capacity to improve student outcomes. BA facilitators mediate when team interactions stray from this focus. BA facilitators might mediate with the entire team during a meeting or between two team members in a private conversation. BA facilitators mediate in a nonjudgmental way that all members recognize as supportive.

Indicators

The BA facilitator focuses team members' attention on those professional and organizational activities that improve student outcomes.

The BA facilitator mediates interactions of team members in a nonjudgmental way if they stray from their priority focus.

The BA facilitator mediates between (two or more) team members in private as needed.

The BA facilitator mediates between (two or more) team members if conflict around ideas or relationships interferes with broader team efforts.

The BA facilitator applies knowledge of self, individual team members, and the team as a whole to the mediation process.

Supporting continuous improvement

Monitoring for improvement involves collecting information on individual or team performance relative to student learning and supporting the development and implementation of professional development or systems change plans.

Indicators

The BA facilitator fosters an understanding of and a value for continuous improvement.

The BA facilitator uses reflective practice tools to structure conversations about continuous improvement.

The BA facilitator supports the team to develop mutually agreed-on priorities for continuous improvement based on desired outcomes for student and team performance.

The BA facilitator develops and implements systems for collecting information that reflect the team's priorities and distributes responsibility for collecting that information across the team.

The BA facilitator guides reflection on themes that emerge from the information, paying particular attention to individual and/or team working patterns.

The BA facilitator relates reflection on working patterns to the desired outcomes for student and team performance.

The BA facilitator guides the formulation of new priorities for continuous improvement.

---

how the BA facilitator supports the team in the implementation of each phase of the BA Model are provided in Chapters 6–9. Finally, the BA facilitator implements a variety of team structures and processes to organize the team and to support the team's ability to create sustainable agreements as described in the next section.

MEETING STRUCTURES

Five team structures help to organize BA meetings.

1. Identifying the meeting purpose
2. Setting a meeting agenda appropriate to the purpose of the meeting

3. Identifying who needs to attend a meeting

4. Identifying meeting process roles

5. Choosing and maintaining a conducive meeting environment

Table 5.4 depicts observable indicators of each of the structures described next.

Table 5.4. Descriptions and indicators of meeting structures

Purposes

Effective teams have different meetings to accomplish different goals. Effective teams have clearly defined purposes for different meetings. When there is a shared understanding of the purpose of the meeting, time is more efficiently utilized doing the work of the meeting.

Indicators

Team members define and agree on the purposes of meetings, such as meetings for case management, unit/lesson planning, and individualized education program (IEP) development.

Team members define and agree on the desired outcomes (products) for the meeting for each topic on the agenda.

Meeting time is utilized to develop action steps that will be taken outside of meeting time.

Agendas

A clearly defined agenda and using the appropriate agenda format based on the purpose of the meeting support the overall effectiveness and efficiency of the meeting.

Indicators

Different agenda formats are defined and used for case management meetings, unit/lesson planning meetings, and IEP meetings.

Agenda items are chosen according to the purpose and desired outcomes for the meeting.

A flexible timetable is developed for addressing each item on a meeting agenda.

Team members address agenda items that are within their capacity to influence.

At the end of each meeting, the next meeting's agenda is planned.

"Meeting evaluation" is an agenda item for all meetings.

Attendance

Meetings are most effective when the right people attend the meeting. This supports the effective and efficient use of each team member's time.

Indicators

Based on the agenda, those who should attend each meeting are identified and invited.

There is an accountability structure in place for attendance at meetings.

There is a structure in place for sharing the decisions and action steps with team members who are unable to attend a meeting.

Roles

Shared leadership of responsibilities within the meeting encourages a sense of community and ownership of the meeting process. Rotation of meeting roles and responsibilities is critical to meeting success.

Indicators

Team members agree on meeting roles.

"Meeting roles" (e.g., facilitator, timekeeper, notetaker) are assigned in each meeting.

Meeting roles are rotated on a regular basis, which reflects a commitment to distributed leadership.

Environment

The environment contributes to the overall productivity of team members as they participate in meetings. Environments that have few distractions and a comfortable arrangement of the table and chairs contribute to team members' abilities to attend to the work of the meeting.

Indicators

The meeting location is chosen to maximize effective and efficient work of the team.

Team members arrange the meeting room environment in accordance with the meeting purpose and agenda.

All team members, including the facilitator, are able to see and hear one another.

The seating arrangement allows team members to focus on flipchart paper or other writing devices and the facilitator.

From Jorgensen, C., McSheehan, M., & Cicolini, N. (2002). *Structures, processes, and skills for teaming that promote learning of general education curriculum content for students with the most significant disabilities.* Durham: University of New Hampshire, Institute on Disability.

Purposes

The BA Model is unique by acknowledging that different meeting purposes require different meeting agendas. There are BA meetings for instructional planning, for case management, for IEP development or review, for problem solving, and for meetings related to specific activities within particular phases of the Model (e.g., the CASTS findings and recommendations meeting). Several BA teams decided to have a BA instructional planning meeting once per week during the first 3 weeks of the month and then to have a meeting during the fourth week of the month solely devoted to case management. By using this strategy, they found that their instructional planning was more efficient because they were not distracted by dealing with case management issues (e.g., ordering equipment or supplies, talking about field trips, addressing issues related to service provision).

Agendas

It follows that meetings held for different purposes should have agendas individually tailored to the desired outcomes from the meeting. Instructional planning meeting agendas provide specific placeholders for the team to 1) review the student's performance during the previous week, 2) hear from the general education teacher about the focus for upcoming lessons, 3) discuss specific supports the student will need to fully participate in and communicate about those lessons, and 4) determine what preparation will need to be done in order to have adapted materials and other supports ready for use in those lessons. Case management meeting agendas focus on issues such as scheduling, service delivery, reports of evaluations, grading, and so forth. Both types of agendas provide prompts for the team to review progress on past to-do items and to generate new action items and the person responsible. A sample instructional planning meeting agenda is presented in Chapter 7.

Attendance

Some people might think that it is desirable for every member of a student's team to be present for every meeting. For teams using the BA Model, there is deliberate care taken to determine which team members need to be at which meetings, accompanied by a strategy for communicating essential information to those who may not be present. Jorgensen, Schuh, and Nisbet (2006) and others have written extensively about the instructional planning process and readers are encouraged to consult those references for details. Instructional planning meetings ought to include those team members who have information about

- The themes and learning goals of upcoming lessons and units
- The routines through which instruction will occur (e.g., whole class, small group, individual investigation)
- The cultural norms of the classroom (including behavioral expectations)
- The vocabulary that will be used during the lesson
- The materials and other resources that will be used by students to support their understanding and demonstration of what they are learning
- The general and individualized instructional approaches that will meet both the student's needs and integrate well with classroom routines
- The standards for performance and how students will be assessed

These meetings are usually attended by the general education classroom teacher, the special education teacher, an English language learners (ELLs) teacher (if appropriate), the paraprofessional (if one is on the team), and one or more related services providers (in our experience, most often the SLP and OT attend depending on the student's needs). The BA facilitator may attend all instructional planning meetings early in the team's use of the BA Model and then attend on a less frequent basis as the team's confidence and skill increase. Attendance at instructional planning meetings by parents/guardians is welcome, as they usually have valuable information that can inform instructional planning (e.g., making the team aware of a passionate interest that may be incorporated into a lesson or unit [Kluth & Schwarz, 2008]).

A case management meeting, which typically occurs less frequently than an instructional planning meeting, is attended by most members of the team, particularly if its purpose is to discuss and make decisions about service provision, transition, participation in large-scale assessments, behavior, or the myriad of other issues that comprise the elements of a student's educational program.

Roles

Thousand and Villa (1992) suggested that members of a collaborative team ought to rotate roles during meetings. They postulated that if each team member had to take his or her turn facilitating a meeting, recording the meeting minutes, keeping team members on topic, and supporting the completion of the agenda items in the allotted time, then the following results would occur: a greater sense of group cohesion, better team meeting behavior, efficient use of the time available for meeting, fewer conflicts, and more sustainable decisions.

Although the research on this aspect of collaborative teaming is largely anecdotal, we do suggest that BA team members rotate roles. In one BA team, the paraprofessional was not attending meetings consistently because it was her responsibility to get the BA student off the bus in the morning (when the meeting was held). Once the team began rotating roles, they realized that all team members would have to share the bus duty in order to ensure that the paraprofessional would be able to fulfill her meeting role.

Environment

Readers will be familiar with the difficulties of trying to have a productive team meeting when the door is constantly opening and closing, when announcements come over the loudspeaker, when there is no wall space for flip chart notetaking, and when team members cannot locate key materials related to the team meeting purpose. Rarely can a separate space in the school be dedicated solely to BA meetings, so it is likely that the team will be using space that also has other purposes. It can be made more hospitable to productive BA team meetings if the following conditions are met.

- The same space is used for every meeting.
- A sign is posted on the door that states, "Team meeting in progress. Interruptions for emergencies only. Thank you!"
- Previous team meeting minutes are available for ready reference.
- There is a way to group adult-size chairs around a common table for face-to-face conversation.
- There is wall space for hanging flip chart paper.

TEAM PROCESSES

Many team processes are used within the BA Model. Although team members may expect the BA facilitator to guide the use of these processes, it is beneficial for all team members to understand them. Table 5.5 presents definitions and observable indicators for each of the following team processes.

- Building community and team identity
- Setting and maintaining group norms
- Building sustainable agreements
- Reflecting on practice
- Resolving conflicts
- Maintaining communication and record keeping
- Collaborating to provide instruction and supports

Table 5.5.　Descriptions and indicators of team processes

Building community and team identity

Establishing and nurturing a sense of community is an ongoing task in an effective and inclusive school. Teams commit to doing community- and team-building activities while they are in their formative stages, when their work together is going smoothly, and when there are conflicts that impede their effective functioning.

Indicators

Team members engage in "get to know one another" activities, including sharing personal stories and professional experiences.

Team members define their roles and responsibilities.

Teams create their own rituals (e.g., birthdays, snacks) and celebrate their successes.

Team members support one another during times of personal stress or crisis.

Team members characterize their interactions with words such as *trust, confidence,* and *confidentiality.*

Setting and maintaining group norms

Each member of the team is held accountable for behavior that contributes to the effectiveness of the whole team when teams establish and maintain norms that govern when and why they meet, how they communicate with one another, how they resolve conflicts, how they make decisions, and how they assure confidentiality.

Indicators

Teams set norms related to group behavior.

Teams develop procedures for personal and group accountability to their group norms.

Building sustainable agreements

Building "sustainable agreements" (Kaner, 1996) is the primary purpose of collaborative teaming for students with intellectual and/or other developmental disabilities (IDD). Effective teams use structured processes for gathering diverse points of view, building a shared framework of understanding, developing workable solutions to problems, developing consensus, reaching closure, and articulating action steps.

Indicators

Teams decide who needs to be involved in which decisions.

Teams use brainstorming and creative thinking activities to gather diverse points of view and ideas.

Teams use strategies to explore possible solutions to problems.

Teams generate alternative solutions when appropriate.

Teams create guidelines that specify the level of agreement or consensus necessary for making different decisions.

Team members use processes such as voting to see how close they are to agreement.

Team members use "decision rules" for coming to closure on decisions.

Team members use efficient processes for determining the action steps necessary for implementing decisions.

Reflecting on practice

Effective teams use student learning as the benchmark for determining their own effectiveness. They continually reflect on all aspects of their professional practice to improve their individual skills and their team efficacy.

Indicators

Teams use reflective practice protocols to solve problems, examine student work, and change systems.

Teams participate in study groups or action research projects to reflect on their practice in light of student learning outcomes, new knowledge, and their own experiences.

Teams evaluate their own effectiveness in a systematic way on a regular basis relative to student learning outcomes.

Teams use reflective practice to improve their individual professional capabilities.

Teams use reflective practice to improve their collective collaboration capabilities.

Resolving conflicts

Conflicts arise within every team. Effective teams acknowledge this and use structured processes to address differences in ideas, repair relationships, improve members' communication skills, and mediate win-win solutions.

Indicators

Teams identify two kinds of conflict—conflict around ideas and conflict around relationships.

Teams openly address each type of conflict as it arises.

When trying to resolve differences, team members state their individual needs and interests clearly rather than arguing for a specific position or point of view.

Teams strive for win-win solutions rather than "I win, you lose" solutions.

Teams respond to conflict around ideas by seeking clarification, engaging in dialogue to understand the ideas, and engaging in discussion to achieve a resolution.

Teams respond to conflict around relationships by identifying the source of conflict, engaging in dialogue to understand the issues related to the relationship, and identifying ways to work together more effectively.

Teams call on the services of an impartial mediator if their effectiveness is diminished because of internal conflicts.

Teams acknowledge the negative effect that interpersonal conflicts have on negotiating student supports and carrying out their professional responsibilities.

Maintaining communication and record keeping

Maintaining communication within a large team requires establishing and consistently using a variety of communication processes.

Indicators

Teams record and share meeting notes or minutes to keep all members, including families, informed.

Teams use electronic communication when appropriate to communicate with one another.

Teams record meeting notes (including chart paper recordings) that capture the clearest statements that summarize important meeting content and process.

Team members communicate with one another outside of meetings to complete team assignments.

Team members communicate with one another prior to meetings regarding upcoming meeting topics.

(continued)

Table 5.5. *(continued)*

Collaborating to provide instruction and supports

Providing effective instruction and support to students with IDD often requires that team members work together in the classroom and in other inclusive school and community environments. Team members use proven coteaching and other collaborative processes to maximize their effectiveness and student learning.

Indicators

When appropriate, related services staff work together with students as they provide direct services.

Team members collaborate to write reports related to student assessments and other aspects of students' educational program.

Team members engage in curriculum planning meetings.

Team members engage in case management meetings.

Team members observe, coach, and give feedback to one another while providing instruction and support to students.

Readers can find abundant resources on many of these team collaboration processes but fewer resources are available to help teams make sustainable decisions. Kaner (1996) and Garmston and Wellman (1999) have developed tools for effective group processes that are relevant for the work of BA teams. Those that are particularly relevant to BA teams are described here, and readers are urged to consult the original sources for additional materials about this subject.

Creating Shared Context

Participants must be able to think from one another's point of view in order for a group to develop sustainable agreements that take everyone's interests into account. They do not have to agree with someone else's perspective, but they do have to understand it. Many groups benefit from using structured thinking activities to help them learn more about each other's frames of reference.

Brainstorming is a specific approach to getting ideas on the table for dialogue and discussion that appears throughout the activities of the BA Model (Chapters 6–10). Brainstorming is a group creativity technique designed to generate a large number of ideas for a possible solution to a problem. In brainstorming, the BA facilitator guides the group, possibly in a round-robin format, to generate a list of possible ideas, focusing on quantity, avoiding criticism of any idea, and encouraging unusual or "outside of the box" thinking (Kaner, 1996). Team members may then narrow the list of ideas to the two or three that they think have the best potential for solving the problem.

Kaner (1996) offered several activities for creating shared context. One draws from the literature on mediation and is called "backing up from solutions to needs." It is a variation of a similar mediation activity that asks participants to distinguish between solutions and interests (Fisher, Patton, & Ury, 1992). The first step in this process is for the BA facilitator to ensure that all team members understand the distinction between solutions and needs. It is helpful to give examples. A solution is, "Julio needs an AAC device right away," and a need is, "Julio needs a way to communicate both socially and academically." A solution is, "The

SLP needs to attend every team meeting," and a need is, "The team needs input from the SLP in order to develop AAC supports for the student's participation."

The process begins with the group generating a list of possible *solutions* to a particular problem or issue. That list is "set aside" and the BA facilitator then asks each member of the group to state his or her *needs* related to the problem or issue. Taking the AAC example further, team members might generate the following list of needs.

- *Veronica, Julio's mom:* I need Julio to be able to tell me how his day at school was.
- *Laurie, the special education teacher:* I need a way for Julio to be able to demonstrate what he knows on our state assessment.
- *Joel, the SLP:* I need assurance from the administration that I will have enough time in my schedule to program the AAC device.
- *Shelley, the OT:* I need to be sure that we are not causing Julio unnecessary anxiety by asking him to learn a new communication system.
- *Maggie, the general education teacher:* I need to be sure that my class is not disrupted when Julio is "exploring" his device by pushing all the buttons.
- *Kathleen, Julio's paraprofessional:* I need to have training in how to use the device.
- *Robert, the school principal:* I need to be sure that we have exhausted all other possible funding sources before putting it in my budget.

After these needs are generated, the BA facilitator then asks the group to return to generating solutions that seek to incorporate a broader range of team members' needs.

Reflecting on Practice

The BA Model includes an emphasis on processes to support a team to examine their practices in supporting the membership, participation, and learning of students with IDD in the general education classroom. Engaging the team in reflective practice contributes to creating a shared context among the team members (Hole & McEntee, 1999). Reflective practice brings individual team member practices to the forefront so that there is shared understanding of what each team member is doing to support the student and the team. Throughout the Model, the BA facilitator engages the team in reflective practice activities, including the CASTS questionnaires, interviews, and observations, and in the meeting to review the CASTS summary and recommendations. The BA facilitator supports the team to critically examine explored supports and accommodations to develop clear descriptions of those supports. The BA facilitator also engages the team in a critical review of data collected related to both student and team members' performance relative to implementing the supports and accommodations.

The process of debriefing observations is an example of reflective practice. The BA facilitator supports team members to make observations of how different supports and accommodations are being implemented. This is often a new, and potentially threatening, experience for many team members. Having a defined process for debriefing the observations is beneficial to avoiding defensiveness among team members. One effective strategy is for the observer to ask the team member who is being observed what it is that he or she would like feedback about and how it would be useful to receive that feedback. Debriefing observations will happen one to one, between the observer and the team member, as well as in team meetings focused on reviewing how things are going.

Reviewing data related to the fidelity of implementing the Model is another example of reflective practice. The BA facilitator coordinates collecting data related to fidelity of implementation and engages the team in a critical review of the data to identify what is working and what might need to be changed. A stepwise process for collecting and reviewing fidelity of implementation data is described in Chapter 8.

Achieving Shared Understanding

Once teams have a number of ideas, they then need to engage in a process to develop a shared understanding of those ideas. Garmston and Wellman stated that "group talk is the organizing ingredient of shared learning, yet it is dangerous and often counterproductive to put adults in a room without frameworks and tools for skilled interaction" (1999, p. 51). They suggest that two kinds of talk—dialogue and discussion—can influence changes in teaching practices and student learning.

Dialogue is "a reflective learning process in which group members seek to understand each other's viewpoints and deeply held assumptions" (Garmston & Wellman, 1999, p. 55). It is the foundation for conflict resolution and leads to shared understanding among all team members, which is a prerequisite for making agreeable and sustainable decisions. During dialogue conversations, team members are asked to suspend judgment and examine the assumptions that underlie their point of view. The BA facilitator supports team members to assume a disposition of *inquiry* rather than *advocacy,* asking for clarification rather than positioning to argue their point of view.

Discussion is different from dialogue in that it utilizes convergent thinking that moves the group toward making a decision. In discussion, the team may be interested in narrowing a list of ideas or options, *prioritizing* those most important, valued, or urgent for action. Prioritizing, as a skill, is required during several phases of the BA Model. For example, in preparation for action in Phase 2, the team prioritizes a set of recommendations they will explore and describe first. One strategy for prioritizing is to have individual team members pick their top options from a list. (To make it an active event, the BA facilitator might give people colored markers or sticky dots to mark their top picks on a flip chart list.) The priorities may at that time be self-evident or may require additional dialogue to understand the different perspectives on what is important to do first. A second round of individuals identifying their top pick(s) can assist in further narrowing the list and prioritizing the actionable items.

Discussion often involves analyzing each possible idea using one of several critical thinking skills (presented in no particular order) that individuals and groups need to have effective discussion (Beyer, 1987).

- Distinguishing between facts and claims
- Distinguishing relevant from irrelevant information
- Determining the accuracy of information and statements

- Determining the credibility of sources
- Identifying unstated assumptions
- Detecting bias
- Identifying logical fallacies and inconsistencies
- Determining the strength of an argument

These thinking skills are used in team discussions and lead to one or more proposals that are considered in the last phase of decision making. The BA facilitator will provide a summary of the dialogue and discussion that leads to one or more proposals that are considered in the last phase of decision making.

Establishing Decision Rules and Levels of Agreement

A variety of decision rules are used (either consciously or by default) in educational settings, including majority rules, delegation, seeking unanimous agreement, one person makes the decision, or even flipping a coin. All too often the process through which decisions are made is unclear or unknown. How many of us have left a meeting saying to ourselves, "Now what did we eventually decide?" or talked to another team member several days later who recalls the final decision differently than we do. Occasionally, this lack of a clear decision is simply puzzling; in other situations, however, it leads to rancor within the team that wreaks havoc on the student's educational program, not to mention team member relationships.

Different types of decisions often require different types of decision rules. For example, decisions related to allocating resources may be ultimately made by an administrator based on recommendations from the team. Decisions about implementing a specific communication or instructional accommodation will likely need buy-in and support of all of the team members. It is important for the team to agree on how a particular decision will be made.

Sometimes following a period of dialogue and discussion, it is helpful for the BA facilitator to take a quick poll of the team members to gauge the amount of agreement or disagreement that exists about a given decision. The results of a quick poll can help the team decide if more dialogue or discussion is needed or if the team is ready to make a decision.

Kaner (1996) provided a model for making a decision that has four distinct steps.

1. Ending discussion
2. Clarifying the proposal
3. Polling the group members for agreement
4. Using the group's decision rule to reach a final decision

Even though using the group's decision rule is the last step in this process, the decision rule must be decided up front. In BA teamwork, we recommend that the most important decisions strive for a high level of agreement across all team members. We recommend using the following levels of agreement rubric (Kaner, 1996).

1. I enthusiastically agree with…
2. I agree with…

3. I agree with..., with a minor clarification and/or edit.

4. I do not agree with... but will go along with the rest of the team if they do, and I will support the decision (e.g., present with a unified front outside of this meeting).

5. I do not agree with... and cannot support it.

6. I do not agree with... and will actively work against its implementation.

This approach is recommended for use when gaining team agreement on CASTS recommendations, agreeing on priorities for Phase 2 activities, agreeing on which student and team supports will continue into Phase 3, agreeing on the sufficiency of data to determine fidelity of implementation, and at many other points in the BA Model implementation. Although each team must decide what level of agreement they will require before moving forward with a particular decision, we recommend that for most BA decisions all team members work toward being at Level 1, 2, or 3. We acknowledge that there are team decisions that do *not* require such high levels of agreement (e.g., what the team will order for lunch), but our experience suggests that decisions are more likely to be sustained when they have high agreement by all team members.

CONCLUSION

In conclusion, the BA team strives to presume one another's honorable intentions, communicate effectively, conduct efficient meetings, develop shared understandings of their student and themselves, and implement sustainable decisions that will promote students' membership, participation, and learning. Chapter 6 describes the first phase of the BA Model—the CASTS.

REFERENCES

Beyer, B. (1987). *Practical strategies for the teaching of thinking.* Boston: Allyn & Bacon.

Fisher, R., Patton, B.M., & Ury, W.L. (1992). *Getting to yes: Negotiating agreement without giving in.* New York: Houghton Mifflin.

Garmston, R.J., & Wellman, B.M. (1999). *The adaptive school: A sourcebook for developing collaborative groups.* Norwood, MA: Christopher-Gordon Publishers.

Hole, S., & McEntee, G.H. (1999, May). Reflection is at the heart of practice. *Educational Leadership, 56*(8), 34–37.

Jorgensen, C., Fisher, D., Sax, C., & Skoglund, K. (1998). Innovative scheduling, new roles for teachers, and heterogeneous grouping: The organizational factors related to student success in inclusive, restructuring schools. In C. Jorgensen (Ed.), *Restructuring high schools for all students: Taking inclusion to the next level* (pp. 29–48). Baltimore: Paul H. Brookes Publishing Co.

Jorgensen, C.M., Schuh, M.C., & Nisbet, J. (2006). *The inclusion facilitator's guide.* Baltimore: Paul H. Brookes Publishing Co.

Kaner, S. (1996). *The facilitator's guide to participatory decision-making.* Gabriola Island, British Columbia, Canada: New Society Publishers.

Kluth, P., & Schwarz, P. (2008). *"Just give him the whale!" 20 ways to use fascinations, areas of expertise, and strengths to supports students with autism.* Baltimore: Paul H. Brookes Publishing Co.

McCarthy, C., McLean, L., Miller, J., Paul-Brown, D., Romski, M., Rourk, J., et al. (1998). *Communication supports checklist for programs serving individuals with severe disabilities.* Baltimore: Paul H. Brookes Publishing Co.

Rainforth, B., York, J, & Macdonald, C. (1992). *Collaborative teams for students with severe disabilities: Integrating therapy and educational services.* Baltimore: Paul H. Brookes Publishing Co.

Thousand, J.S., & Villa, R.A. (1992). Collaborative teams: A powerful tool in school restructuring. In R.A. Villa, J.S. Thousand, W. Stainback, & S. Stainback (Eds.), *Restructuring for caring and effective education: An administrative guide to creating heterogeneous schools* (pp. 73–108). Baltimore: Paul H. Brookes Publishing Co.

Villa, R., & Thousand, J. (Eds.). (1995). *Creating an inclusive school.* Alexandria, VA: Association for Supervision and Curriculum Development.

Using the Beyond Access Model

Phase 1

Comprehensive Assessment of Student and Team Supports (CASTS)

Implementing the BA Model begins with completing a CASTS (see Figure 6.1). CASTS is a process for gathering information about the perspectives of each team member[1] that serves as a basis for implementing the BA Model. It differs from other assessments used to identify the capabilities of students with IDD in that it takes stock of student performance in the context of current school and team practices and how these practices align with a preestablished set of best practices associated with the BA Model. The process also differs from other assessments in that it includes a process for promoting shared understanding of the findings and recommendations among the team members and a process for shared decision making by the team regarding next steps. We have all been part of teams in which individual members were working at cross purposes because there was not shared understanding or agreement about a particular instructional approach. The CASTS process is designed to support shared understanding and commitment among the team members to the student's educational program priorities and the instructional and support strategies that will help best achieve the desired results of membership, participation, communication, and learning.

Two essential questions frame the CASTS:

1. What supports are in place that promote the student's full membership, participation, communication, and learning of general education core academics within the general education classroom?
2. How does the team currently work together to promote these outcomes?

More detailed questions addressed during the CASTS can be found in Table 6.1.

---

[1]Any reference to a student's IEP team includes parents/guardians.

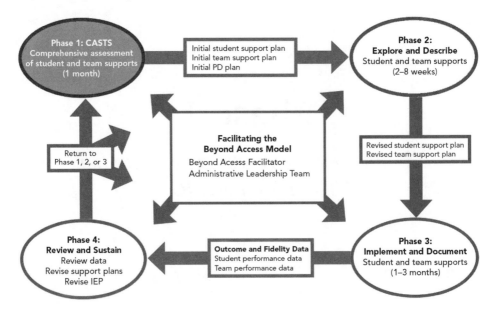

Figure 6.1. Beyond Access Model Phase 1: Comprehensive Assessment of Student and Team Supports (CASTS). (From McSheehan, M., Sonnenmeier, R.M., & Jorgensen, C.M. [2009]. Membership, participation, and learning in general education classrooms for students with autism spectrum disorders who use AAC. In D.R. Beukelman & J. Reichle [Series Eds.] & P. Mirenda & T. Iacono [Vol. Eds.], *Augmentative and alternative communication series: Autism spectrum disorders and AAC* [p. 427]. Baltimore: Paul H. Brookes Publishing Co.; adapted by permission.) (Key: IEP, individualized education program; PD, professional development.)

As described in the following CASTS activities, information is gathered from a variety of sources including reviews of records and work samples, question-naires, observations, and interviews. The BA facilitator guides the CASTS process with participation by all team members and select building- and district-level general and special education administrators. The information gathered is compared with the BA Model Best Practices Rating Scale (see Appendix A). Common and discrepant perspectives across team members are identified and noted in the summary of the CASTS findings. A set of CASTS recommendations is drafted by the BA facilitator for the team to consider. A final set of recommendations that are agreed on by all team members is used as the focus for activities in Phases 2–4.

PHASE 1 DISPOSITIONS

Certain dispositions—attitudes and behaviors—are needed by both the BA facilitator and the student's team members to obtain the optimal CASTS outcomes.

Beyond Access Facilitator Dispositions

The dispositions needed by the BA facilitator include 1) withholding judgment of the information that is gathered, 2) maintaining the confidentiality of information and opinions provided by team members, 3) having an openness to discovering multiple perspectives, 4) resisting the temptation to provide suggestions for chang-

Table 6.1. Sample Comprehensive Assessment of Student and Team Supports (CASTS) questions

---

Who is the student? What is his or her medical and educational history and the elements of his or her current educational program? What is his or her family constellation?

How do team members describe the student's membership in the general education classroom and other school environments?

How do team members describe the student's participation in general education instruction?

How do team members describe the student's current knowledge and skills in core academic subject areas? What assumptions about the student's innate abilities are held by team members?

How do team members envision the student's future after high school?

What supports (accommodations and modifications) are being provided to the student to support his or her membership, participation, and learning?

How do team members describe their team collaboration?

What team- and school-level structures and processes support the team's effective collaboration?

How do the student's educational program and the team's collaboration align with BA Model core Best Practices?

What do team members need to learn in order to meet the needs of the student and improve the student's membership, participation, and learning and the team's collaboration?

---

ing the student's education program *prior to* gaining agreement from all team members on the findings and recommendations of the CASTS, and 5) holding a perspective of striving for excellence and continuous improvement of practices.

Withholding Judgment

As completing a student assessment requires us to withhold judgment until all information is gathered and reviewed, so, too, must the BA facilitator withhold judgment during the CASTS process. The BA facilitator may discover information during the CASTS that goes against his or her philosophy of inclusive education, reveals attitudes or practices that seem outdated, or unearths flaws in the general or special education system. The BA facilitator must be clear about his or her role in guiding the CASTS. His or her role is not to evaluate the job performance of team members, not to render judgment about the child-rearing practices of the student's parents, and not to monitor the team or school's accountability to IDEA 2004 regulations. Comments or body language that communicate either positive ("I'm impressed with your use of assistive technology to support Theresa's writing.") or negative feedback ("I'm disappointed there are limited accommodations and modifications being provided to the student.") do not serve the goal of building the team's trust in either the BA facilitator or the CASTS process. The BA facilitator can best communicate interest in learning about an individual's perspective when observing and interviewing team members by asking for examples, restating what has been said to ensure understanding, and making general comments ("You have worked hard on this.").

Maintaining Confidentiality

Confidentiality of information should be stressed at the beginning of the CASTS process and any time the BA facilitator interacts with team members during the CASTS. Trust is essential if the BA facilitator is going to understand the current status of team collaboration and how supports currently are provided to the student. Team members must be assured that the identity of the informant will not be revealed to other team members (without express consent of the informant) when the CASTS findings are presented to the team. The BA facilitator might frame the confidentiality assurance in this way:

> "I want to assure you that any information you provide to me during the CASTS process will not be reported in a way that reveals who provided that information. When the CASTS findings are presented to the team, I will report information as coming from 'one,' 'a few,' 'many,' or 'all' team members. If a particular piece of information would be easy to trace back to you, then I will ask your permission before reporting it to the team. For example, if you report that 'The SLP promised that she would schedule an AAC evaluation by the end of September,' I will report that information as 'One or more team members are concerned about the delay in getting an AAC evaluation completed for the student.' Do you have any questions or concerns about how confidentiality will be handled?"

It is also important that the BA facilitator immediately address any breach of confidentiality and/or any concerns about confidentiality that arise during the CASTS process.

Openness to Discovering Multiple Perspectives

When gathering information about the educational program of a student with intensive support needs, it is inevitable that different team members will view similar events or situations from different perspectives. A parent may think that the team is not being aggressive enough in pursuing the use of AT with his or her child, whereas other team members are satisfied with the progress that is being made given the challenges of identifying, ordering, and learning to use new technology. A paraprofessional may feel that decisions are being made by other team members without consulting him or her, whereas an administrator may be concerned about who on the team has the right to know particular pieces of confidential information that relate to certain decisions. The BA facilitator is most effective when he or she focuses not on discovering objective facts of a situation or on which team member is "right," but rather on understanding how team members came to hold their individual perspectives. Probing questions that serve to clarify are helpful in understanding differing perspectives among team members.

Resisting Temptation to Make Recommendations

Whoever serves in the role of BA facilitator is likely to be an experienced and respected expert in educating students with IDD. His or her usual role within the school may be to provide suggestions to other team members for improving students' educational programs and learning outcomes. During the CASTS process, however, that natural inclination to offer advice must be resisted. There are two primary reasons why this disposition is so important to the successful completion of the CASTS. First, until the CASTS process is completed, the BA facilitator will not know the "whole story," and any premature recommendations might not take into account important information that will be collected later on. Second, an essential feature of the BA Model is its focus on developing high levels of agreement across team members as a way to enhance shared understanding and shared commitment to any particular action.

An experience of this book's first author underscores the importance of resisting the temptation to make recommendations prematurely. After observing a student over the course of a school day, the author noticed that the student frequently held printed text very close to his face. This student wore thick glasses, and the author wondered why text had not been enlarged for the student or why he was not using a visual magnification device. The author approached an administrator and remarked, "I think we need to get a vision consultation immediately to find out what is going on." The administrator called the special education teacher to her office and asked the same question. To the chagrin of the author, the special education teacher told the administrator that earlier in the year the team had consulted a vision specialist who did an evaluation and determined that the student's corrected vision was within normal limits. The team felt that the student was using the feel and smell of the paper as a source of sensory stimulation. Henceforth, the author was very careful about jumping to conclusions or making recommendations before the entire CASTS process has been completed.

Commitment to Excellence and Continuous Improvement of Practices

The last disposition that must be held by the BA facilitator during the CASTS relates to supporting team members to make changes in their usual ways of viewing a student and implementing his or her educational program. The BA facilitator needs to present an attitude that communicates a collaborative effort to strive for excellence and continuous improvement of team practices to support improved student outcomes. This will be communicated throughout the CASTS process (and through all phases of the BA Model). The commitment to improvement will be an explicit step in the orientation process with the ALT (see Chapter 10). All members of the IEP team will be required to register agreement with expanding their knowledge and practices.

Team Member Dispositions

In addition to the BA facilitator's disposition in leading the team during the CASTS, team members themselves must bring a positive attitude and associated behaviors to make the CASTS process successful. Team members' dispositions include 1) honesty, 2) the commitment of time, 3) reflective thinking, and 4) openness to change.

Honesty

Honesty by team members is a valued disposition during the CASTS process. We would be naïve to think that team members will reveal every fact or feeling about a student's educational program and their collaboration with other team members. Engaging in CASTS provides a rare opportunity for team members to raise issues that, if resolved, may contribute to enhanced student learning and increased satisfaction with the collaborative teaming process. CASTS questionnaires and interviews provide an opportunity for team members to be honest about their own fears and uncertainties. Very few educators were prepared in college to provide educational services to students with IDD, and even fewer have had access to sufficient ongoing professional development to keep pace with the ever-expanding knowledge base regarding AT, AAC, and greater demands for accountability. One of the questions on the CASTS questionnaire asks, "What professional development and support do you need in order to advance your knowledge and skills and to engage in productive collaborative teaming relative to this student?" Team members who provide honest answers will have those answers considered in making recommendations for professional development activities and, as a result, are more likely to feel that the BA Model is really making a difference for them and for their students.

Commitment of Time

Engaging in the CASTS process can take up to two months of focused attention. The BA facilitator's time contribution is the greatest of all the team members, but everyone needs to devote time to providing documents for review, completing the CASTS questionnaires, participating in an individual interview, and attending the CASTS findings and recommendations meeting. Team members who approach these time requirements with a generous rather than a begrudging attitude may find that they are more open to discovering new and helpful information about the student and themselves.

Reflective Thinking

In our experience, the majority of educators who use the BA Model appreciate the opportunity for deep reflection provided by the CASTS process. We have heard comments such as, "It was really nice to be asked what I think about this student's educational program in an atmosphere where I didn't need to worry how my comments will be received." Other team members have remarked, "This is the first time I have ever really thought about what the future might look like for this student and considered how important my role is in helping her to achieve a quality of life after school" and "I never realized how much my assumptions were impacting how I approach my job. Just engaging in this process has prompted me to change some things that I am doing." In fact, our analysis of the CASTS process with students' educational teams revealed that, even in the absence of any direct recommendations, many team members made changes in their practice as a result of being asked why they do what they do (McSheehan, Sonnenmeier, Jorgensen, & Turner, 2006).

Openness to Change

Change is difficult for many people. Being asked to change can be threatening and provoke anxiety, particularly when team members feel as if they are barely keeping their heads above water with their regular responsibilities. They wonder, "How will this affect me?" "Will I have the knowledge and skills necessary to take on this new endeavor?" "Will we get the support we need from our administration?" "Will this innovation go the way of many others that fell by the wayside after the first initial excitement has died down?"

Individuals engage in change in different ways. Within a team of six or seven people, one or two are likely to be the "leapers"—they are eager to try out new practices because they have confidence in their abilities to learn and adjust. And there are likely to be one or two people on any team who fear change and will do almost anything to maintain the status quo. Rather than berating these individuals, their natural reluctance can be utilized to uncover potential pitfalls to trying new things, and their cautiousness can actually help balance those who are too eager to move forward without thoughtful consideration of consequences.

Engaging the BA Model requires focused energy to accommodate different personality styles and temperaments. It is not only the responsibility of the BA facilitator, but it also involves team members attending to one another through the process. The CASTS process appeals to those who are wary of change because it is designed to take a careful look at "what is" before moving to "what might we change." As described in subsequent chapters, the BA Model supports team members to engage in a thoughtful process of change. In Phase 2—Explore and Describe—team members try out new practices "just for a short period of time" before making a stronger commitment to a given practice. In Phase 3—Implement and Document—team members strive to implement student and team supports with increasing fidelity, and in Phase 4—Review and Sustain—they review fidelity and efficacy data to determine if the student's demonstrated performance is a valid indicator of communication and learning.

PHASE 1 CASTS OUTCOMES

There are four outcomes from conducting the CASTS: 1) a synthesis of CASTS findings, 2) team member agreement with those findings, 3) a set of recommendations for exploring new student and team supports in Phase 2, and 4) team member agreement with those recommendations.

Synthesis of CASTS Findings

The BA Best Practices (see Chapter 2) serve as the benchmark for doing a discrepancy analysis with the team's current educational practices. The BA facilitator reviews all of the data collected through the CASTS process and identifies any discrepancies between the data and the BA Best Practices. The BA facilitator also looks for discrepancies among team member responses to the CASTS questionnaires and interview, observations made, and a review of artifacts. Next, the BA facilitator synthesizes the findings from the CASTS and writes a summary that will be shared with the team members.

Draft CASTS Recommendations

The BA facilitator develops a set of draft recommendations based on the summary of the CASTS findings. These draft recommendations address both student and team supports and team member professional development, which will be explored in Phase 2.

Team Agreement with CASTS Findings

This step in the BA Model distinguishes it from other models of consultation or technical assistance in that a high level of agreement is sought from all team members regarding the CASTS *findings* before proceeding with *recommendations*. In our experience, providing recommendations to a team about making significant changes in their practice is often met with resistance or rejection precisely because the team has not been supported to achieve shared understanding of "what is" prior to being asked to engage in "what might be" thinking and action. It is very common for a consultant to issue a set of recommendations and then return several weeks later to find that few of the recommendations have been implemented as suggested. It is tempting to explain this lack of follow-through as stubbornness or lack of commitment to the student's best interests, when it may be a normal reaction to poor understanding and management of the adult learning and systems change process. How can we expect team members to adopt new practices if they do not agree with our reporting and analysis of their current reality?

Dispositions of withholding judgment and striving for excellence and continuous improvement are particularly beneficial during the team review of CASTS findings. If a team's current practices fall short of the BA Best Practices, then this segment of the CASTS findings meeting may promote feelings of defensiveness from some team members. The BA facilitator uses a variety of group process skills and his or her knowledge of the change process to acknowledge team members' feelings and to reiterate that the team will have control over the recommendations that are selected for Phase 2. The BA facilitator also emphasizes that the BA Model was designed to not only consider the effect of new practices on the student, but also to consider and plan for the team support needed to utilize and sustain those new practices. The presence of building- and district-level administrators at the CASTS meeting is absolutely required if team members are to have assurance that they will receive the necessary administrative support as they proceed.

Agreement with CASTS Recommendations

After team members have reached agreement with the CASTS findings, the BA facilitator presents the draft recommendations for student and team supports and team member professional development. Rather than presenting recommendations from a posture of "You should do X because I say so," the BA facilitator again is careful to provide a nonjudgmental comparison of current versus best practices as the rationale for a recommendation. For example, BA Best Practices suggest that students who are unable to meet their academic and social communication needs by using spoken words[2] need AAC and AT supports. During the team meetings when findings and recommendations are presented, the BA facilitator might say

> "The CASTS findings—based on a review of John's records, examination of his IEP, the classroom observation, and reports from team members— reveal that John does not currently have an effective means of communicating during instruction and social situations. When comparing this current situation to BA Best Practices, it is recommended that the team engage the state's Assistive Technology Center team to conduct a comprehensive AAC and AT assessment to explore features of an SGD that would be most functional for John, for staff to participate in professional development related to supporting John's use of AAC, and then for us to pursue a 2-month trial of a device to determine if it does indeed promote John's membership, participation, communication, and learning."

---

[2]This does not refer, of course, to students who are deaf and hard of hearing who do not also experience IDD.

Some teams are able to address both the findings and recommendations in one meeting; others need to have two meetings. By the end of the recommendations meeting, team members will have clarified, edited, and added to the recommendations, and levels of agreement will have been tallied. Recommendations achieving high levels of team agreement then move on to Phase 2. The BA facilitator revises the original findings and recommendations document (if necessary) and sends a final copy to each team member.

The description of CASTS activities presents detailed instructions for presenting and then seeking team member agreement with the CASTS findings and recommendations.

PHASE 1 CASTS ACTIVITIES

Thirteen activities comprise the CASTS. Each activity, its related product, and the individuals involved are depicted in Table 6.2. Guidelines for completing each activity are then presented. Activities are presented in an order found to be helpful from our initial research and fieldwork. As familiarity with conducting a CASTS increases, you will find that synthesizing and drafting findings are not necessarily discrete steps and may actually occur throughout the CASTS activities. Blank forms and a sample CASTS summary are included on the accompanying CD-ROM.

Activity A: Review the Student's Historical Records

The purpose of this step is to understand how previous evaluators and team members described the student's abilities and how they thought about the provision of supports. An understanding of what has been "known" in the past provides a context from which to understand current practices regarding the student's membership, participation, and learning of general education curriculum within the general education classroom.

Outcome
The BA facilitator uses content analysis methods (Bogdan & Biklen, 1998) to create a written summary of the records that were reviewed. This summary will not be shared with other team members but will be used to inform the findings and recommendations.

Instructions
After acquiring the appropriate written permission from the student's parents/guardians, the BA facilitator reviews the student's cumulative educational record, which includes evaluation reports (e.g., achievement, communication, occupational and physical therapy, psychology, medical) and IEPs from previous years. The focus of this review is to glean information from the records that informs the context of the student's current educational program. This will include information about 1) the student's past educational placements; 2) participation in statewide assessments; 3) relevant medical information; 4) the types of instructional, behavioral, and communication supports that have been used in the past; 5) the types and locations of related services the student has received; 6) whether the student has participated in extended year programming; 7) past descriptions of the student's abilities, potential, and needs based on previous evaluations; and

Table 6.2. Comprehensive Assessment of Student and Team Supports (CASTS) activities, products, and individuals involved

Activity	Product	Individuals involved
A: Review the student's records	Summary of student's records	Beyond Access (BA) facilitator
B: Review the student's current educational program and artifacts	Field notes	BA facilitator
C: Review team and school artifacts	Field notes	BA facilitator
D: Administer team member questionnaires (including BA Outcomes Survey)	Discrepancy analysis of similarities and differences among team member responses, discrepancy analysis between team member responses and BA Best Practices, synthesis, and summary of questionnaire data	BA facilitator All team members Building principal, building- and/or district-level special education administrators
E: Complete BA Best Practices Rating Scale	Discrepancy analysis between team member input via questionnaires and other CASTS data with Likert scale responses to BA Model Best Practices Rating Scale	BA facilitator With input, as needed, from building principal, building- and/or district-level special education administrators
F: Conduct a "Day in the Life" observation of the student at school	Field notes and "Day in the Life" summary (Jorgensen, Schuh, & Nisbet, 2006)	BA facilitator
G: Conduct home visit and family interview(s)	Summary of family constellation and key questions and concerns	BA facilitator Parents/guardians
H: Observe a team meeting	Field notes regarding the current status of the team's use of best practices in collaborative teaming	BA facilitator Team members
I: Conduct team member interviews	Field notes	BA facilitator Team members Building principal, building- and/or district-level special education administrators
J: Conduct follow-up interviews and observations (if necessary)	Field notes	BA facilitator Select team members Building principal, building- and/or district-level special education administrators
K: Synthesize and summarize CASTS findings	Written summary of the synthesis of findings and exemplars	BA facilitator
L: Draft CASTS recommendations	Written draft recommendations	BA facilitator
M: Share CASTS findings and recommendations with the team and achieve agreement	Meeting agenda, written summary of findings and draft recommendations, summary of team discussion, and team agreement ratings	BA facilitator Team members Building principal, building- and/or district-level special education administrators

From McSheehan, M., Sonnenmeier, R., Jorgensen, C.M., & Turner, K. (2006). Beyond communication access: Promoting learning of the general education curriculum by students with significant disabilities. *Topics in Language Disorders, 26*(3), 266–290; adapted by permission.

8) any other information that is relevant to the student's membership, participation, and learning within the general education classroom.

Next Steps

As the BA facilitator reviews the student's historical record, he or she begins to formulate guiding themes and questions to support the next activity (review of the student's current educational program). These themes and questions might include examining the current program for consistency with or changes from past recommendations, discrepancies between what is found in the cumulative record and what the BA facilitator has been told thus far about the student and team, discrepancies among individual reports, and other areas in need of further examination.

Activity B: Review the Student's Current Educational Program and Artifacts

The purpose of this step is to understand the student's current educational program by focusing on the student's membership, participation, and learning within the general education classroom. This review will include identifying 1) the student's learning goals from the general education curriculum and the student's IEP, 2) how these goals are supported through instructional materials, 3) communication supports and student work samples, 4) how instructional materials promote the student's full access to and engagement with the general education curriculum, and 5) how the student is able to demonstrate what he or she knows given the current communication and instructional supports.

Outcome

The BA facilitator uses content analysis methods (Bogdan & Biklen, 1998) to create a written summary of the records and artifacts that were reviewed. This summary will not be shared with other team members but will be used to inform the findings and recommendations.

Instructions

The BA facilitator reviews the instructional materials, supports, and work samples that reflect the student's current communication and learning. Instructional materials include lesson plans, basal readers, textbooks, handouts, maps, and so forth. Supports include adapted materials, behavioral support plans, communication boards or books, and so forth. Work samples can include worksheets, quizzes and tests, projects, writing samples, data forms from learning trials, videotape of the student using supports, photographs of the student's communication device and/or supports, videotape of the student using his or her communication device and/or supports, and any other artifacts of student work. Samples of materials should be gathered across all core academic subjects and classes.

The BA facilitator summarizes the key findings and questions that arise from the review of these communication supports, instructional materials, and work samples.

Next Steps

The BA facilitator reviews the synthesis and summarizes key findings and questions from the review to develop the questionnaire to be completed by all team members and for individual team member interviews.

Activity C: Review Team and School Artifacts

The purpose of this step is to determine which organizational or systemic factors at the team, school, and district level are supporting or impeding the team from working effectively to support the student's membership and participation in general education instruction in the general education classroom. Information gathered will be used during ALT meetings as a starting point for discussions of how to support IEP teams to use the BA Model effectively (see Chapter 10).

Outcome

The BA facilitator uses content analysis methods (Bogdan & Biklen, 1998) to create a written summary of organizational or systemic factors that 1) are aligned with the BA Model Best Practices; 2) impede students' membership, participation, and learning and team collaboration; and 3) are absent. This summary will not be shared with other team members but will be used to inform the findings and recommendations.

Instructions

The BA facilitator gathers and synthesizes findings from 1) samples of team meeting minutes, 2) the school's mission statement, 3) buildingwide classroom management or behavior procedures, and 4) schoolwide initiatives that might influence the student's educational program.

Next Steps

The summary will be used in the CASTS findings report as part of the school's description.

Activity D: Administer Team Member Questionnaires

The purpose of having team members complete written questionnaires is to gather information regarding their views on the student's characteristics and learning styles and present levels of performance and perceptions of competence, the current educational program, the effectiveness of team collaboration, and the student's future after school.

Outcome

The BA facilitator uses content analysis methods (Bogdan & Biklen, 1998) to compile a written synthesis of all team member responses to the questionnaires. This will not be shared with other team members but will be used to inform the CASTS findings and recommendations.

Instructions

The BA facilitator develops a questionnaire based on the guiding questions from the BA start-up meeting, related conversations, and information gleaned from the student's records. All team members respond independently to the same questions about both the student and the team. Questions are individualized based on issues raised during the initial interviews and from the review of the student's historical record and current educational program. Questions that reveal information about the student's current membership, participation in the general education classroom, and learning are included on the Student and Team Outcomes Survey (Appendix 7.1). Team members are also asked to make suggestions regarding supports to improve the student's membership, participation, and learning and team collaboration. Team members are asked to complete the questionnaires and return them within a week. Having team members fill out an online digital version of the questionnaire facilitates efficient synthesis of all questionnaire responses. A sample CASTS questionnaire is presented in the chapter appendix.

Team member responses to the questionnaire are then reviewed, and team agreement and divergent perspectives are identified. Suggestions that the team members have for improving the student's membership, participation, and learning, and the team's collaboration are summarized.

Next Steps
Findings from the questionnaires will be incorporated into the draft of CASTS findings and recommendations, which will be shared with the team at the conclusion of the CASTS. Issues of concern from the synthesis of questionnaires that need to be probed more fully in the team member interviews should be identified.

Activity E: Administer Beyond Access Best Practices Rating Scale

The purpose of this step in the CASTS is for team members to rate their own knowledge and practices relative to key indicators of the BA Best Practices.

Outcome
The responses to the Likert-scale items on the BA Best Practices Rating Scale are summarized using descriptive statistics. Patterns of responses and selected data from the survey summary will be shared with team members, protecting the anonymity of any team member whose response may be easily identifiable.

Instructions
Each team member is asked to complete the BA Best Practices Rating Scale (using a secure and confidential online survey format if possible). Team members are assured that their identities will be kept confidential and only summary data will be presented. The current BA Best Practices Rating Scale is presented in Appendix A.

Next Steps
When all participants have completed the survey, descriptive statistical information is calculated as a way of providing summary information to the team. This includes the range of responses and the mean or mode of responses per category of BA Best Practices.

Activity F: Conduct a "Day in the Life" Observation of the Student at School

The purpose of the "Day in the Life" observation is for the BA facilitator to get a firsthand look at how the student's educational program is implemented throughout the school day and the degree to which current educational practices are aligned with BA Best Practices. The BA facilitator tries to experience the day from the perspective of the student, presuming competence and contrasting the student's educational experience to that of typical peers. Data collected from the observation enable triangulation of information across three information sources—the IEP, team member report, and observation—to inform the CASTS findings and recommendations. This activity is not designed to assess the student's abilities or the skills of the adults working with the student.

Outcome

A summary is written and arranged in chronological order for each major time block in the student's day at school, including the BA facilitator's reflections on the discrepancy between the student's educational experience and that of typical peers.

Instructions

1. *Schedule the observation*—Determine which time blocks on which days are most representative of a "typical day at school" for the student and his or her general education classmates. Avoid Mondays, Fridays, and days on which field trips, assemblies, or large-scale assessments are scheduled. Reconfirm the observation with participants the day before the observation.

2. *Prepare for the observation*—Review the focus questions presented in Figure 6.2. Add any questions that arose from the previous CASTS steps that might be answered during the observation.

3. *Conduct the observation*—At the beginning of each observation period, confirm with the teacher in charge that it is still permissible to do the observation at that time. If unexpected changes in the schedule have arisen, then make an on-the-spot decision about whether rescheduling is necessary. Accompany the student (from an unobtrusive distance whenever possible) throughout the school day from arrival until dismissal. Make field notes on paper or using a laptop computer. Do not engage the student or the adults. Respond to questions such as, "What are you doing in this class today?" with, "I am observing a typical day in the life of a student." Record notes that reflect answers to the observation questions and note any issues that might need later clarification.

4. *Concluding an observation*—At the end of each time block, briefly thank the teacher in charge and move on to the next period or activity. No feedback or judgments regarding observations are provided at the time of the observation.

5. *Determining additional class observations*—Continue with observations until a complete, representative "day in the life" of this student has been observed. In cases in which a student is not present for significant portions of the general education classroom activities, it will be helpful to observe those classroom activities so the BA facilitator can see what the *desired* typical day might look like for the student. If the student is not present for any instruction in a specific academic area (e.g., this student does not presently attend a general education math class, which is why the IEP team has initiated use of the BA Model), then it is essential to conduct observations in that academic area to be able to describe the academic, instructional, and social expectations as well as to identify potential supports that may be helpful for the team and for the student's membership, participation, and learning in that setting.

This observation involves accompanying a student with significant disabilities through his or her day strictly as an observer. The purpose of the task is to experience the school day from the perspective of the student, to increase your understanding of the factors that influence the student's educational experiences, and to provide some information about how the student's program aligns with Beyond Access Best Practices.

Etiquette

Make arrangements to observe when it is convenient for the teacher and other staff. If you are told that the student is experiencing a particularly difficult day and your presence might interfere, reschedule the observation. If classmates ask why you are there, explain the purpose of the observation.

   Introduce yourself to the teacher you are observing. Tell the teacher that you are doing a "day in the life" observation as part of the planning process for supporting the student to be a successful member of the classroom. Reconfirm that it is still a good day and time to observe.

Focus Questions

Use the following questions to focus the observation. (The "you" in the following questions refers to the student you are shadowing.)

How do you get to school?

How similar or dissimilar is your day to that of students without disabilities?

Is your schedule just like other students who are your age or in your grade?

In class, are you treated the same as or different from other students?

Do you receive pull-out instruction outside of the general education classroom?

What is this instruction like?

What do you miss by being out of the general education classroom?

Is your seat with the other students in the general education classroom?

Do you have the same materials?

Do you have the same access to the classroom, the learning materials, and the teacher's instruction as the other students do?

Does the teacher call on you?

Are you assigned to groups like the other students?

How are the class expectations personalized for your learning needs?

How are your relationships with other students? Adults?

How do people communicate with you?

What kinds of conversations are you involved in? Academic? Social?

Do you have a way to communicate every minute of the day?

Figure 6.2.   Guidelines for a "Day in the Life" observation. (From Jorgensen, C.M., Schuh, M.C., & Nisbet, J. [2006]. *The inclusion facilitator's guide* [pp. 221–223]. Baltimore: Paul H. Brookes Publishing Co.; reprinted by permission.)

(continued)

Figure 6.2. *(continued)*

How do people talk about you?

Do they speak directly to you?

When people are talking about you, do they include you in the conversation, or do they talk about you as if you aren't there (or aren't listening or understanding)?

Do people treat you as if you are smart and valuable?

How is support provided to you?

Do you have opportunities to be helpful to other students?

If you didn't have a disability, would you be happy at this school?

Conclusion
After your observation is complete, write a summary about how this student's educational program aligns with Beyond Access Best Practices.

Next Steps
Summarize the observation notes at your earliest convenience so that you do not forget small details or impressions. Organizing your notes using the time of day or the observation questions as headings can be helpful. As you summarize and synthesize your field notes, keep in mind what you observed that was consistent with and discrepant with indicators of membership, participation, and learning.

Activity G: Conduct Home Visit and Family Interview(s)

The purpose of the home visit is to see the student in his or her home environment and to determine if there are significant differences between the way that the student interacts at home compared with school (e.g., communicates, engages with siblings, participates in typical routines). The home visit is also integral to the development of a partnership between home and school. Given that significant changes to a student's educational program may be recommended (e.g., in the student's daily schedule, in the provision of related services, in the type of communication supports), parent/guardian buy-in is critical.

Outcome
Field notes and reflections, synthesized using content analysis methods, will inform the CASTS findings and recommendations but will not be shared with other team members.

Instructions
The observer should schedule the home visit at the convenience of the family. It may be preferable to conduct the home visit and parent/guardian interview at two different times, although parent preference to do both during the same visit should be accommodated. The visit may last between one and several hours.

During the observation portion of the home visit, the observer does not interact in any substantive way with the student or the family. It is important to reassure the family that their parenting is not being judged and that the purpose is "seeing your son or daughter in his or her natural home environment." Some home visitors take notes during the visit; others write notes following the visit. The observer should use judgment to determine which method will be most comfortable for the family.

If the home visit and parent/guardian interview are conducted together, then there should be a distinct part of the visit that is observation, followed by the interview segment. Assure the family that confidentiality will be maintained.

Next Steps

A written summary of the home visit—both the observation and family interview—are used to inform the CASTS findings and recommendations.

Activity H: Observe a Team Meeting

The purpose of observing a team meeting is to obtain baseline data on team members' communication skills and the meeting structures and processes that are being used prior to introduction of the BA Model.

Outcome

Field notes are recorded regarding what goes on during a typical team meeting, including the use of meeting structures and processes, team member roles, decision-making processes, and impressions of the existence of team conflict. Findings from the observations of the team meeting contribute to the CASTS findings and recommendations.

Instructions

This observation should take place at a regularly scheduled team meeting, if one exists. If a student's team does not have regularly scheduled team meetings—and only meets to write progress reports or to develop the student's IEP—then this step of the CASTS is not completed. It is important for the BA facilitator to tell the team that they are not being evaluated but that the observation will provide information that will be used to plan the professional development that will be provided during Phases 2, 3, and 4 of the Model. The BA facilitator should not participate in the team meeting and should take notes on the elements of collaborative teaming that reflect the BA Best Practices, such as team members' communication skills, use of a meeting agenda, team members' roles during the meeting, the content of the discussions, how decisions are made, how time is managed, and how decisions are translated into action plans.

Summarize your field notes as soon as possible after the observation. Include information about 1) use of an agenda, 2) clarity of meeting purpose, 3) content of meeting, 4) time management, 5) decision-making processes identified and used, 6) communication, 7) action plans proposed and agreed on, and 8) behavior of people as they left the meeting.

Next Steps

After the team meeting observation, the BA facilitator is poised to conduct team member interviews to clarify information and ask additional probing questions to understand each person's perspective regarding the student's educational program and the team's collaboration.

Activity I: Conduct Team Member Interviews

The purpose of interviewing each team member is twofold. First, it provides an opportunity for the BA facilitator to establish a positive relationship with each team member. Second, team members will often reveal more and different information when talking in person compared with what they will write on a questionnaire. Conducting interviews after reviewing the team members' responses to the questionnaire and observation data (i.e., "Day in the Life" of the student at school, team meeting, home visit) allows the BA facilitator to ask questions about the emerging themes (similarities and differences) among the various sources of data.

Outcome
Field notes that highlight the team member's comments, insights, and concerns are reviewed. Initial impressions of data that are consistent and discrepant with BA Best Practices are identified.

Instructions
Team member interviews are done after the written questionnaires have been completed and read by the BA facilitator. Prior to the interview, potential questions should be generated to reflect 1) clarifications needed based on written responses to the questionnaires, 2) follow-up queries to any questions that were not answered, 3) extended questioning about a written response, and 4) an invitation to discuss anything that was not reflected in the individual's written responses, including observations and other data collected thus far.

It is important, again, to emphasize that information gathered during an interview will be kept confidential (i.e., the content of what the interviewee reports may be shared with the whole team but the informant's name will not be revealed). The interviewer should take notes during the interview. Many people can type faster than they can write, so using a laptop is acceptable. We often tell interviewees that we will be taking notes as we talk, and we apologize up front for not maintaining eye contact. Sample team member interview questions are included in Table 6.3.

Summarize your interview notes at your earliest convenience so that you do not forget small details or impressions. Then, synthesize the notes across team members, keeping in mind what was reported that was consistent with and discrepant with indicators of membership, participation, and learning, and team collaboration. Determine the areas in which the team is in agreement and areas in which there are divergent perspectives about the student or the team. Summarize the suggestions that the team members have for improving the student's membership, participation, and learning, and the team's collaboration. Quotes may be used as exemplars to reflect the differences in perspectives across team members. If a quote might indirectly reveal the person's identity, then seek permission from that person to use the quote.

Next Steps
These findings are then incorporated into the draft CASTS findings shared with the team at the conclusion of the CASTS. Based on the interviews with all team members, identify the issues that need to be addressed in the CASTS recommendations.

Table 6.3. Sample Comprehensive Assessment of Student and
Team Supports (CASTS) interview questions

Could you tell me a little bit about your background as a _____?

How do you see your role on [student's] team?

How are things going so far this year?

How do you plan for what [student] will do in your class?

Tell me more about what's working and what's not.

When you completed your questionnaire, you left blank the question, "What are the three most important things for the student to learn this year in general education classes?" Could you talk about that?

What parts of the day seem to be going well and what's challenging?

How does a typical [challenging activity named above] activity usually proceed?

What else seems to be difficult?

Let's shift now to talking about how your team is working together. What's working well? What's difficult?

When [paraprofessional, etc.] does come in to your classroom to support [student], how does that work?

Is [student] getting the same assignments as the other kids? How do you handle that?

Is there anything else you would like to share about [student] and the Beyond Access Model?

Activity J: Conduct Follow-Up
Interviews and Observations (if Necessary)

The purpose of follow-up interviews and observations is to gain more information about the student's participation, communication, and performance during instruction and to clarify information gathered from the team member interviews and emerging themes across all previous CASTS activities. A common need for a follow-up observation might be if the initial observation was conducted at a time when there was a substitute teacher, when the school schedule was interrupted by an assembly or other unanticipated event, or when the student was having an "off" day. A common reason to conduct a follow-up interview is to probe more deeply into an issue that did not become apparent until all of the interviews were completed.

Outcome
Field notes of additional information will be integrated into the CASTS findings and recommendations.

Instructions
The instructions for follow-up interviews and observations are the same as for the initial ones. Team members should be informed that the BA facilitator needs additional information in order to get a complete picture of the current educational

program in order to accurately report the findings and generate comprehensive recommendations.

Next Steps

At this point in the CASTS, the BA facilitator assembles all of the materials and syntheses gathered thus far in preparation for synthesizing and summarizing the findings in preparation for the CASTS team meeting.

Activity K: Synthesize and Summarize CASTS Findings

The purpose of synthesizing all of the CASTS data into a set of findings is to provide the team with a comprehensive picture of the student's current educational program relative to the BA Best Practices. Both science and art are involved in writing the summary of the findings. The BA facilitator needs to be especially skilled at identifying themes in the findings and presenting them in a way that illustrates the "big picture" of the student's educational program, supported with examples from relevant CASTS activities. Perhaps the most challenging situation arises when the team's current educational practices are highly discrepant from the BA Best Practices.

Outcome

The outcome from this step is a written draft of findings that is shared at a team meeting. If there are clarifications, additions, or edits to the draft findings, then these are incorporated into a final findings document.

Instructions

The BA facilitator organizes the data from each CASTS activity into the following general outline.

- Description of the school
- Who is this student (e.g., personality, likes, dislikes, strengths, challenges)?
- Student's current membership, participation, and communication in general education instruction in the general education classroom
- Alignment between current practices and BA Best Practices
- Team member ratings of the student's proficiency in academic content areas
- Supports currently being provided to the student
- Recommendations generated by the team for improving the student's membership, participation, communication, and learning
- Team membership
- Team collaboration (i.e., communication skills, meeting structures, team processes)
- Recommendations generated by the team for improving team collaboration

Next Steps

Based on the synthesis of CASTS findings, themes will emerge that will suggest student and team supports to explore and describe during Phase 2 and team professional development.

Activity L: Draft CASTS Recommendations

The purpose of this step is for the BA facilitator to generate draft recommendations based on the synthesis of the CASTS findings.

Outcome
The outcome from this step is a written draft of recommendations that is shared at a team meeting. If there are clarifications, additions, or edits to the draft recommendations, then these are incorporated into a final document.

Instructions
Based on the summary of CASTS findings, write draft recommendations for Phase 2: Explore and Describe. Recommendations may be organized based on the following outline:

- Best practice recommendations
  Presume competence
  Membership and belonging
  Participation
  Learning
  Communication
- Recommendations for student supports
- Recommendations for team supports
- Recommendations for professional development
- Proposed team member responsibilities during Phase 2

The BA facilitator uses the following guidelines to draft the recommendations.

- Draw from evidence-based practices to generate recommendations for new student and team supports.
- Draw recommendations from themes that appear in multiple sources of data.
- Look for unique and creative ideas that have not been tried before.
- Make recommendations that will build the team's capacity by focusing on intermediate outcomes that are likely to lead to the ultimate student outcomes.
- Encourage the team to keep using effective practices and to enhance fidelity of implementation.
- Capitalize on individual team member strengths.
- Focus on new student and team supports that are likely to show impact in a short period of time.
- Ensure that student supports can be implemented within general education instruction in the general education classroom.

- If possible, align recommendations with other school improvement or reform initiatives (e.g., Response to Intervention, service learning).

- Consider the resources that will be needed in order for the team to implement student and team supports.

- Anticipate what specific and focused professional development will be needed by the team in order to implement the recommendations.

Next Steps

Schedule a team meeting to present the findings and recommendations. Ensure that all team members can attend, including parents/guardians and members of the ALT. Reserve a meeting room that will be free of interruptions. Order light snacks and beverages. Arrange for interpreters, staff substitutes, transportation, or other accommodations to ensure that all members are able to fully participate for the entire meeting.

Activity M: Share CASTS Findings and Recommendations with the Team and Achieve Agreement

The purpose of the CASTS findings and recommendations meeting is to achieve a high level of team member agreement with those findings and recommendations.

Outcome

Prepare final versions of the findings and recommendations and ensure high levels of agreement by team members.

Instructions

The BA facilitator strives to present the findings without judgment or interpretation in a way that represents the current reality of the student's educational program and the team's collaboration. The BA facilitator uses his or her judgment in presenting an accurate and fair balance of information that may be viewed as complementary by the team members and information that may be viewed as critical, always using the BA Best Practices as the benchmark for comparison. It may be helpful for the BA facilitator to preface the presentation of findings with the following statement.

> "As you know, the BA Model is based on a number of values- and evidence-based practices that have been shown to have a positive effect on students' membership, participation, communication, and learning of the general education curriculum in the general education classroom. The purpose of the CASTS is to gather a 'picture in time' of how Scott's current educational program compares with those best practices. There will be ample opportunity for you to ask questions, to clarify and add information, and to rate your level of agreement with the findings. We will strive for a high degree of shared understanding about these findings before we consider any recommendations for the next phase of the BA Model. It will be up to you to decide what recommendations you would like to focus on during the next phase of the

Model. The information shared here today will remain confidential within the team."

The findings are presented in a way that is accessible to all team members, including the student's parents/guardians and the student if he or she is present. If English is the student or parent/guardian's second language, then ensure that all text materials are presented in English and in the student or parent/guardian's first language.

The findings and subsequent recommendations can be presented in one or two team meetings. If both the CASTS findings and recommendations are to be considered in one team meeting, then 2 hours should be allotted. Two 1-hour meetings can be held as an alternative. A template for a meeting agenda to share the CASTS findings and recommendations with the family, educational team, and administrative leadership team is presented in Figure 6.3.

We have found it effective to present the findings and recommendations in a PowerPoint presentation, with all team members having a hard copy in front of them. The draft document is not distributed prior to the meeting, and the draft is collected at the end of the meeting so that any edits or additions can be incorporated into a final document. It is helpful to have another person present take notes on any discussion, clarifications, edits, and additions and to record team agreement ratings. We also recommend recording team member agreement ratings for each section of the findings and the recommendations, posted on a piece of flip chart paper for everyone to see (see template in Figure 6.4). This record of agreement ratings is typed and kept with other BA Model documents in the filing system managed by the BA facilitator.

During a CASTS findings and recommendations meeting, team members engage in a consensus building process in which they 1) add any missing and highly relevant information to the findings, 2) seek clarification or propose revisions to any inaccurate information, and 3) register their level of agreement with the statement "these findings reflect the diverse perspectives of our team at the present time." It is important to clarify with the team that they are not being asked to *agree* with all of the findings but rather to rate their agreement with the "snapshot of the student and team" that the findings represent. Team members use the 6-point agreement scale (depicted in Chapter 5) to register their agreement.

We recommend that only those findings that receive a 1, 2, or 3 rating are formally accepted by the team and used as a basis for considering the recommendations for subsequent activities in Phases 2–4. Any findings that receive a 4, 5, or 6 rating need to be edited or dropped from further consideration.

Next Steps

At the conclusion of the findings and recommendations meeting(s), the BA facilitator edits either or both documents to reflect clarifications, edits, and additions offered by team members. He or she provides a copy of the final documents to all team members and keeps one in his or her BA files. It may be helpful for the BA facilitator to laminate a copy of the recommendations and team member responsibilities and post it in the room where the team has their instructional planning meetings (maintaining student confidentiality of course). The recommendations for professional development are translated into a plan (what, who, when) at the beginning of Phase 2.

PURPOSE

Review findings and recommendations from the Comprehensive Assessment of Student and Team Supports (CASTS)

Agree on findings, recommendations, and responsibilities for Phase 2 of the Beyond Access (BA) Model

MEETING PROCESSES

To foster both full participation and efficiency use the following guidelines: no side talk, no story telling, use fingers to do ratings.

We will take notes during the meeting.

Any changes will be made and a final copy returned to team members.

Everything discussed and presented here will remain confidential within the team.

PRESENTATION OF KEY FINDINGS (STUDENT AND TEAM)

Initial polling

Clarify, edit, add

Levels of agreement (provided in a separate handout)

PRESENTATION OF KEY RECOMMENDATIONS (STUDENT AND TEAM)

Initial polling

Clarify, edit, add

Levels of agreement

PRESENTATION OF PROFESSIONAL DEVELOPMENT RECOMMENDATIONS

Initial polling

Clarify, edit, add

Levels of agreement

TEAM MEMBER RESPONSIBILITIES DURING PHASE 2—EXPLORE AND DESCRIBE

Initial polling

Clarify, edit, add

Levels of agreement

WRAP UP AND NEXT STEPS

EVALUATE THE MEETING

What worked?

What didn't work?

What could be done differently next time?

Any "ah-ha" moments?

ADJOURN!

Figure 6.3. Meeting Outline to Share the CASTS Findings and Recommendations.

Team Member Agreement Ratings

Instructions

Record each team member's level of agreement using the following scale:

1 = I enthusiastically agree with...

2 = I agree with...

3 = I agree with..., with a minor clarification and/or edit.

4 = I do not agree with...but will go along with the rest of the team if they do, and I will support the decision (e.g., present with a unified front outside of this meeting).

5 = I do not agree with...and cannot support it.

6 = I do not agree with...and will actively work against its implementation.

CASTS section/team member	Parent/ guardian	General education teacher	Special education teacher	Para-professional	Speech-language pathologist	Occupational therapist	Principal	Special education administrator	Other team members
FINDINGS									
School description									
Who is the student?									
Membership and participation in general education									
Reading skills and attributes									

Team Member Agreement Ratings *(page 2 of 3)*

CASTS section/team member	Parent/ guardian	General education teacher	Special education teacher	Para-professional	Speech-language pathologist	Occupational therapist	Principal	Special education administrator	Other team members
Writing skills and attributes									
Math skills and attributes									
Science skills and attributes									
Social studies skills and attributes									
Current supports									
Team description									
Team planning									

Figure 6.4. Template for recording Team Member Agreement Ratings. (Full-size version included on the accompanying CD-ROM.)

(continued)

Figure 6.4. *(continued)*

CASTS section/team member	Parent/guardian	General education teacher	Special education teacher	Para-professional	Speech-language pathologist	Occupational therapist	Principal	Special education administrator	Other team members
Team collaboration									
Other findings									
RECOMMENDATIONS									
General best practices									
Student									
Team									
Professional development									
Team member responsibilities									

Team Member Agreement Ratings *(page 3 of 3)*

BEYOND ACCESS

POSSIBLE DELAYS TO SUCCESS IN PHASE 1

The challenges that can arise in successfully completing the CASTS include 1) scheduling difficulties and timely completion of the activities, 2) team member concerns about confidentiality inhibiting their participation or contributions, 3) premature judgments or suggestions prior to gaining team agreement on findings and recommendations, and 4) difficulty reporting sensitive information back to the team.

The CASTS activities that need to be scheduled first are those that are dependent on team members' schedules (i.e., home visit, "Day in the Life" observation, interviews, the findings and recommendations meeting[s]), and then time should be built in for the BA facilitator to review the data from one set of CASTS activities prior to engaging in the next. For example, doing the review of the student's historical and current records informs the development of the team member questionnaire, analyzing the team member responses to the questionnaire informs the content of the team member interviews, and so forth. The BA facilitator confirms each scheduled appointment in writing and provides a reminder the day before.

Team member concerns about confidentiality may inhibit their willingness to be honest and open during the CASTS. We have found that team members provide more information during the interviews than they do on the written questionnaires. The BA facilitator needs to take great care to follow through on his or her assurance of confidentiality to build the team's confidence in him or her.

The BA facilitator may be tempted to provide suggestions to team members during the CASTS process. To avoid yielding to this temptation, he or she should use phrases such as, "That is interesting," "Could you provide more details," and "I'd like to wait until I've completed the CASTS before recommending anything new," rather than, "I wonder if you might try . . ." "Have you thought about . . ." or "I've found it helpful to . . ." when observing or interviewing team members.

The last challenge to success during the CASTS may arise if the BA facilitator is hesitant to report what may be perceived as critical information. Garmston and Wellman (1999) reminded us that there are two kinds of conflict that occur between people—interpersonal conflict and conflict around ideas. In the spirit of transparency and to model effective ways to deal with conflict, the BA facilitator might preface the presentation of findings and recommendations by acknowledging and describing both kinds of conflict. The BA facilitator assures team members that conflict can be helpful if it is managed carefully and if team members presume one another's positive intentions. The BA facilitator notes that dedicated and competent professionals are likely to disagree with one another about many issues related to the "best" way to support students with IDD to achieve the ultimate indicators of membership, participation, communication, and learning and that the team will be supported to manage those disagreements to prevent their disintegration into interpersonal conflict.

DEALING WITH CHANGE

Engaging in the CASTS process can be energizing, exciting, and validating for some team members. For others the process may evoke feelings of defensiveness, incompetence, or worry about the extra work that they perceive will be required of them. Team members who are innovators and early adopters of innovations are likely to leave the CASTS meeting and start trying new ideas the very next day. Others will present an attitude of "I'm not changing until you can prove that it will be better than what I am doing now and won't take any more time." The BA facilitator might conduct a short activity based on the Concerns Based Adoption Model (Hord, Rutherford, Huling-Austin, & Hall, 1987) to help team members identify their own reactions to change and to validate both the enthusiasm of the "leapers" and the caution of those who will "wait and see." Readers may find resources from Senge (2006) and Garmston and Wellman (1999) particularly helpful in supporting their team members through the change process.

CONCLUSION AND TRANSITION TO PHASE 2

The CASTS is the foundation for the process steps of the BA Model, just as presuming competence is the foundation of all other best practices related to students' inclusion. The CASTS findings and recommendations inspire team members to be courageous in going beyond their comfort zones and usual ways of doing things.

Chapter 7 describes Phase 2 of the BA Model, in which the team explores and describes new supports for both the student and the team and engages in professional development to increase their knowledge and skills of BA Best Practices needed to implement those supports accurately and consistently.

REFERENCES

Bogdan, R., & Biklen, S.K. (1998). *Qualitative research in education: An introduction to theory and methods* (3rd ed.). Boston: Allyn & Bacon.

Garmston, R.J., & Wellman, B.M. (1999). *The adaptive school: A sourcebook for developing collaborative groups.* Norwood, MA: Christopher-Gordon.

Hord, S.M., Rutherford, W.L., Huling-Austin, L., & Hall, G.E. (1987). *Taking charge of change.* Alexandria, VA: Association for Supervision and Curriculum Development.

Individuals with Disabilities Education Improvement Act (IDEA) of 2004, PL 108-446, 20 U.S.C. §§ 1400 *et seq.*

Jorgensen, C.M., Schuh, M.C., & Nisbet, J. (2006). *The inclusion facilitator's guide.* Baltimore: Paul H. Brookes Publishing Co.

McSheehan, M., Sonnenmeier, R., Jorgensen, C.M., & Turner, K. (2006). Beyond communication access: Promoting learning of the general education curriculum by students with significant disabilities. *Topics in Language Disorders, 26*(3), 266–290.

Senge, P.M. (2006). *The art and practice of the learning organization.* New York: Doubleday/Currency.

Comprehensive Assessment of Student and Team Supports (CASTS) Questionnaire

CASTS Questionnaire *(page 2 of 9)*

The student learns best when:

The student has difficulty when:

What is the one thing you like best about the student?

How do you see the student communicating in 5 years? In 10 years?

Comprehensive Assessment of Student and Team Supports (CASTS) Questionnaire

Instructions

Please answer the following questions as a way for us to gather information about 1) your student/child and your efforts to support him or her in school and at home and 2) you, the team, and the supports in place for your work. Each member of the individualized education program (IEP) team, including family members, should complete this form. Additional individuals who might have vital information but are not presently part of the IEP team may complete the form. Not all questions will apply to every person completing the form. Please write N/A to indicate you will not be answering the question.

Note to the Beyond Access Facilitator: Space is provided to insert additional questions related to the student and/or team prior to distribution of the CASTS Questionnaire.

Student's name: _____   Date: _____

Person completing the questionnaire: _____

Role in the student's life: _____

How long have you worked with or known the student? _____

The following questions are focused on the student.

Who is the student? What is he or she good at doing? What are his or her strengths?

Who does the student enjoy being around? Who are the student's friends?

Appendix 6.1. Comprehensive Assessment of Student and Team Supports (CASTS) Questionnaire. (Full-size version included on the accompanying CD-ROM.)

CASTS Questionnaire (page 3 of 9)

What is your opinion about the student's ability to learn general education academics?

What are the three most important things for the student to learn this year in general education classes?

List the student's accommodations and modifications in each subject area.

Content area	Accommodations	Modifications
Reading		
Writing		

CASTS Questionnaire (page 4 of 9)

Content area	Accommodations	Modifications
Math		
Science		
Social studies		

What might improve the student's participation in the general education class in academic content areas' general education instruction?

Reading:

(continued)

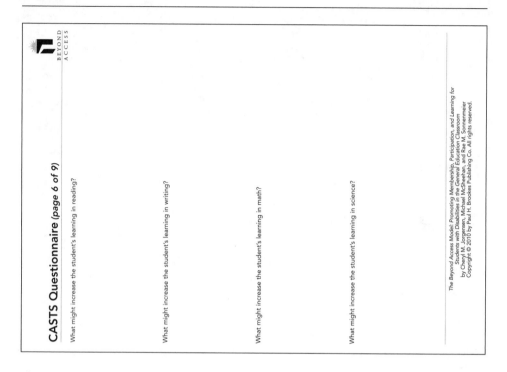

CASTS Questionnaire *(page 6 of 9)*

What might increase the student's learning in reading?

What might increase the student's learning in writing?

What might increase the student's learning in math?

What might increase the student's learning in science?

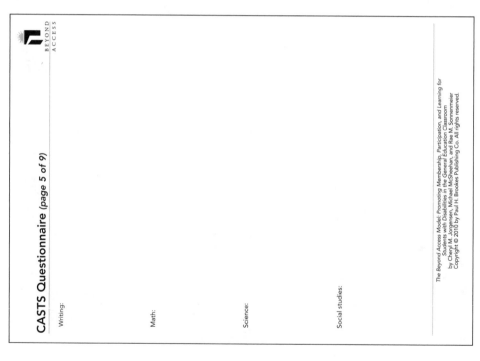

CASTS Questionnaire *(page 5 of 9)*

Writing:

Math:

Science:

Social studies:

CASTS Questionnaire (page 8 of 9)

The following questions are focused on the team—the adults working with the student.

Our team does its best work (i.e., collaborating, planning, communicating) when:

Our team does not do well when:

List some things you think need to be in place for the team in order to support the student to more fully participate and learn in general education class activities and in school.

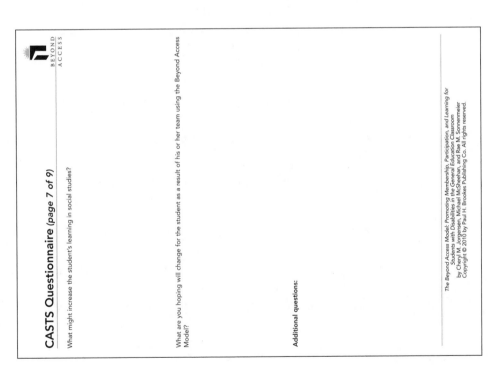

CASTS Questionnaire (page 7 of 9)

What might increase the student's learning in social studies?

What are you hoping will change for the student as a result of his or her team using the Beyond Access Model?

Additional questions:

(continued)

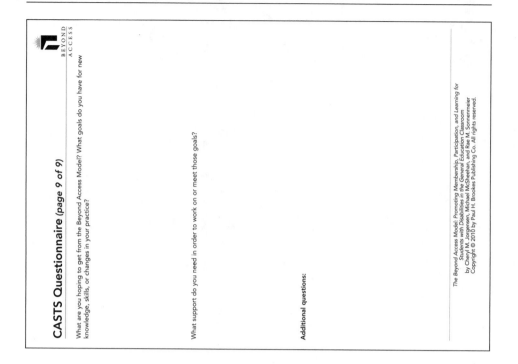

CASTS Questionnaire *(page 9 of 9)*

What are you hoping to get from the Beyond Access Model? What goals do you have for new knowledge, skills, or changes in your practice?

What support do you need in order to work on or meet those goals?

Additional questions:

Phase 2

Explore and Describe
Student and Team Supports

Based on the recommendations for supports agreed on by the team during the CASTS (Phase 1 baseline assessment), the team explores and describes student and team supports during Phase 2 (see Figure 7.1) of the BA Model to enhance 1) student membership in the general education classroom (e.g., having a desk, getting assigned a classroom job, being called on for attendance); 2) student participation in and communication about academic activities and instructional routines in the general education classroom (e.g., generating messages during brainstorming, looking at an adapted book during silent reading, selecting from an array of answers to respond to a multiple-choice question); 3) student demonstration of learning (e.g., giving answers about setting and character during guided reading, completing worksheets, writing essays); and 4) team collaboration (e.g., effective meeting structures, decision-making processes, team communication skills). The supports are explored and described in a way that maintains high expectations and presumed competence in the student's ability to be a member of the general education classroom, to participate in and communicate about academic activities and instructional routines within the classroom, and to demonstrate learning. In Phase 2, the team also engages in professional development to enhance their knowledge and skills in areas specifically needed to explore and describe the supports during Phase 2. See Table 7.1 for an example of one team's professional development plan.

EXPLORATION

We begin by describing one team's successful Phase 2 exploration, including all of the steps they took related to a student, Steven's, participation in a partnered reading activity with a classmate. We describe the dispositions of team

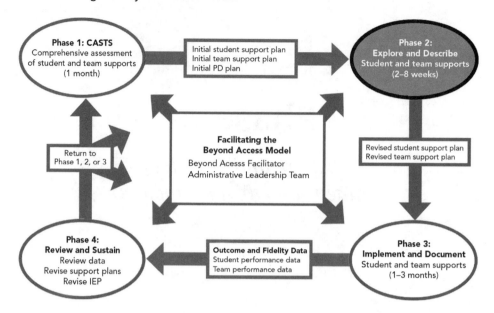

Figure 7.1. Beyond Access Model Phase 2: Explore and Describe. (From McSheehan, M., Sonnenmeier, R.M., & Jorgensen, C.M. [2009]. Membership, participation, and learning in general education classrooms for students with autism spectrum disorders who use AAC. In D.R. Beukelman & J. Reichle [Series Eds.] & P. Mirenda & T. Iacono [Vol. Eds.], *Augmentative and alternative communication series: Autism spectrum disorders and AAC* [p. 427]. Baltimore: Paul H. Brookes Publishing Co.; adapted by permission.) (*Key:* CASTS, Comprehensive Assessment of Student and Team Supports; IEP, individualized education program; PD, professional development.)

members and the BA facilitator needed to implement Phase 2 and the desired outcomes of this phase of the Model. Then, a detailed description of the activities that comprise Phase 2 is presented. We end with two additional examples of teams' implementation of Phase 2, one successful example (for Emily) and one challenging example (for Thomas).

Example of Successful Phase 2 Exploration: Partner with Classmates During Reading

Step 1: Specify Recommendation to Be Explored
The CASTS revealed that Steven's interaction with books was primarily guided by a one-to-one interaction with his paraprofessional. She provided the physical support of holding the book, turning pages, tracking text with her index finger, and reading aloud to Steven. Most other students in class were either reading independently, chatting in pairs as they read, or conferencing with the general education classroom teacher. The CASTS recommendation was to explore the use of partner reading for the whole class during the reading block, pairing Steven with a classmate.

Step 2a: Determine Conditions
The team discussed how the majority of supports provided to Steven by the paraprofessional during reading could be provided by a classmate. A possible unintended consequence of having peers provide supports could be a deleterious ef-

Table 7.1. Sample of a team's Beyond Access professional development plan

Topic/best practice	Learning activities	Practice activities	Reflection activities
High expectations and presuming competence for learning	**Read** *Least Dangerous Assumption:* (Jorgensen, 2005b) *I am Intelligent* (Biklen & Duchan, 1994) *"There's No Way This Kid's Retarded"* (Kasa-Hendrickson, 2004) **Watch** Users of AAC on YouTube videos (e.g., Amanda Baggs)	**Analyze** Student's AAC device and other communication supports for evidence of age-appropriate social and academic vocabulary. Add vocabulary if necessary. IEP section on present levels of performance to determine if assessment results are qualified with respect to student's communication difficulties	**Review and discuss** Classroom videotape showing adult interactions with student and student interactions with classmate. Analyze for voice inflection and breadth of topics of conversation.
Augmentative communication	**Read** *Speaking Up and Spelling it Out* (Fried-Oken & Bersani, 2000) **Watch** Videotapes of proficient AAC users **Listen** Invite guest speakers who use AAC to a workshop. Ask them to share their experiences before they got their device.	**Practice** Design AAC supports for specific social and academic participation. **Explore** Student use of AAC supports **Review and analyze** Videotape of conversations between student and classmates	**Log on** To AAC users group and monitor conversation. Develop list of effective supports for students who use AAC. **Reivew and reflect** Videotape of student using exploratory AAC supports
Instructional planning	**Read** *An Inquiry-Based Instructional Planning Model for Diverse Classrooms* (Jorgensen, 2005a) *Instructional Planning Process* (Chapter 5; Jorgensen, Schuh, & Nisbet, 2006) **View** Videotape of inclusive classroom where a student is participating in a lesson with supports	**Complete** Instructional planning forms from Jorgensen, et al. (2006) Graphic organizer for writing Visual supports for academic routines and daily schedule	**Review** Analyze student performance data. Determine how supports need to be enhanced and revise support plan. Gather data on supports and student performance and analyze again.

Key: AAC, augmentative and alternative communication; IEP, individualized education program.

133

fect on the classmates' performance. The team felt there was minimal risk for that and agreed that they would monitor for such an effect through observations and checking in with classmates on the process. No student would be forced to partner with any particular classmate; the same held true for Steven. Steven and his classmates would have some choice in selecting their partners. With approximately 3 reading blocks per week that could be structured for partner reading, the team felt that 2 weeks would be sufficient time to get a general impression of the effect of this support.

Step 2b: Choose Indicators

By creating a classwide emphasis on pairs during this reading block, and preparing classmates to provide Steven with the necessary assistance should they be paired with him, it was expected that Steven's membership (sense of belonging, decreased reliance on paraprofessional) and participation (percentage of time engaged in the same instructional routine as classmates) would increase.

Step 3: Verify Capacity for Implementation

With some coaching, it was felt that a classmate could learn to position a book so that both the classmate and Steven could see the pages, track text with his or her index finger, and read aloud with Steven. The team decided that the paraprofessional would model how to position the book, turn the pages, track text with an index finger, and read aloud with Steven. Once she provided a model, the paraprofessional would fade her support, monitor the interaction between Steven and his classmate, and coach the pair as needed.

Step 4: Initiate Exploration

The teacher introduced the change in the format for the reading block, specifically mentioning that everyone would have an opportunity to read in pairs. She described how when you read in pairs, it is helpful to show your partner what and how you are reading. She modeled for the class how to hold a book, turn pages, and track the text being read aloud. She probed with the class how the tracking might be helpful to them and their partners. The teacher suggested pairs for the first several days and then allowed more self-selection over time.

Step 5: Adjust Recommendation

In Steven's case, the team was getting an initial impression that the recommendation held promise for enhancing his membership and participation during the reading block. Therefore, an adjustment was not necessary at this time, and the exploration continued.

Step 6: Discuss and Reflect on Key Indicators

The team discussed how the partner reading strategy would affect Steven's membership and participation. The team was unanimous in their opinion that the partner reading strategy was increasing both.

Step 7: Adjust Recommendation Based on Step 6

Given that the new strategy was having a positive effect on Steven's membership and participation, no adjustments were necessary.

Step 8: Share Impressions

During the first session that Steven read with a classmate, the partner asked the classroom teacher, "Doesn't Steven read with Mrs. Jones?" The teacher explained they were trying something new and that Mrs. Jones and she would be on hand if there were any concerns. By the end of the fourth session, it was clear to the teacher and Mrs. Jones that a classmate could quite readily manage the supports of positioning the book so that he or she and Steven could see it, turning pages, tracking text with his or her index finger, and reading aloud. No student showed a negative consequence. Steven appeared quite pleased to be reading with a classmate. A probe of Steven's listening comprehension showed that his participation with the classmate supports was consistent with his participation when supports were provided by the paraprofessional.

Step 9: Make a Decision

The team recommended that the partner reading move to Phase 3 for more specific data collection, and they also realized they would now need to explore a way for Steven to read *to* his classmates.

Phase 2 Dispositions

During Phase 2, team members are encouraged to embrace a "Let's try it and see how it works" approach. This approach encourages the team to be creative and open minded, particularly if a team member is unsure about how a given strategy might work. The short period of time needed for exploring and describing any particular recommendation from the CASTS (typically between 2–8 weeks depending on the support to be explored and described) may be helpful to team members who are not inclined to commit to a novel approach for an extended period of time. In addition, the approach in this phase is inclusive. All team members, regardless of their professional certification or expertise, are encouraged to render a gut-level opinion of how the supports are designed or implemented and whether they hold promise for enhancing student learning. No one person is required to be an expert in AAC, instructional design, or collaborative teaming in order to provide input to the process.

This same mindset of "Let's try it and see how it works" also applies to exploring and describing different meeting processes and team collaboration strategies. For example, a team may explore meeting on a more regular basis; using an agenda; rotating responsibilities during meetings for notetaking, keeping time, and facilitating the meeting; and limiting discussions strictly to instructional planning. After a few weeks of using these teaming structures and processes, the team will render a gut-level opinion about whether the new ways of working together are making a positive difference for them and for the student.

Phase 2 Outcomes

The products of Phase 2 are a new set of recommendations for each CASTS recommendation that the team agreed to explore and describe. There are four possible recommendations that the team may make:

1. Extend the exploration of the recommended support "as is" for a longer period of time
2. Adapt the recommended support and extend the exploration period
3. Abandon the recommended support because it does not seem to show promise
4. Adopt the recommended support and carry it forward into a more formal implementation and documentation period during Phase 3

The team selects one of these four recommendations based on dialogue and discussion of their experience with trying out the recommended support for the prescribed time period. The team needs to be mindful of how a Phase 2 recommendation may affect the larger goals of enhanced student membership and participation in the general education classroom. In some cases, a particular recommendation may show initial promise for enhancing the student's academic performance but have the unintended consequence of reducing the amount of time that the student is spending in the general education classroom with his or her typical peers. Thus, judgment about whether to continue a particular recommended support must always be checked against the broader goals of increasing students' membership, participation, communication, and learning with typical classmates in the general education classroom. The Student and Team Outcomes Survey (see Appendix 7.1) depicts the outcomes that BA teams measure on a quarterly basis to determine how the broad goals associated with presuming competence, membership, participation, communication, learning, and collaborative teaming are being advanced throughout each phase of the BA Model.

Phase 2 Activities

Following a brief description of each step of Phase 2, another example of a successful Phase 2 exploration will be presented. In addition, an example that represents common challenges that may occur during Phase 2 will be described. Although all team members share responsibility for working together in Phase 2 to try out the agreed-on recommendations from the CASTS, the BA facilitator assumes a leadership role in coordinating and supporting the team to accomplish each step described next.

Step 1: Specify Recommendation to Be Explored
At the onset of Phase 2, the team confirms which student and team support recommendations from the CASTS they will begin to explore and describe. Likely examples for exploration in Phase 2 include 1) specific AAC/AT features; 2) instructional accommodations and supports; 3) increased time in the general education classroom; 4) a shift from adult to peer supports; 5) changes in meeting structures, decision-making processes, and teaming skills; and 6) changes in the

location of service delivery from a special education environment to the general education classroom.

Shortly after the CASTS meeting is completed, the BA facilitator convenes a team meeting in which the members prioritize which recommendations will be tried first. The BA facilitator guides polling by team members using the levels of agreement described in Chapter 5. If there is no clear agreement about whether a particular recommendation will be tried (despite it having received positive agreement during the CASTS), then the BA facilitator leads the team in dialogue to understand why particular team members are hesitant to follow through with a CASTS decision.

Perhaps there is reluctance due to concerns about demands on the team members' time. Perhaps team members need concrete assurance from administrators that the necessary supports will be available to the team (e.g., time for meetings, software purchases, professional development workshops) as they move through Phase 2. After this dialogue and discussion, the BA facilitator again polls the team members, and a final list of agreed-on priorities are selected for exploration in Phase 2. Those recommendations that did not rate the highest priority for exploration will be explored later. Figure 7.2 depicts a shortened version of a planning form for recording the results of the prioritization discussion.

Step 2a: Determine Conditions

The BA facilitator guides the team to determine the specific conditions that will guide the exploration of a particular recommendation, including the following:

- Who will be involved in the trial
- Where the trial will be implemented
- When during the day or week it will occur
- How the student or team will explore the new strategy
- What indicators will suggest that the recommended support is successful
- How unintended consequences will be addressed
- How long the recommendation will be tried before being formally evaluated

The BA facilitator uses a planning template similar to the one depicted in Figure 7.3 to guide the team's dialogue and decisions about these conditions.

CASTS recommendation	Priority rating (1 = now, 2 = next, 3 = later)	Timeline/notes
General best practices		
Student		
Team		
Professional development		

Figure 7.2. Prioritizing CASTS Recommendations for Phase 2 Exploration.

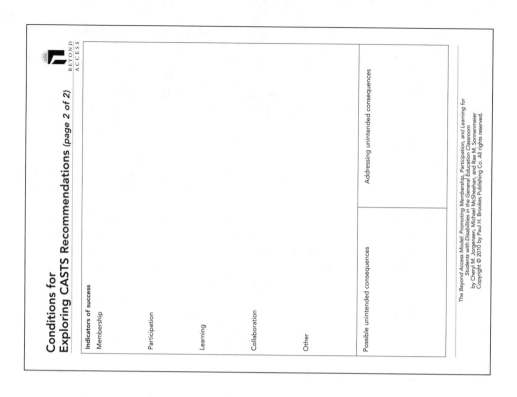

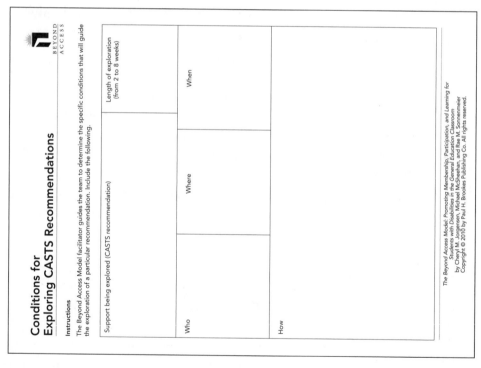

Figure 7.3. Conditions for Exploring a CASTS Recommendation. (Full-size version included on the accompanying CD-ROM.)

Step 2b: Choose Indicators

At this step, the team also decides what indicators of membership, participation, learning, and team collaboration will be used to check the effect of the trial recommendation.

Step 3: Verify Capacity for Implementation

The BA facilitator guides the team to determine if the individuals involved in trying out the recommendation have the basic capacity to implement it or if they need professional development or technical assistance before beginning the trial. As you will recall, the CASTS produces a set of recommendations for the team's professional development. Professional development addresses both declarative knowledge (i.e., knowing the facts or concepts, knowing what supports will be helpful, the ability to describe a support) and procedural knowledge (i.e., knowing the *how*, developing skills for implementation, putting something into practice, implementing with skill to achieve a particular result). The professional development needs to increase both the declarative and procedural knowledge related to fostering membership, participation, communication, learning, and team collaboration. In addition, professional development enhances team members' knowledge and skills in areas of other best practices such as unit/lesson planning and augmentative communication.

If professional development is provided by someone who is not part of the student's team, then it is important for the professional development to be targeted to the specific needs of the student or team and to provide specific examples to the team of how to utilize the new declarative and procedural knowledge within the Phase 2 exploration. For example, following a workshop on using modeling as an instructional approach to increase the student's use of AAC, the team might meet for a reflective practice session led by the BA facilitator to confirm their understanding of modeling and to discuss how modeling can be applied in the context of their general education classroom for this student. If a workshop is provided on emergent literacy for students with IDD, then the team might meet to confirm what emergent literacy skills the student is demonstrating and to discuss how to embed the general strategies from the workshop into the classroom teacher's literacy curriculum and instruction. The role of the BA facilitator is to work with building and district administration to identify and engage the professional development providers, orient those providers to the needs of the student and team, translate the information as it relates specifically to the student and team, and ensure that information from the professional development event is integrated into the team's daily practice.

Step 4: Initiate Exploration

The team initiates the exploration of the recommended support for the determined period of time. The template in Figure 7.3 is posted in a prominent spot where the team has its regular planning meetings. As the team engages in conversations about upcoming lessons and the supports needed for the student to participate, there is intentional focus on the Phase 2 recommendations being explored. For example, if a Phase 2 recommendation is to ensure that the student has vocabulary on his or her AAC device related to discussion of current events in social studies class, then a standing agenda item for each team meeting is discussing current events in the news, providing the vocabulary needed by the student to engage in class discussion, and assigning the responsibility to a team member to program that vocabulary into the device.

Step 5: Adjust Recommendation

The team makes adjustments in implementing the recommended support if immediate positive results are not observed. Implementing this step is where the art and science of teaching come together. Clearly, it is not possible to recommend a cookbook approach to the process of good diagnostic teaching; however, some guidelines can help the team engage this step in a thoughtful way. Each time a support is explored with a student or the team, the team members involved ask themselves the following questions.

- Did we implement the support as we planned?
- What were the conditions under which the support was implemented?
- Did the student show interest and/or engagement that was different from his or her usual reaction?
- Is it possible that the student's performance was affected by his or her health, behavioral state, time of the day, or other factors?
- How might we change one or more conditions the next time the support is tried in order to increase the likelihood of its success?

In Phase 2, it is important to recognize that both the student and the team are learning new ways of doing things, and a certain level of discomfort is to be expected. Team members must be careful not to judge an explored support as not promising until they have become comfortable implementing it with the student or team.

Step 6: Discuss and Reflect on Key Indicators

The BA facilitator supports the team's ongoing discussion of and reflection on indicators of the student's membership, participation, communication, and learning and the team's collaboration. This step is a reminder for the team to constantly be engaged in reflection about the implementation and effect of using the new support. These discussions occur "on the spot" by the team members who are with the student as the recommended support is being implemented, as well as during team meetings. The role of the BA facilitator is to ask probing questions of the team during instructional planning meetings as a way to gather formative information that will flesh-out the description of the recommended support. As the team clarifies and enhances their description of the recommended support and reflects on the findings from the initial exploration, they are checking to see that they actually do have the capacity to implement the recommended support.

Step 7: Adjust Recommendations Based on Step 6

The BA facilitator supports the team to continue to make adjustments to the conditions under which they are exploring the new support. This is done to ensure sufficient opportunities in sufficient contexts to inform their description of the recommended support and their impressions of its promise for enhancing student membership, participation, communication, and learning.

Step 8: Share Impressions

The BA facilitator asks team members to share their impressions about the effect of the recommended support. The BA facilitator supports the team to achieve a shared understanding of what has been tried (i.e., formulating the team's description of the support) and team members' gut-level judgments about the usefulness of the recommended support. This entails the team discussing their experiences during the exploration, seeking to understand other team members' experiences with using the strategy, and summarizing all members' experiences and impressions.

Step 9: Make a Decision

The BA facilitator supports the team to make a decision about the recommendation. As mentioned previously, the four possible decisions for each explored support are as follows:

1. Extend the exploration of the recommended support "as is" for a longer period of time
2. Adapt the recommended support and extend the exploration period
3. Abandon the recommended support because it does not seem to show promise
4. Adopt the recommended support and carry it forward into a more formal implementation and documentation period during Phase 3

The role of the BA facilitator is to guide the team's discussion and dialogue to a point in which there is shared understanding of the trial of each recommendation. The planning template depicted in Figure 7.4 records team members' votes from the four possible choices listed previously. The team moves into Phase 3 for those recommended supports that they agree to adopt for a more formal implementation and documentation period.

Example of a Successful Phase 2 Exploration: Weekly Instructional Planning Meetings

Step 1: Specify Recommendation to Be Explored

Emily's team consisted of a special education teacher, a third-grade general education teacher, an SLP, an OT, and a paraprofessional (who supported Emily and another student in the classroom). Prior to the team's initiation of the BA Model, they met as a full team yearly to write Emily's IEP and quarterly to generate reports on Emily's progress toward achievement of her IEP objectives. Emily's literacy instruction was provided by the special education teacher in a resource room, although Emily did join her third-grade class for self-selected reading time. To en-

Team Member Decisions About Recommended Supports

Instructions

Record each team member's decision regarding the CASTS recommendation being explored. The four possible decisions include:

- Extend the exploration of the recommended support "as is" for a longer period of time.
- Adapt the recommended support and extend the exploration period.
- Abandon the recommended support because it does not seem to show promise.
- Adopt the recommended support and carry it forward into a more formal implementation and documentation period during Phase 3.

Team member	Extend	Adapt	Abandon	Adopt
Parent/guardian				
General education teacher				
Special education teacher				
Paraprofessional				
Speech-language pathologist				
Occupational therapist				
Principal				
Special education administrator				
Other team members				

Figure 7.4. Team Member Decisions About Recommended Supports. (Full-size version included on the accompanying CD-ROM.)

hance Emily's access to the general education curriculum in the general education classroom, a recommendation was made for the team to engage in a 45-minute weekly instructional planning meeting in which they would discuss and plan for Emily's participation in the general education Four-Blocks literacy program. Although exploration of this recommendation entailed several subrecommendations, we will describe just three.

Step 2a: Determine Conditions

The entire team agreed to participate in the weekly team meeting, which was scheduled for Fridays from 7:40 A.M. to 8:25 A.M. It was held in the special education teacher's resource room. The BA Model instructional planning meeting agenda was used to guide the discussion, provide a template for recording the meeting minutes, and record team member responsibilities in a to-do list (see Appendix 7.2). The team agreed to try the instructional planning meeting structure 8 times, 1 time weekly for 2 months.

Step 2b: Choose Indicators

Some desired outcomes from this exploration were that all team members attend and participate in the instructional planning meeting, meeting minutes contain a summary plan for Emily's participation in Four-Blocks, and a to-do list specify what needs to be done to prepare and implement supports for Emily's participation. The BA Model indicators related to this example included increased percentage time in class, increased percentage time in academics, increased percentage time participating in academics, and improved team collaboration.

Step 3: Verify Capacity for Implementation

The building principal was engaged to assist with scheduling the meeting. A buildingwide paraprofessional (non-IEP team member) was enlisted to provide support for Emily to get off the bus and take her to the classroom so that Emily's paraprofessional could stay for the entire team meeting. The OT—whose services were contracted from a regional special education collaborative agency—changed her schedule so that she spent a longer block of time in the school on Fridays to enable her to attend the team meeting. Because this team had never engaged in whole-group instructional planning, a related CASTS recommendation was made to provide them with a workshop on instructional planning, team decision making, and facilitating. Following the workshop, the BA facilitator (another special education teacher in the school who had prior experience facilitating team meetings) led two team meetings to model the process.

Step 4: Initiate Exploration

Over the course of the 2-month exploration, the team adopted many new dispositions and habits, including the following:

- Arriving on time
- Not engaging in small talk at the beginning of the meeting
- Following the "no discussion" rule during announcements
- Only talking about instructional planning during the meeting, not other general or case management issues
- Not having side conversations
- Completing to-do items agreed to in previous meetings
- Using the levels of agreement scale to support sustainable decisions

Step 5: Adjust Recommendation

After three meetings, the team discussed the difficulty that the notetakers were having with recording all of the meeting discussions. The team decided that they would try not recording the whole discussion but instead note important topics with bullet points.

Step 6: Discuss and Reflect on Key Indicators

A team discussion on how well the instructional planning process was going revealed that there were two incidents in which team members were not in attendance for the entire planning meeting. The special education teacher missed a portion of one meeting because she was called away to address another student's in-school illness, and the paraprofessional missed one meeting because the staff member assigned to meet Emily at the bus was absent from school and no substitute had been hired. Prior to beginning the BA Model, several team members had expressed concern about Emily remaining in the general education classroom for literacy instruction because supports for her active engagement had not been developed. After several weeks of the new instructional planning process, team members noted that their new focus on planning for Four-Blocks made them more confident in having Emily stay in the general education classroom.

Step 7: Adjust Recommendation Based on Step 6

The team made two adjustments to the continued exploration of the weekly team meeting based on their Step 6 reflections. The special education teacher spoke with the school guidance counselor and nurse and found them willing to address any "student emergencies" that arose while the special education teacher was in the team meeting. To address the problem with consistent and reliable coverage for the paraprofessional's attendance at the meeting, they instituted a written plan specifying "back-up" responsibilities for the paraprofessionals involved in escorting students from the bus to their classrooms so that the paraprofessional involved in the team meeting did not have to be enlisted.

Step 8: Share Impressions

After they had met for 2 months using the new structure and process, Emily's team shared impressions that suggested the instructional planning process was successful.

- With the two aforementioned exceptions, team members were attending the weekly instructional planning meetings.
- Minutes were generated for each meeting and included a summary plan for Emily's participation in Four-Blocks.
- A to-do list was created at the end of each meeting, listing specific team members and the tasks they would do to prepare support materials for Emily's participation in Four-Blocks lessons.

Step 9: Make a Decision

At the conclusion of the 8-week exploration, the team discussed their impressions regarding the effectiveness of the team meeting. They all agreed to adopt the 45-minute weekly instructional planning meeting and move it into Phase 3 for more formal implementation and documentation.

Example of a Challenging Phase 2 Exploration: Enhance Vocabulary on a Speech-Generating Device

Step 1: Specify Recommendation to be Explored

During the CASTS it became evident that Thomas was using some of the nine items currently available on his SGD. None of the vocabulary, however, was related to academics. Thus, for example, when classmates were calling out answers in class, Thomas could not participate in a similar way. The CASTS recommendation was to increase the availability of academic-related vocabulary on Thomas's SGD.

Step 2a: Determine Conditions

The team discussed in which activities this recommendation might first be explored. They agreed that brainstorming situations in which classmates were calling out information that was not in response to quiz questions or probes for comprehension and instead was an activity to prime them for a discussion of a particular topic might be a preferred place to start. That way, Thomas could activate his SGD without any negative consequence of getting an answer wrong. In this situation, Thomas would not have to select a particular vocabulary item from his SGD display; rather, he could select any item and be participating successfully.

Over the next 2 weeks, for a total of four activities, the general education teacher would provide the SLP (i.e., the person who knew the most about how to program messages into the device) with the topic (e.g., recalling events from a book the class has been reading) and some suggested vocabulary (i.e., five events from the book). The SLP would program the device, using her judgment in selecting the vocabulary arrangement and symbol representation for each target on the SGD display. The paraprofessional would preview the new page with Thomas.

Step 2b: Choose Indicators

The hope for trying out this recommended support was to increase Thomas's participation and communication in instructional activities in which classmates were calling out information. In the specific activities targeted for exploration, likely indicators of positive effect included a number of observable behaviors from Thomas (e.g., activation of the SGD during the brainstorming instructional block, increased visual attention to the activity or source of instruction, positive affect such as smiling), from classmates (e.g., positive comments about Thomas's new participation), and from the general education teacher (e.g., adding Thomas's comment to the written list of events from the book).

Step 3: Verify Capacity for Implementation

When the paraprofessional saw that new vocabulary had been programmed into Thomas's SGD, she knew where it fit in the context of ongoing instruction because of the weekly team planning meetings and her daily meetings with the general education teacher. Although new to Thomas's team, the SLP had attended a workshop on programming this SGD. She felt that it was reasonable to expect that she could do the programming because of the limited vocabulary being explored in the four activities. She was concerned about her time commitments but was willing to dedicate two 30-minute blocks over the next 2 weeks for this exploration.

Step 4: Initiate Exploration

At the end of the first week, the general education teacher had provided the SLP with the topic and vocabulary for one brainstorming activity. The information was provided the day of the activity, and the SLP did not have enough time to program the SGD. For the second week, the general education teacher identified two brainstorming activities occurring later in the week in which this recommendation could be explored. On Monday, she gave the necessary information to the SLP, who programmed the device on Tuesday. On Wednesday, the paraprofessional previewed the vocabulary with Thomas just before the class activity was about to start. The paraprofessional noticed that the new items on the SGD display only spoke the label on the target, not the full vocabulary needed for the activity (e.g., instead of producing the sentence, THE CHILDREN GO THROUGH THE DOOR IN THE WARDROBE FOR THE FIRST TIME, the SGD produced WARDROBE DOOR).

Step 5: Adjust Recommendation

The paraprofessional consulted with the general education teacher and decided to proceed with the exploration based on the modified speech generated by the device. They chatted with Thomas and described the dilemma and how the situation would be accommodated for that day. During that activity, Thomas did select items from the SGD, and the teacher expanded the modified speech to full sentences that she wrote on the class list of summary events. One selection from the preprogrammed messages that Thomas selected was an event from the book that another classmate already stated and was already on the list at the front of the room. The teacher thanked Thomas for the contribution and pointed out that it was on the list.

The results were shared during the team meeting at the end of that week. During a brief discussion of the results and dilemmas, the SLP noted that she would benefit from additional training on device programming and was doubtful that training could occur for a few weeks. An interim solution included the SLP reviewing the device manual to see if she could problem-solve how to program the device to produce a complete sentence instead of only the symbol label. They agreed that the initial results, even with the on-the-spot accommodations, appeared positive because Thomas was able to contribute academic content during an instructional activity. Classmates were observed to have a positive response to Thomas's use of the SGD in the activity.

Step 6: Discuss and Reflect on Key Indicators

This scenario represents a common occurrence during a Phase 2 exploration—conflicting results during the trial. The team discussed that Thomas gave two different responses to the addition of new vocabulary on his SGD. During a class brainstorming activity to predict possible upcoming events in a book, Thomas selected messages from the SGD, calling out information and having the teacher write his ideas on the board with other classmates' ideas. During a brainstorming recall of events from the most recent chapter the class read (during assigned silent reading blocks and for homework), Thomas made no selections and was observed to be rocking in his chair and pushing the SGD away. This resulted in him being taken out of the classroom for a period of calming and making him miss important opportunities for social and academic participation.

Step 7: Adjust Recommendation Based on Step 6

The results from these two attempts to explore the new support were shared during the next team meeting. Team members were pleased to hear the success of the first attempt. It seemed consistent with the earlier trial and led to the impression that "increasing the availability of academic-related vocabulary on Thomas's SGD" (at least for the function of calling out answers during brainstorming activities) should proceed to Phase 3.

Thomas's behavior in the last trial was of concern. Did this mean that the recommendation needed further exploration? Was this just "a bad day" for the student, or was something else at play? The BA facilitator reminded the team to apply the least dangerous assumption of presumed competence to the interpretation of Thomas's behavior. She recommended that the team think about what might cause a typical student to be distracted during an instructional activity. Through further reflection and discussion, the team realized that Thomas had missed three of the four silent reading blocks during which classmates were reading the chapter that was part of the trial activity. (He was pulled out of class for other therapies at those times.) The special education teacher shared that the homework reading may not have been completed because the family had been hosting an out-of-town guest (Thomas's grandfather) for the week. It became apparent that, in this context, Thomas's behavior made sense. He was most likely communicating his lack of familiarity with the chapter and his discomfort with being expected to contribute in an activity for which he was not prepared.

Step 8: Share Impressions

When the team had provided Thomas with new vocabulary on his SDG and supported his participation in several instructional activities, they decided to share their impressions and make a decision regarding their future actions related to programming his SGD. The team noted Thomas's heightened interest in using his SGD, his classmates' positive comments regarding his participation, and their team's gut-level feeling that Thomas had more to tell them than might be assumed from his disability label and past psychoeducational evaluations.

Step 9: Make a Decision

Taking the entire Phase 2 experience into consideration, the team voted to advance the recommendation to "increase the availability of academic-related vocabulary on Thomas's SGD (for the function of calling out answers during brainstorming activities) to Phase 3.

POSSIBLE DELAYS TO SUCCESS IN PHASE 2

Some delays to success in Phase 2 may arise and may be related to prioritizing the CASTS recommendations (e.g., team members may struggle with which recommended supports to explore first) or becoming distracted by other dilemmas that may arise (e.g., addressing challenging behavior might start to feel like the priority while the exploration of new supports takes a back seat, implementing a new schoolwide program may take away from the team's allocated instructional planning time). There may be delays in getting the required professional development, and the team may be hesitant to try certain student- or team-level practices without sufficient training. Alternately, teams may explore too many things at once and be unable to differentiate which supports are making a difference, or they may experience burnout. Teams may stay in Phase 2 too long and never move on to formalizing decisions as to a support's efficacy.

DEALING WITH CHANGE

Exploring the initial priorities from the CASTS is often the turning point for a team because the first signs of evidence emerge that the team can increase a student's membership, participation, and learning of academics in the general education classroom. It may be the first time a team has truly worked together on common goals for the student. It may also be the first time that the general education teacher sees the student as "his or her student." Phase 2 may also evoke challenging situations and emotions. Teams may feel overwhelmed with fulfilling their typical roles and responsibilities to all students while at the same time committing to go the extra mile to try out new instruction, supports, and ways of working together. Team members may experience a "crisis of confidence" if they feel a sense of inadequacy with respect to new practices. If certain recommendations do not seem to show promise, then the team may feel disappointment. If the team does not sense a strong administrative commitment and follow through, then they may feel disillusionment. A skilled BA facilitator will acknowledge team members' feelings, remind the team that any change creates a temporary disequilibrium, and encourage them to celebrate their and the student's accomplishments. He or she also will maintain regular communication with the ALT to advocate for the supports that the team needs in order to do their jobs well. Chapter 10 describes in detail the role of the ALT in supporting teams who are using the BA Model.

CONCLUSION AND TRANSITION TO PHASE 3

The team shifts their activities in Phase 3 to focused implementation and documentation of the CASTS supports that have shown promise at the conclusion of Phase 2.

REFERENCES

Biklen, D., & Duchan, J. (1994). "I am intelligent": The social construction of mental retardation. *Journal of The Association for Persons with Severe Handicaps, 19*(3), 173–184.

Fried-Oken, M., & Bersani, H.A. (Eds.). (2000). *Speaking up and spelling it out: Personal essays on augmentative and alternative communication.* Baltimore: Paul H. Brookes Publishing Co.

Jorgensen, C. (2005a). An inquiry based instructional planning model that accommodates student diversity. *International Journal of Whole Schooling, 1*(2), 5–14, 46.

Jorgensen, C.M. (2005b). The least dangerous assumption: A challenge to create a new paradigm. *Disability Solutions, 6*(3), 1, 5–9, 13.

Jorgensen, C.M., Schuh, M.C., & Nisbet, J. (2006). *The inclusion facilitator's guide.* Baltimore: Paul H. Brookes Publishing Co.

Kasa-Hendrickson, C. (2004). "There's no way this kid's retarded": Teachers' optimistic constructions of students' ability. *International Journal of Inclusion Education, 8*, 1–15.

Student and Team Outcomes Survey and Agenda/Minutes for Instructional Planning Meetings

Student and Team Outcomes Survey

Student's name: _____ Grade: _____

Quarter: ☐ CASTS ☐ 1 ☐ 2 ☐ 3 ☐ 4 Date: _____

Rater's name: _____ Rater's role: _____

Overview

The Student and Team Outcomes Survey focuses on indicators related to the following:

1. Student's membership, participation, and learning of the general education curriculum in the general education classroom

2. Collaborative teaming practice

3. Other indicators identified by the team during the Comprehensive Assessment of Student and Team Supports (CASTS) process

All team members complete a rating of these indicators at baseline (CASTS) and on a quarterly basis. The ratings on these indicators are summarized and reviewed during a team meeting to monitor and to evaluate the overall efficacy of the Beyond Access (BA) Model.

Indicators of the student's membership in the general education classroom

1. Check the box that represents the approximate percentage of the school day that the student currently spends in the general education classroom:

   ☐ 0%–10% ☐ 10%–20% ☐ 20%–30% ☐ 30%–40% ☐ 40%–50%
   ☐ 50%–60% ☐ 60%–70% ☐ 70%–80% ☐ 80%–90% ☐ 90%–100%

2. Check the box that represents the approximate percentage of the school day that the student currently spends on the same schedule (i.e., making the transition from class to class and lesson to lesson) as classmates in the general education classroom:

   ☐ 0%–10% ☐ 10%–20% ☐ 20%–30% ☐ 30%–40% ☐ 40%–50%
   ☐ 50%–60% ☐ 60%–70% ☐ 70%–80% ☐ 80%–90% ☐ 90%–100%

Indicators of the student's participation in the typical activities of the general education classroom

3. Fill in the approximate percentage of time that the student is present and an active participant for lessons and/or activities in the following content areas in the general education classroom:

Content area	Student present (%)	Active participant (%)
Reading		
Writing		

The Beyond Access Model: Promoting Membership, Participation, and Learning for Students with Disabilities in the General Education Classroom
by Cheryl M. Jorgensen, Michael McSheehan, and Rae M. Sonnenmeier
Copyright © 2010 by Paul H. Brookes Publishing Co. All rights reserved.

Student and Team Outcomes Survey (page 2 of 5)

Content area	Student present (%)	Active participant (%)
Math		
Science		
Social studies		

4. Check the box that represents the percentage of the school day that the student currently is in the same instructional routines (e.g., small-group activities, large-group instruction, one-to-one activities, independent seatwork) as classmates:

   ☐ 0%–10% ☐ 10%–20% ☐ 20%–30% ☐ 30%–40% ☐ 40%–50%
   ☐ 50%–60% ☐ 60%–70% ☐ 70%–80% ☐ 80%–90% ☐ 90%–100%

5. Check the box that represents the percentage of the school day that the student currently has the means and supports to communicate about the same topics within the same instructional routines commensurate with classmates:

   ☐ 0%–10% ☐ 10%–20% ☐ 20%–30% ☐ 30%–40% ☐ 40%–50%
   ☐ 50%–60% ☐ 60%–70% ☐ 70%–80% ☐ 80%–90% ☐ 90%–100%

6. Indicate the degree to which the student currently has the means and supports to meet the following communication needs within instructional routines commensurate with classmates. Note the types of assistive technology (AT)/augmentative and alternative communication (AAC) used for various means (speaking, writing, reading, listening; e.g., speech-generating device is used for sharing information; graphic organizer software is used for writing).

	Infrequently	Sometimes	Most of the time	Always
Speaking (voice output; e.g., asking questions, sharing information)				

The Beyond Access Model: Promoting Membership, Participation, and Learning for Students with Disabilities in the General Education Classroom
by Cheryl M. Jorgensen, Michael McSheehan, and Rae M. Sonnenmeier
Copyright © 2010 by Paul H. Brookes Publishing Co. All rights reserved.

Appendix 7.1. Student and Team Outcomes Survey. (Full-size version included on the accompanying CD-ROM.)

8. How proficient is the student in each of the following academic areas relative to *grade-level expectations/general achievement standards*?

Content area	Very low proficiency	Low proficiency	Fair proficiency	High proficiency	Very high proficiency
Reading					
Writing					
Math					
Science					
Social studies					

Indicators of effective and efficient collaborative teaming

9. How often does the team (or a subteam) meet for the purposes of instructional planning?

☐ Never meet for instructional planning
☐ Rarely meet for instructional planning
☐ Sometimes meet for instructional planning
☐ Often (more than once a month) meet for instructional planning
☐ Regularly (once a week or more) meet for instructional planning

10. Check the box that represents how effective instructional planning meetings are to plan the student's membership and participation within lessons to learn the general education curriculum.

☐ Hardly ever effective
☐ Occasionally effective
☐ Sometimes effective
☐ Most often effective
☐ Always effective

	Infrequently	Sometimes	Most of the time	Always
Writing (e.g., producing a written or printed product)				
Reading (e.g., decoding, comprehending)				
Listening (e.g., understanding teacher and others, following directions)				

Indicators of student learning

7. How many opportunities did the student have during this quarter to hand in *learning products* compared with classmates, and how often does the student complete the work assigned in the following academic areas?

Content area	Number of assignments given to entire class	Number of assignments given to the student	Number of assignments student handed in
Reading			
Writing			
Math			
Science			
Social studies			

(continued)

Student and Team Outcomes Survey *(page 5 of 5)*

11. Check the box that represents how *efficient* instructional planning meetings are to plan for the student's membership and participation within lessons to learn the general education curriculum.

   ☐ Hardly ever an efficient use of time

   ☐ Occasionally an efficient use of time

   ☐ Sometimes an efficient use of time; sometimes not

   ☐ Most often an efficient use of time

   ☐ Always an efficient use of time

12. Check the box that represents how well the team *collaborates* to plan for the student's membership and participation within lessons to learn the general education curriculum (e.g., listening, providing strategies for resolving conflict, establishing decision-making rules).

   ☐ Hardly ever effective team collaboration

   ☐ Occasionally effective team collaboration

   ☐ Sometimes effective team collaboration; sometimes not

   ☐ Most often effective team collaboration

   ☐ Always effective team collaboration

Other indicators to be monitored

Note: Based on BA Model Best Practices, these indicators are developed and agreed by the team during each CASTS of the BA Model and updated as needed (with full team agreement). Examples might include the following:

- Increasing the academic vocabulary available to student

- Increasing the adapted books available to student

- Increasing the coaching provided by and for various team members

Agenda/Minutes for
Instructional Planning Meeting (*page 2 of 6*)

3. Announcements (5 minutes)

4. Update on instructional planning results (10 minutes)
    *   How did the student do last week?

    *   How well did our support plans work? Did we deliver supports accurately and consistently?

5. Instructional planning (30 minutes)
    Which subject is the focus for planning today?
    ☐ Math   ☐ Science   ☐ Reading   ☐ Writing   ☐ Social studies

Agenda/Minutes for
Instructional Planning Meeting

Date: _____   Facilitator: _____

Notetaker: _____   Timekeeper: _____

In attendance:

1. Set agenda (2 minutes)

2. What has the student learned this week? (5 minutes)

Appendix 7.2. Agenda/Minutes for Instructional Planning Meeting. (Full-size version included on the accompanying CD-ROM.)

Agenda/Minutes for
Instructional Planning Meeting *(page 4 of 6)*

BEYOND ACCESS

When (activity/routine)	Typically, all students... (observable things they DO)	Student can show this by... (same or alternative means)	Supports student may require to enhance participation and learning	Preparation by team (what, who, by when)

6. **Assessment and grading**

(Note: This item is added to the agenda if the team has concluded, at the end of Phase 4, that effective supports have been implemented with fidelity. At this point, the team has high confidence that the student's performance is an authentic measure of his or her learning.)

Agenda/Minutes for
Instructional Planning Meeting *(page 3 of 6)*

BEYOND ACCESS

When (activity/routine)	Typically, all students... (observable things they DO)	Student can show this by... (same or alternative means)	Supports student may require to enhance participation and learning	Preparation by team (what, who, by when)

7. To do (3 minutes)

What	Who	When

8. Next meeting (2 minutes)

Date: _____   Time: _____

Location: _____

Agenda items: _____

9. Evaluate the meeting (3 minutes)

- What worked?

- What didn't?

- What will we do differently next time?

- Any "ah-ha" moments?

Phase 3

Implement and Document Student and Team Supports

During Phase 3 (see Figure 8.1), the team systematically improves their capacity to implement student and team supports and gathers data on those supports that showed promise in Phase 2. During Phase 2, team members utilized a "Let's try it and see how it works" approach. During Phase 3, team members begin to formalize and systematize their efforts by continuing to implement the recommended supports, documenting team members' fidelity of implementation of supports, and documenting efficacy of supports relative to student and team outcomes. In an era of evidenced-based practice and accountability for results, documenting fidelity of implementation and efficacy of supports is strongly recommended.

This chapter provides definitions of *fidelity of implementation* and *efficacy* and discusses their importance in Phase 3 of the BA Model. In each of the two arenas of documentation—fidelity of implementation and efficacy—the team must consider the following: What are useful data? How will team members collect data? How will team members ensure the data are being collected? How much data are enough?

Following the description of each arena of documentation, we present an example of a team's Phase 3 implementation, including all of the steps the team members took. Then, we describe the dispositions, outcomes, and activities for documenting fidelity of implementation and efficacy. Although the chapter presents fidelity of implementation first, followed by a discussion of efficacy, in practice, these two processes occur simultaneously. The chapter concludes with a discussion of possible delays to success and strategies for dealing with change.

FIDELITY OF IMPLEMENTATION

Fidelity of implementation (or simply *fidelity*) is defined as the use and delivery of a support in the way in which it was designed to be used and delivered by an

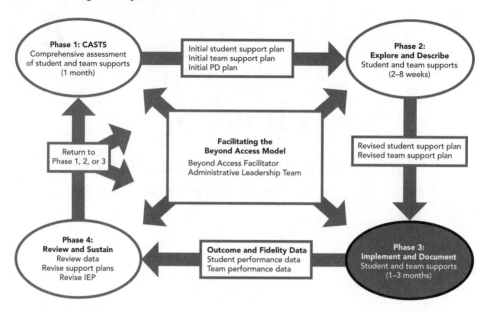

Figure 8.1. Beyond Access Model Phase 3: Implement and Document. (From McSheehan, M., Sonnenmeier, R.M., & Jorgensen, C.M. [2009]. Membership, participation, and learning in general education classrooms for students with autism spectrum disorders who use AAC. In D.R. Beukelman & J. Reichle [Series Eds.] & P. Mirenda & T. Iacono [Vol. Eds.], *Augmentative and alternative communication series: Autism spectrum disorders and AAC* [p. 427]. Baltimore: Paul H. Brookes Publishing Co.; adapted by permission.) (*Key:* CASTS, Comprehensive Assessment of Student and Team Supports; IEP, individualized education program; PD, professional development.)

individual or multiple team members. Fidelity is enhanced through professional development and documented by the person implementing the support or by trained observers. It is necessary to ensure fidelity across team members and in multiple settings in order to be confident that the recommended supports are having the desired result.

Fidelity is evaluated using a fidelity of implementation checklist. Improving fidelity involves expanding the modeling, coaching, and other forms of professional development initiated in Phase 2 to increase the confidence, knowledge, and skills of team members to implement supports accurately and consistently. Teams seek to answer not only the question, "Are we implementing the supports in the way they were intended or recommended?" but also to further articulate their impressions from Phase 2 by answering the question, "What is required to successfully implement the supports with fidelity across multiple team members during the situations in which the supports are needed?"

Phase 3 is designed to help teams move beyond gut-level professional judgment and avoid the trap of judging that something is effective without knowing whether it has been implemented correctly. This stepwise approach that enhances and documents fidelity concurrent with documenting efficacy aligns well with the principles underlying the least dangerous assumption of presuming students' competence. Unless and until students are provided with accurate and consistent supports (operationalized as fidelity of implementation), then teams cannot have confidence in data that purport to measure "what students know." In order to do this, team members learn new skills to bring quality and consistency to their practice through documentation.

The team might address fidelity of implementation of student supports by having team members self-report, conducting classroom observations of team members, or analyzing videotapes of lessons. To address fidelity of implementation of team supports, the team might complete evaluations of meetings, survey team members on the nature of their collaborative efforts (e.g., How often are service providers modeling for the paraprofessional? Do team members perceive those as positive and helpful interactions?), keep track of the percentage of the time that planned instructional supports are actually created and provided to the students, and/or have a trained observer sit in on meetings and complete a fidelity of implementation checklist.

Example of Fidelity of Implementation: Self-Selected Silent Reading

In Phase 2, the team explored using the support of adapted books to increase Steven's participation in self-selected silent reading. Previously, Steven was taken off to the side in the classroom during self-selected silent reading, and the paraprofessional or special education teacher read to him. After the team made adaptations to the book (i.e., placed pages of a book in see-through page protectors and attached page "fluffers" to separate the pages), team members found that Steven needed a way to 1) select a book from the self-selected bookshelf, 2) position the book for viewing, and 3) turn pages in the book. The team implemented additional supports, including adding strings to books on the bookshelf within Steven's reach to support self-selection of a book, positioning an easel on his desk so the selected book could be positioned for viewing, and gluing Popsicle sticks to pages in the books to support turning the pages.

In addition, the team found that Steven needed a way to request someone's attention if he needed assistance and a way for him to ask questions if he did not understand or needed clarification about a word or event in the book. They also described that it was difficult to not return to former practices of selecting a book for him and reading to him, particularly if there was limited time for self-selected reading. Some team members asked, "If the students only have a limited time for reading, then wouldn't it be better for us to just read the book to him rather than wait for him to gain access to the book himself?" Additional supports that the team implemented included recording messages in Steven's SGD to request someone's attention and to ask questions related to the book. Members of the team also agreed to monitor Steven's book reading from a distance and intervene as needed to provide additional support for him to participate in self-selected silent reading.

Initial results from three probes across 2 weeks gave team members the impression that Steven could participate in self-selected reading when the previous supports were provided. Their experience in Phase 3 is described next, following the steps for fidelity of implementation.

Step 1: Formalize Support Description into a Checklist
The team confirmed the description of the supports and formalized the essential components into a checklist so that team members could document implementation. A sample checklist of supports for Steven to engage in self-selected silent reading is presented in Figure 8.2.

Components for self-selected silent reading	Present	Absent	Notes
Steven is well-positioned in his wheelchair.			
Steven selects a book from the bookshelf—pulls string on the side of the book.			
Book is positioned for viewing—easel made available on Steven's desk.			
Page turners—Popsicle sticks and page fluffers are attached to individual pages.			
Steven requests attention with messages programmed in speech-generating device (SGD).			
Steven asks questions with messages programmed in SGD.			
Adults remain at a distance and approach when requested by Steven.			

Figure 8.2. Checklist for documenting the fidelity of implementation of Steven's supports in Phase 3.

Step 2: Determine Conditions

- *Settings*: Steven will use these supports in the general education classroom during self-selected reading and will sit in his wheelchair in a location of his own choosing.
- *Who*: The general education teacher, paraprofessional, and special education teacher need to implement these supports. Other team members are not typically in the classroom during this time.
- *Fidelity level*: The team estimates the level of fidelity required by various team members based on their need to implement the supports.

  Awareness: SLP, OT, PT, nurse

  Partially proficient: not applicable

  Proficient: paraprofessional

  Expert: general education teacher, special education teacher
- *Fidelity measures*: The three team members who will implement the supports will complete the fidelity checklist. The person completing the checklist will note who the primary person was implementing the supports, even if it was him- or herself. If one person filled out the fidelity checklist based on observation of another team member's implementation, then the two would debrief shortly following the observation of the activity and note whether each support was provided or not provided and make any comments that might be interesting for the team to discuss.

- *Time line/quantity of data collection*: The team established a 3-week time line for collecting the fidelity data, with the expectation that a minimum of 10 opportunities for self-selected reading would occur during that period.

Step 3: Verify Capacity for Implementation

Using team member self-ratings (see Table 8.1) and dialogue, the team determined that resource handouts on how to physically adapt books (which the team already had on file) would be sufficient for the components related to physically adapted books. The SLP was confident she could program messages into Steven's SGD that would allow him to request assistance and ask questions about the text of the book. In part, this would be accomplished by duplicating messages already in his device and organizing a single-page display for self-selected reading. They predicted one display would meet these communication needs. The three team members implementing this support reported they were already skilled enough with AAC to support Steven in this activity.

Step 4: Initiate Implementation with Fidelity Documentation

Within a week, the SLP had the new communication display programmed and available to Steven. She oriented him to the new page and let him know when it would be used. The paraprofessional and special education teacher continued to make physical adaptations to other books based on their skills from the initial exploration and following the instructions on the resource handouts. During self-selected reading, the general education teacher reminded Steven that he, like others, would be reading on his own. If he needed assistance, he should use his device to call someone over to help.

Step 5: Adjust Implementation and Fidelity Documentation

At the team meeting the following week, the paraprofessional brought three completed checklists, and the three team members who had been present during implementation reported their impressions. As the discussion progressed, it became apparent to the BA facilitator that people were filling out the fidelity of implementation checklist based on Steven's performance rather than on whether the support was provided. For example, if Steven self-selected a book, then the person completing the fidelity checklist checked "present," and if Steven did not

Table 8.1. Sample ratings of individual team members' capacity to implement a support in Phase 3

Capacity rating	Description
Awareness	I know what the support is and am able to identify it when seeing it implemented.
Partially proficient	I can implement most but not all of the components of the support when coached to do so.
Proficient	I can independently implement the necessary components of the support.
Expert	I can independently implement the necessary components of the support and am skilled at teaching others to implement it.

ask for assistance, the person checked "absent." The BA facilitator clarified for the team that the checklist items are to document if the support was provided, not if Steven used the support or if using the support elicited the target behavior from Steven. This confusion is common, and the dialogue clarified the team's understanding of the differences between fidelity and efficacy. The team revised the checklist to better represent the focus on provision of supports (rather than a focus on Steven's performance). The team proceeded the following week with the initial plan for fidelity data collection.

Step 6: Discuss and Reflect on Fidelity of Implementation
As fidelity data were collected, the team continued to take advantage of both informal and scheduled opportunities to discuss and reflect on the emerging findings. The three team members implementing these supports gave each other feedback on implementation. They also updated the team during weekly instructional planning meetings, and the BA facilitator led team members' ongoing discussion of and reflection on the emerging findings by encouraging discussion around the following questions.

- Have we implemented the support as we planned? What went well? What was missing?
- What were the conditions under which the support was implemented? How might that have affected fidelity?
- How might we change one or more ways that we implement the support next time in order to increase fidelity?

The team realized that the time pressures of self-selected reading often resulted in books being selected for Steven and someone positioning the book for him. When those two steps were completed for Steven, he was able to engage the rest of the supports and was participating in self-selected reading in class.

Step 7: Adjust Implementation and Fidelity Documentation Based on Step 6
The BA facilitator encouraged the team to consider adjusting the components of the supports to make the first two steps optional. Although these were important for Steven's independence, they did not appear essential for increasing participation in self-selected reading. The team disagreed with this and felt the purpose of self-selected reading was not preserved without these first steps. The BA facilitator invited the general education teacher to reflect on the time pressures she saw as the barrier to completing the first two steps. As the team discussed this further, team members agreed that the time pressure might be alleviated by allowing Steven to begin selecting his book 1–2 minutes earlier than other classmates, as long as that did not result in him missing other portions of class instruction. The BA facilitator and OT suggested they might be more helpful in solving this problem if they observed self-selected reading. Over the next week, they observed and noticed that one cause of the delay came when Steven had to navigate around classmates who were crowded around the bookshelf at the same time. They agreed that the problem would be alleviated if Steven could select his book before his classmates.

Following these adjustments, the team agreed to extend the fidelity data collection by another week. This created an additional five opportunities for implementation of the self-selected reading supports with Steven. The team anticipated that having him select his book 1–2 minutes before his classmates would correct

Components for self-selected silent reading	Present	Absent	Notes
Steven is well-positioned in his wheelchair.			
Steven is prompted to go to the bookshelf 1–2 minutes early.			
Strings are attached to the sides of books so that Steven can pull a string to select a book.			
Book is positioned for viewing—easel made available on Steven's desk.			
Page turners—Popsicle sticks and page fluffers are attached to individual pages.			
Messages are programmed in speech-generating device (SGD) so that Steven can request attention.			
Messages are programmed in SGD so that Steven can ask questions.			
Adults remain at a distance and approach when requested by Steven.			

Figure 8.3. Revised checklist for documenting the fidelity of implementation of Steven's supports in Phase 3. Revisions reflect input from Steps 5–7.

the problem of team members skipping the first two steps of the checklist and would preserve the other components of the supports. The supports checklist was revised accordingly based on discussions in Steps 5–7. (see Figure 8.3).

Step 8: Summarize Data
The BA facilitator summarized the fidelity data following the additional week of documentation. The summary demonstrated that the team met the conditions from Step 2 by allowing Steven to select his book in advance of classmates.

Step 9: Make a Decision
With the data summarized, the team met and determined there were sufficient fidelity data for a formal review by the team. All team members agreed at a Level 2 (see Chapter 5). With sufficient data for a formal review, the team moved into Phase 4 to review the data and make a decision about the next steps.

The emphasis of Steven's team on documenting fidelity of supports for self-selected reading provides an example of the steps involved in this part of Phase 3. Team members collaborated to clarify the purpose of data collection and to improve their practices with the ultimate goal of enhancing Steven's participation. Next, the dispositions that helped the team successfully complete this portion of the Model are discussed.

Fidelity of Implementation Dispositions

Team member dispositions for this part of Phase 3 include 1) flexibility to be both a learner and a teacher, 2) vulnerability in self-reflection, 3) a willingness to make one's practice public, 4) shared responsibility for evaluating both individual and collective team efforts, and 5) presuming the competence of one's colleagues.

All team members need to be aware of what others are doing and how they are doing it. Having agreed-on tools for measuring fidelity and having shared responsibilities in data collection will help increase the team's capacity to implement supports with greater consistency. This brings team members' practices out of the private therapy room or closed-door classroom and into the open. Garmston and Wellman wrote about this as *deprivatized practice.* "When practice is deprivatized, teachers visit one another's classrooms to observe master teaching, to coach each other, to mentor, and to problem solve in the living laboratory of instructional space" (1999, p. 18). This disposition is not only essential to a professional community but also helps improve fidelity. Bringing practice out in the open contrasts with operating in isolation, which may "buffer mediocrity and hide high performers from those who might learn from their modeling, consultation, and coaching" (p. 18).

Deprivatized practice is consistent with the professional development begun in Phase 2 and continued in Phase 3, which begins to focus more on coaching and reflective practice to increase shared understanding and implementation consistency among team members. If one team member has expertise that needs to be developed in others, then that team member steps up to assist others in learning that skill.

During Phase 3, the concept of presuming competence appears not only in relation to the student but also in relation to team members. Do I view my colleagues as people capable of learning what I know and can do? How might I best support their learning based on presuming they are competent to learn?

The data collection of Phase 3 requires that the team be clear about what is important, focus their attention on details, observe one another's practice, engage in reflective discussion, and hold themselves accountable to protocols and to each other. Follow-through is central to Phase 3 success. Phase 3 involves a process of moving from implicit to explicit practices.

Fidelity of Implementation Outcomes

The product from this portion of Phase 3 will be a summary of fidelity of implementation data. When teams take action to improve fidelity, they increase the confidence with which they can view student learning data as a valid measure of student performance. In addition, they increase their shared understanding of a student's educational program, their capacity to implement supports among team members in multiple settings, and their confidence in their ability to educate a student with IDD in general education classrooms and other inclusive environments.

Fidelity of Implementation Activities

Although all team members share responsibility for working together in Phase 3 to implement and document the agreed-on recommendations from the CASTS, the BA facilitator assumes a leadership role in coordinating and guiding the team to accomplish each step described next for each support. For ease of description in this section, we will refer to support in the singular. We recognize that some supports cannot be disentangled or many need to be documented as a "bundle" with another support or supports.

Step 1: Formalize Support Description into a Checklist

At the outset of Phase 3, the team confirms the description of the support that team members want to ensure is being implemented with fidelity. From Step 8 in Phase 2, there should be an initial description generated from team members based on their experiences with and impressions from exploring the support. Before proceeding with implementation, it is necessary for the team to formalize and confirm the support description so team members know what they are implementing and documenting. Essential components of the support description should be provided in a checklist so that the team can check to make sure that all essential components of the support are being implemented with fidelity.

Step 2: Determine Conditions

Not all team members may need to implement each support with high fidelity. For example, everyone may take a turn facilitating meetings, and thus everyone needs to be proficient with implementing that team support. Alternately, only the general education teacher, paraprofessional, special education teacher, and SLP might have the opportunity to facilitate guided reading, so only those team members need to demonstrate proficiency with implementing support during guided reading. The PT might never be in class for guided reading and therefore might only need to be aware of its use and related outcomes.

When initiating Phase 3 for fidelity of implementation, team members discuss in which settings the support is needed, who will be implementing the support, what level of fidelity is required by which team members, what type of fidelity measures are the best fit for data collection, and how much fidelity data need to be collected. The BA facilitator guides the team in completing the fidelity of implementation planning template (Figure 8.4), including the following:

- *Settings*: The situations and places in which the support is needed.
- *Who*: The team members who are likely to implement the support.
- *Fidelity level*: The level of fidelity of implementation of the support needed by the various members of the team. Individual team members may have a different level of fidelity based on the likelihood of their implementation of the support. Teams may decide to tailor the levels of fidelity for a specific support based on student and/or team needs. We recommend the following four levels of fidelity be used in this step:

  Awareness: Team member knows what the support is and is able to identify it when seeing it implemented.

  Partially proficient: Team member implements most but not all of the components of the support when coached to do so.

  Proficient: Team member independently implements the necessary components of the support.

  Expert: Team member independently implements the necessary components of the support and is skilled at teaching others to implement it.

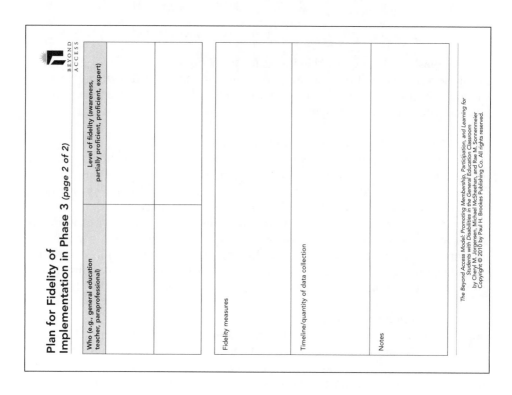

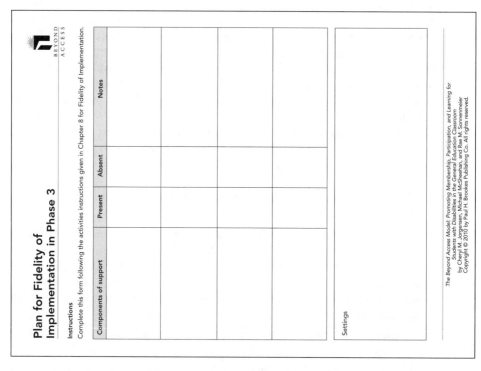

Figure 8.4. Plan for Fidelity of Implementation in Phase 3. (Full-size, three-page version included on the accompanying CD-ROM.)

- *Fidelity measures*: Self-reports, one-to-one observation, and video review are likely data sources for fidelity. Self-reports using checklists are completed during or immediately following implementation of the support (see example in opening scenario of this chapter). One-to-one observations utilize the same checklist but are completed by an observer. Video reviews are conducted by individual or several team members who are trained to identify the essential components of a support as it is implemented.

- *Time line/quantity of data collection:* Documentation of fidelity at the degree of specificity described in these directions is not likely (nor recommended) to be maintained by a team for extended periods of time. The team establishes a reasonable time line for and a quantity of documentation of fidelity. The team sets data collection goals based on team members' best judgment of how much data will be required for them to make fidelity determinations. For the purposes of improving fidelity, team members might document and adjust their implementation until a majority of the team members implementing the support have reached the needed level of fidelity (awareness, partial, proficient, or expert), set a predetermined amount of time (e.g., 4 weeks) during which they will collect fidelity data, or establish a time line based on completion of a specific set of activities (e.g., upon completion of two half-day trainings and three observation with coaching sessions per team member). The time lines and quantity of data are estimated and may be adjusted based on experience as team members initiate these activities.

Step 3: Verify Capacity for Implementation

After thoroughly describing the support and specifying the conditions under which it will be implemented, the BA facilitator guides the team to assess current team member capacity. Using team member self-ratings and dialogue, the team determines what professional development is required by individual team members for them to meet the conditions set forth in Step 2. For example, the SLP might be the only team member who knows how to program a student's SGD. The SLP rates her fidelity as partially proficient in that she still relies on the device manual to guide her through the programming steps. The conditions set forth in Step 2 might indicate that all team members need to have basic skills in programming new vocabulary on the SGD. Thus, a formal presentation from someone with expertise with the student's SGD may be necessary, with team members then coaching each other and sharing the device manual to foster their proficiency with this support.

Step 4: Initiate Implementation with Fidelity Documentation

The team implements the support and collects fidelity data. The team does so with attention to the conditions, roles, and measures identified in Step 2. For example, if part of the fidelity data collection involves the SLP observing other team members as they provide communication supports, then those observations are scheduled.

Step 5: Adjust Implementation and Fidelity Documentation

The team makes adjustments in implementing the support and the fidelity documentation procedures as needed. The team discusses the fidelity data to ensure that team members are collecting what is needed to assess how well the support is being implemented. If the data are not useful in addressing fidelity, then changes will need to be made in the fidelity data collection plan.

Step 6: Discuss and Reflect on Fidelity of Implementation

As fidelity data are collected, there are both informal and scheduled opportunities to discuss and reflect on the emerging findings. Continuing with the example from Step 4, the SLP might not only complete the fidelity of implementation checklist for a specific support, but also might debrief with the person being observed to provide that team member with immediate feedback on his or her performance relative to the essential components of the support. During regularly scheduled meetings (of the full team or subcommittees of the team), the BA facilitator guides the team members' ongoing discussion of and reflection on the emerging findings. As fidelity is documented, the team members involved in the implementation ask themselves the following questions:

- Have we implemented the support as we planned? What went well? What was missing?

- What were the conditions under which the support was implemented? How might that have affected fidelity?

- How might we change how we implement the support next time in order to increase fidelity?

In Phase 3, as with Phase 2, it is important to recognize that both the student and the team are learning new ways of doing things, and a certain amount of awkwardness and uncertainty is to be expected. Team members need time to build their confidence and skills in providing the supports. Team members are careful not to judge each other's capabilities to implement a support if there has not been adequate professional development. Team members must also be careful not to judge a support as not promising before they have become comfortable implementing it with the student or team. To do so would confound efficacy with fidelity.

Step 7: Adjust Implementation and Fidelity Documentation Based on Step 6

The BA facilitator supports the team to continue to make adjustments to the conditions under which team members are implementing and documenting the support. This is done to ensure sufficient opportunities in sufficient contexts in order to inform their fidelity of implementation of the recommended support. These adjustments are based on the emerging findings of the team members' documentation of fidelity and their experiences implementing the support (see questions in Step 6). The BA facilitator encourages team members to provide and receive ongoing professional development, as needed, that will include modeling and coaching by team members during in-class activities and during planning meetings. With ongoing professional development, team members adjust their implementation to reach their fidelity goals.

Step 8: Summarize Data

The BA facilitator is constantly monitoring with team members to determine if they are reaching the goals set out in Step 2. When the conditions, particularly the time line and quantity of data conditions, are met, the BA facilitator (or other team member who is the point person for a particular support) summarizes the fidelity data. The summary demonstrates 1) how the team met the conditions for implementing the support with fidelity (Step 2) and 2) how the fidelity data are sufficient for decision making to move the support to Phase 4 (as illustrated in the example of the exploration of self-selected silent reading).

Step 9: Make a Decision

With the data summarized, a team discussion is scheduled to determine if there are sufficient fidelity data for a formal review by the team. The BA facilitator guides the team to make a formal decision about the sufficiency of the data collected using the levels of agreement (see Chapter 5). If the team agrees there are sufficient fidelity data for a formal review, then the team initiates the activities outlined in Phase 4 with this data summary. If there is not agreement among the team members that there are sufficient fidelity data for a formal review, then the team determines how much additional data collection is needed or what additional professional development is required to improve fidelity, within a specified time frame. Steps 4–8 are repeated, and another team meeting is held to review the additional fidelity data for the specific support to determine if the team is now in agreement to move to Phase 4.

EFFICACY

Efficacy involves collecting data that show whether the supports that are implemented (with increasing fidelity) are having the desired outcomes for the student and for the team. Chapters 2 and 4 provide descriptions of ultimate and intermediate outcomes. Baseline data on these outcome measures are gathered during the CASTS using the Student and Team Outcomes Survey (see Appendix 7.1). The team seeks to answer, with confidence and supporting documentation, the following questions: By using these supports, are we increasing our presumed competence of the student and increasing collaborative teaming by the adults (intermediate outcomes)? By using these supports, are we increasing membership, participation, and learning for the student (ultimate outcomes)? This will involve designing and agreeing on the data collection methods, collecting the data, and analyzing the data to confirm if the desired outcomes are, in fact, being realized. We must confirm or refute our impressions with sufficient documentation.

Calculator's (1999) discussion of efficacy in AAC relates well to the BA Model. He highlighted the necessity of demonstrating meaningful outcomes in the context of participation in daily living without waiting for proficient use of an AAC system (or, we would add, any other support). "These individuals [with disabilities who are being provided with AAC services] cannot be expected to wait for access to events they value while they, and others, engage in training over extended periods of time. Initial benefits should be obvious in the short term" (1999, pp. 5–6). Calculator went one step further by suggesting that participation is *necessary* for proficient use of an AAC system. The BA Model is similarly based on the notion that membership and participation are *necessary* for demonstrating learning of academic content in the general education classroom. Teams using the BA Model do not wait for all the perceived prerequisites or fidelity of implementation of all supports to be fully in place before they begin to measure the effect of those supports. Our initial research on the effect of the BA Model suggests that presumed competence, collaborative teaming, membership, participation, and learning will increase from conducting the CASTS (Phase 1) and exploring and describing (Phase 2), prior to establishing desired levels of fidelity of implementation in Phase 3 (Jorgensen, McSheehan, & Sonnenmeier, 2007; McSheehan, Sonnenmeier, Jorgensen, & Turner, 2006; Sonnenmeier, McSheehan, & Jorgensen, 2005). Finally, Calculator acknowledged that

> Some may prefer a cleaner, more orderly, perhaps unrealistic world in which single causes consistently yield predictable, unidirectional effects. Perhaps a more realistic proposition would suggest that any outcome of AAC [and of efforts to foster membership, participation, and learning] is a combined, transient, cumulative effect that arises from several co-occurring variables, any one or combination of which can exert a differential impact on an individual's success with AAC [and inclusive education], at any given moment. (1999, p. 7)

Using efficacy data to evaluate the effect of the BA Model is a prime example of the somewhat messy process of documenting outcomes that occurs in real school settings rather than under easily controlled experimental conditions.

Efficacy Dispositions

Team member dispositions for documenting efficacy include the same attributes described in the previous section on fidelity of implementation, plus three additional ones: 1) the ability to pay attention to detail while keeping the "big picture" in mind, 2) resiliency when the team's current efforts are not resulting in the desired student outcomes, and 3) a steadfast commitment to the least dangerous assumption of presumed competence.

Using data to inform instructional decision making has long been a strength of special education. In the age of heightened accountability, documenting all students' learning is linked to the determination of annual yearly progress as required by NCLB. The challenge is to collect data that are sensitive enough to detect small changes in student behavior without losing focus on the bigger picture of students' membership, participation, and learning.

The second disposition needed by BA teams engaged in gathering efficacy data is best described as resiliency. For many students with IDD, it takes many months or even years of sustained work by committed parents and educators to achieve significant, observable progress in communication and learning. If the first set of efficacy data do not show changes in the desired student outcomes, then the team members need to embrace an attitude that says, "Well, it didn't work when we tried that support, so let's go back to the drawing board and see what we can try next. We are confident that if we work together effectively, we'll get closer to success next time."

Finally, holding fast to the least dangerous assumption of presumed competence that the student can and will learn and communicate is the disposition that will sustain teams when their efforts do not prove efficacious. This disposition, perhaps more than any other, has helped many parents and professionals remain

Table 8.2. Sample of efficacy data based on quarterly administration of the Student and Team Outcomes Survey

Outcome indicator	Baseline (CASTS)	Quarter 1	Quarter 2	Quarter 3
Percentage of day in classroom	30–40	60–70	70–80	70–80
Percentage of day on same schedule	0–10	20–30	30–40	60–70
Means to communicate with voice output	Infrequently	Infrequently	Sometimes	Most of the time
Frequency of instructional planning	Never	Often	Regularly	Regularly

Key: CASTS, Comprehensive Assessment of Student and Team Supports.

optimistic and committed to, as Gold (1978) put it, try another way. Given the power that our expectations have on student motivation and learning, never giving up is perhaps the best gift we can give our students (Jorgensen et al., 2007).

Efficacy Outcomes

Summary data based on the quarterly administration of the Student and Team Outcomes Survey (see Table 8.2 for an example) are the second major product from Phase 3 activities. These efficacy data provide the necessary documentation for moving into Phase 4, in which the IEP team conducts a formal review to see if the data demonstrate that implementation of planned supports are having their intended effect.

Efficacy Activities

The activities for baseline data collection are described in Chapter 6. Ongoing efficacy data collection is completed using the Student and Team Outcomes Survey (Appendix 7.1) on both ultimate and intermediate outcomes—membership, participation, learning, and team collaboration. We recommend these outcome measures be collected every 2–3 months, aligned with grade and IEP progress reporting periods. Once collected, the student and team outcomes data will be used in Phase 4 for a formal review of efficacy.

POSSIBLE CHALLENGES TO SUCCESS IN PHASE 3

There are two primary reasons why teams experience challenges to successfully using the BA Model during Phase 3. The first challenge is managing the data that are being generated from the fidelity and efficacy documentation. Some BA teams have found it useful to organize these data in digital files or printouts in a binder that can be referenced each time the team meets. The contents might include:

Phase 1: CASTS

- CASTS Questionnaire (see Appendix 6.1)
- Student and Team Outcomes Survey baseline findings (see Appendix 7.1)
- Team Member Agreement Ratings (see Figure 6.4)

Phase 2: Explore and describe

- Prioritizing CASTS Recommendations for Phase 2 Exploration (see Figure 7.2)
- Team meeting minutes during Phase 2 (see Appendix 7.2)
- Descriptions of each support being implemented
- Conditions for Exploring CASTS Recommendations (see Figure 7.3)
- Team member decisions about recommended supports (see Figure 7.4)
- Updates from the Student and Team Outcomes Survey (see Appendix 7.1)

Phase 3: Implement and document

- Plan for Fidelity of Implementation in Phase 3 (see Figure 8.4)
- Team meeting minutes from Phase 3
- Updates from the Student and Team Outcomes Survey (see Appendix 7.1)
- Record of decision making for each support (e.g., abandon, revise, move to Phase 4)

Phase 4: Review and sustain

- Checklist for Documenting Fidelity of Implementation (see Appendix 10.1)
- Student and Team Outcomes Survey summaries (see Appendix 7.1)
- Record of decision making for supports (e.g., efficacious, sustainable, referrals to the ALT)
- Record of decision making for addressing CASTS recommendations not yet explored
- Record of professional development

  Professional development recommendations from CASTS

  Agendas or other records of professional development activities

> Recommendations for ongoing professional development to improve fidelity

- Evidence of learning

> Summaries of present levels of performance in academic areas (with relevant work samples)

> Team member ratings on confidence in student's demonstration of learning

The second challenge to success is the tendency to judge that the student is not learning before sufficiently exploring a wide array of supports and ensuring adequate fidelity has been achieved. Changing long-standing assumptions about the learning potential of students who have been labeled with IDD or perceived as *low functioning* represents a steep learning curve for many people. If, after many weeks or a few months of sustained effort by the team, students are not showing higher levels of engagement and learning, then teams may be quick to assume that the student will never learn. Each team member has a responsibility to support his or her teammates in maintaining high expectations as exploration, fidelity, and efficacy data are considered together.

DEALING WITH CHANGE

During Phase 3, team members may experience a variety of emotions. They may be joyful about their student's enhanced membership, participation, and learning and proud of their growing competence as a collaborative team. Conversely, they may experience a sense of frustration and disappointment if their supports do not result in changes in student outcomes or if there is unresolved team conflict. Positive outcomes are certainly cause for celebration, and taking time to recognize each team member's hard work and commitment is important. A personal note of thanks or a piece of candy on one's keyboard makes team members feel valued and appreciated.

When difficulties are faced by the team during Phase 3, the BA facilitator might employ one of several possible strategies for relieving tension and addressing team members' concerns in a respectful way. The BA facilitator might suggest that the team devote one of its planning sessions to generating a list of "what is going well" as well as "what are the struggles." This list is a tangible reminder that challenges are almost always balanced by some successes. The second strategy that the BA facilitator might employ is asking a colleague who is not on the team to provide an outside perspective on the particular challenge the team is facing. It is easy for all of us to experience tunnel vision when viewing a familiar problem, and asking for advice from another person with a fresh perspective can sometimes reveal a new idea to try. The third strategy for dealing with Phase 3 difficulties is to focus the team's attention on one difficulty at a time. It can be overwhelming to address simultaneously all of the support needs of some students with IDD, and addressing one issue at a time may provide a brief respite for the team to recover its energy. Again, the BA facilitator takes the lead in engaging in these problem-solving activities.

CONCLUSION AND TRANSITION TO PHASE 4

When the team has high agreement that the fidelity and efficacy data are sufficient, the focus transitions to Phase 4. During Phase 4, the team answers three questions:

1. Given the current fidelity with which we are implementing this support, are we confident that the evidence of student learning represents a reliable and valid measure of the student's achievement?

2. Has a support implemented with high fidelity proven its efficacy in improving the student's membership, participation, and learning?

3. For those supports that have proved efficacious, what do we need in order to sustain it over time?

REFERENCES

Calculator, S. (1999). AAC outcomes for children and adults with severe disabilities: When seeing is believing. *Augmentative and Alternative Communication, 15,* 4–12.

Garmston, R.J., & Wellman, B.M. (1999). *The adaptive school: A sourcebook for developing collaborative groups.* Norwood, MA: Christopher-Gordon Publishers.

Gold, M. (1978). *Try another way: Training manual.* Austin, TX: Marc Gold & Associates.

Jorgensen, C.M., McSheehan, M., & Sonnenmeier, R. (2007). Presumed competence reflected in the educational programs of students with IDD before and after the Beyond Access professional development intervention. *Journal of Intellectual and Developmental Disabilities, 32*(4), 248–262.

McSheehan, M., Sonnenmeier, R., Jorgensen, C.M., & Turner, K. (2006). Beyond communication access: Promoting learning of the GE curriculum by students with significant disabilities. *Topics in Language Disorders, 26*(3), 266–290.

No Child Left Behind Act of 2001, PL 107-110, 115 Stat. 1425, 20 U.S.C. §§ 6301 *et seq.*

Sonnenmeier, R.M., McSheehan, M., & Jorgensen, C.M. (2005). A case study of team supports for a student with autism's communication and engagement within the GE curriculum: Preliminary report of the Beyond Access Model. *Augmentative and Alternative Communication, 21*(2), 101–115.

Phase 4

*Review and Sustain
Student and Team Supports*

During Phase 4 (see Figure 9.1), a comprehensive review of progress made on implementing the CASTS recommendations is conducted within three arenas of decision making: 1) student and team supports (that were carried over from Phase 3), 2) CASTS recommendations not yet explored, and 3) team professional development. Phase 4 also involves engaging the ALT to consider and take action with regard to team-level and schoolwide structures and supports for sustaining efficacious practices.

This review and involvement with the ALT sets the context for the ultimate review activity, the reason why the BA Model came to be in the first place: To ensure the team is confident that the student is not only gaining access to but also demonstrating learning of the general education curriculum in the general education classroom.

This chapter begins with a comprehensive example to illustrate considerations in implementing Phase 4 of the BA Model. Then, it describes the dispositions, outcomes, and activities for Phase 4, followed by examples in practice. The chapter concludes with a discussion of possible challenges to success and strategies for dealing with change.

PHASE 4 EXAMPLE

IEP members for Ben, a fifth-grader, reflected on all that had been accomplished and all that had yet to be explored as they approached the end of the first year of implementing the BA Model. From the original CASTS recommendations, they identified several new ways of enhancing Ben's membership and participation in the general education classroom that they determined to be efficacious and sustainable—without ALT intervention. The Student and Team Outcomes Survey

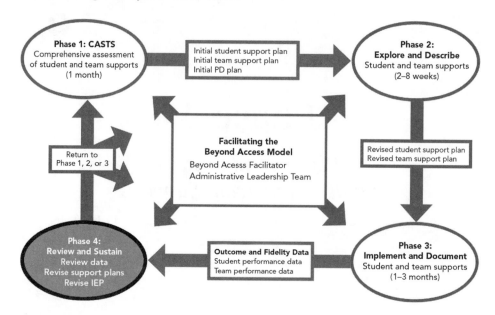

Figure 9.1. Beyond Access Model Phase 4: Review and Sustain. (From McSheehan, M., Sonnenmeier, R.M., & Jorgensen, C.M. [2009]. Membership, participation, and learning in general education classrooms for students with autism spectrum disorders who use AAC. In D.R. Beukelman & J. Reichle [Series Eds.] & P. Mirenda & T. Iacono [Vol. Eds.], *Augmentative and alternative communication series: Autism spectrum disorders and AAC* [p. 427]. Baltimore: Paul H. Brookes Publishing Co.; adapted by permission.) (*Key:* CASTS, Comprehensive Assessment of Student and Team Supports; IEP, individualized education program; PD, professional development.)

reflected an increase in Ben's membership and participation in the general education classroom. Changes in Ben's supports included the following:

- Emotional supports (e.g., three positive statements to Ben for every one comment of critical feedback)
- Physical supports (e.g., seating him toward the front of the room, repositioning him frequently between his wheelchair and stander)
- Material supports (e.g., symbol-enhanced worksheets)
- Communication supports (e.g., using an SGD during instruction to share academic information)
- Personalized instruction (e.g., using Ben's interests as the context for examples provided during whole-class instruction)

The outcomes surveys also reflected positive increases in collaborative teaming. Changes in team collaboration that contributed to the success in supporting Ben and were determined to be efficacious included the following:

- Meeting regularly
- Focusing on instructional planning during meetings
- Coaching one another on how to best support Ben in class
- Attending professional development workshops together as a team

These team practices required some intervention and leadership from the ALT, including the following:

- Release time
- Professional development
- Encouragement to "try something new"

Given all the successes, several team members were anxious to make determinations about what Ben was learning. As the team reviewed findings from the multiple administrations of the Student and Team Outcomes Survey, average ratings of Ben's performance relative to grade-level expectations showed Ben was perceived as performing below grade level in all academic areas.

As team members discussed their confidence level in the evidence of Ben's learning, a concern about Ben's communication supports arose. Creative communication supports for Ben continued to be a struggle within the team as some team members felt he was communicating "well enough" for someone with his disabilities, whereas other team members, who were also questioning how much to expect from Ben's communication, were attempting to apply the vision of "communication commensurate with same age peers." If Ben's communication performance was because of a lack of exploring sufficient AAC supports, then several team members wanted to continue using the BA Model through the next year and explore more communication supports. This was viewed by some team members as a barrier to "completing" their use of the BA Model.

After extensive dialogue guided by the BA facilitator, team members reconciled their agreement about Ben's learning and continuation with the BA Model. They reviewed the initial CASTS and found several recommendations in the area of AAC that had yet to be explored. This would require additional professional development and coaching in AAC. The BA facilitator noted, on review of the BA Best Practices Rating Scales, that many team members' knowledge of AAC might be enhanced through an outside AAC consultant with expertise in supporting the use of AAC with a student such as Ben in the general education classroom. Team members agreed to this and to prioritize this professional development to begin over the summer so they could begin the next school year with fresh ideas for enhancing Ben's communication.

PHASE 4 DISPOSITIONS

Four dispositions are needed by team members when engaging in Phase 4 activities: 1) having high expectations for the student and the team—focusing on excellence, 2) being patient—not rushing to judgment about whether students are learning, 3) keeping the end in mind—remembering that the goal of the BA Model is moving students *beyond* access to authentic learning of the general education curriculum in the general education classroom, and 4) knowing when the team needs support in order to sustain effective practices—the ability to distinguish between problems that are within the team's ability to manage them and when input and action from the ALT are required.

Having High Expectations

How do teams know if the outcomes in membership, participation, and learning demonstrated by the student are "good enough?" How do team members know if they are providing supports in a "good enough" manner? If the student reaches "proficiency," then does the team breathe a sigh of relief? When do teams stop trying to help students learn more? Although there are no hard and fast rules or formulas for calculating whether a particular level of student or team performance represents high-quality achievement, the following questions can guide teams to think deeply about this question:

- Is the student demonstrating learning of academic content that has not previously been observed?
- Is the student's rate of learning faster than was observed previously?
- Is the team observing changes in the ultimate indicators of membership and participation?
- Does the student seem happier at school?
- Are others treating the student with greater respect for his or her accomplishments?
- Is the gap narrowing between the student's academic and communication performance and that of typical classmates?
- If the student did not have an IDD, would team members (including parents) be satisfied with the student's performance?

Enthusiastic "yes" responses to these questions may indicate that the team has held high expectations for their practice and for the student's achievement. Uncertain or definite "no" answers do not mean that the student or team has failed, but rather may indicate that there is more work to be done.

Being Patient

Whether the Phase 4 activity of team confidence ratings regarding student learning is engaged 3 months or 3 years following the CASTS, teams are likely to feel some urgency in answering the question, "What does this student know?" They have been working hard to improve their own declarative and procedural knowledge, they may be reaping the benefits of new team collaboration processes and structures, and they may be eager to learn if their efforts are bearing fruit. Despite this natural sense of urgency, teams are advised not to make a premature assessment of what the student knows. This will take discipline and patience. Even if the fidelity of implementing supports needs improving and the data support returning to Phase 2 or 3, teams can take pride in and celebrate what has been accomplished.

Moving Students *Beyond* Access

Phase 4 discussions of efficacy of supports always need to be referenced to the primary vision of the BA Model; that is, moving students toward authentic learning and demonstration of grade-level academic knowledge and skills within the general education classroom and promoting an effective and efficient communication system that allows the student to communicate in a way commensurate with same-age peers. When teams embody this disposition, they are able to differentiate between incremental but unimportant changes in student performance and meaningful improvement in the ultimate outcome indicators of membership, participation, and learning.

Knowing When the Team Needs Support

During Phase 4 activities, teams are prompted to ask not only whether a particular support is efficacious, but also whether it is sustainable. Educational history is replete with examples of innovations that received ample support during start up and showed promise for improving student learning, but were not sustainable over time. When this happens, some team members will assume personal responsibility and continue to strive for excellence, whereas others may misdirect their resentment to the students, saying, "See, I told you that he couldn't learn the general education curriculum." Others might direct their frustrations toward their colleagues, "If only we had a competent SLP who knew something about AAC."

An effective team learns to recognize when it needs support from the ALT in order to sustain effective supports over time. The BA facilitator assumes a leadership role by learning to spot signs of team burnout, by monitoring to ensure that certain team members are not trying to be heroic by taking on more responsibilities than they can effectively manage, and by discerning when the ALT needs to be consulted when managing a problem is outside the team's purview or beyond its available resources.

PHASE 4 OUTCOMES

The outcomes of Phase 4 include a comprehensive review of the status of implementing the CASTS recommendations. This will lead to several decisions and actions, including the following:

- A decision to sustain an effective practice
- A decision to return to a previous phase of the Model to continue exploration, implementation, and documentation of a support prior to determining its efficacy
- A request to the ALT for action to support sustainability of efficacious student and team supports
- A decision to explore, implement, and document supports not yet tried
- Additional professional development
- Team member confidence ratings with regard to the evidence of student learning

PHASE 4 ACTIVITIES

The next section describes the steps involved in each of the four activities of Phase 4. An example of the activity in practice follows each description.

Activity A: Review and Determine Efficacy and Sustainability of Supports

Decisions about supports from Phase 3 address whether supports are efficacious and sustainable. If team members decide a support is efficacious, then they will communicate one of the three recommendations for sustainability with the ALT by 1) continuing to use the support and sustain it without specific ALT intervention, 2) continuing to use the support and request the ALT take action to support sustainability, or 3) putting the support on "hold" until there is an ALT sustainability intervention. If supports are not seen as efficacious, then the team determines why that might be and formulates a recommendation to either discontinue use of the support (and re-engage Phase 2 to explore new supports) or make adjustments to the implementation of the original support (and reengage either Phase 2 or Phase 3).

Step 1: Review Data
At the end of Phase 3, the BA facilitator has prepared summaries of the fidelity and efficacy data collected to date. The team reviews those summaries.

Step 2: Dialogue About Trends in Fidelity and Efficacy Data
The team reviews the fidelity and efficacy data together with an eye toward uncovering themes or trends in the data (e.g., Are supports provided with fidelity? Are supports creating the desired intermediate and ultimate outcomes? Is there something else that might explain the outcomes?). The team is attempting to build shared understanding of the data through this dialogue. Team members seek agreement on what the data mean—what stories the data are telling. The BA facilitator monitors this dialogue to see if the team is building agreement to answer the following questions: Is there evidence of both fidelity and efficacy? Is there one without the other? If so, why might that be?

Step 3: Determine Efficacy
The BA facilitator polls the team members to move them toward determining the efficacy of the supports (in the context of fidelity dialogue). The BA facilitator polls the group to see where people are leaning. Is the support efficacious or not? If the group polls clearly in support of one determination or the other (i.e., efficacious, not efficacious), then the BA facilitator uses levels of agreement to determine if the group is at a Level 3 or higher (see Chapter 5). If so, the formal decision making moves to determining what action is appropriate for the support. If not, the BA facilitator either identifies and addresses the concerns of individuals whose agreement ratings are at a Level 4 or lower until all members are at a Level 3 or higher or returns the team to dialogue (Step 2).

Step 4: Determine Action
If team members agree the support is *not* efficacious, then the BA facilitator guides team members to determine if they will 1) improve fidelity (engaging more professional development), 2) adjust the support and reengage Phase 2 or Phase 3, or 3) discontinue this support and reengage Phase 2 to explore another support that might address the same need. If a support is discontinued, then team members are advised to reflect on why it may have been ineffective. This will inform their selection of another support to address the needs to enhance student or team performance.

If the support is determined to be efficacious, then the BA facilitator guides team members to determine if they will 1) continue using the support and no ALT intervention is needed, 2) continue using the support and request the ALT to provide support for sustainability, or 3) put continued implementation of the support on "hold" until the ALT can intervene regarding sustainability. Just because a support is effective does not mean the team can continue to implement it without there being a deleterious effect on the team (this will be highlighted in an example later in the chapter). For example, when we determined that Jay's participation in general education instruction and learning of grade-level content from novels was enhanced by adapting grade-level novels to a lower reading level while preserving the essential content, it required several hours for one person to adapt the novel using the general education teacher's unit/lesson plans and end-of-chapter quizzes as the guide. The several hours required by one team member to maintain fidelity with the original plan of adapting each novel was not sustainable. Although each team member was willing to adapt a novel, eventually the extra time would likely result in burnout or would not be replicable the following year (at a different school with different team members). It was necessary to engage the ALT to develop a long-term plan to continue this practice or look for alternate solutions.

A referral to the ALT is made by the BA facilitator with team input. The ALT is provided with a brief summary of the fidelity and efficacy data, a description of the challenges that the IEP team is experiencing relative to sustaining effective supports, and the team's request for specific action. For example:

Dear ALT,

For the past 3 months, Jenna's team has been using a trial version of Kidspiration graphic organizer software to enhance her writing skills. Team members have achieved high fidelity in providing her with the supports necessary for her effective use of the software in her third-grade classroom. We have reviewed six samples of Jenna's writing and found that she has made significant improvement in four key areas: 1) writing about more varied topics, 2) using a topic sentence to begin a paragraph, 3) providing supporting details, and 4) showing increased confidence and accuracy in reading what she has written to her classmates. Our trial subscription of the software is scheduled to expire in 1 week, and the school's IT manager has informed us that there is no money in the current budget to purchase a site license so that the software can be loaded into Jenna's laptop, the classroom computer, and the computer in the Writing Center where Jenna receives speech-language services. In order for us to sustain these supports and positive student learning outcomes, we request that the ALT identify a funding source for the software and authorize its purchase. We would be happy to meet with you to review the data supporting this request. Thank you for your consideration, and we look forward to hearing from you prior to our monthly team meeting with Jenna's parents, scheduled for 2 weeks from this Friday.

Sincerely,
Jill Stephenson
Jenna's case manager and BA facilitator

Phase 4 Example of Activity A

Hector was a first-grade student with autism. During the CASTS, his participation in small-group guided reading was documented, and it primarily consisted of him responding to adult-directed interactions (e.g., "Show me the ___", "Which one is the ___?"), with adults using constant time delay or simultaneous prompting. Throughout Phases 2 and 3, his team explored and implemented using adult modeling of Hector's SGD to determine if that support would increase Hector's participation (as measured by his use of the device to make comments and ask questions) during small-group guided reading lessons.

Step 1: Review Data

After reviewing the fidelity data collected in Phase 3, Hector's team reviewed the efficacy data depicted in Table 9.1. The team also reviewed a graph that recorded the number of times Hector used his AAC device to make comments and ask questions during small-group guided reading. (Both self-initiations and responses to obligatory turns were measured.) At baseline, Hector was using his device two times during a lesson. (The number of comments and questions from a classmate

Table 9.1.   Example of changes in Student and Team Outcomes Survey over time based on quarterly administration

Outcome indicator	Baseline	Quarter 1	Quarter 2
Student membership			
Percentage of day in classroom	40–50	60–70	60–70
Percentage of day on same schedule	10–20	40–50	40–50
Student participation			
Percentage of time present/percentage of time active			
Reading	50/25	70/40	70/60
Writing	10/50	30/40	50/40
Math	50/50	70/60	70/75
Science	70/50	80/60	80/80
Percentage of day in same instructional routines	25	50	60
Percentage of day with means and supports to communicate	20	50	50
Means and supports to communicate			
Speaking	Infrequently	Sometimes	Sometimes
Writing	Infrequently	Infrequently	Sometimes
Reading	Infrequently	Sometimes	Most of the time
Listening	Infrequently	Sometimes	Most of the time
Team collaboration			
Frequency of instructional planning	Never	Often	Often
Effective meetings	Hardly ever	Occasionally	Sometimes
Efficient meetings	Hardly ever	Occasionally	Occasionally
Effective team collaboration	Hardly ever	Occasionally	Sometimes

without disabilities in this lesson was approximately 10.) At data point 1, he made one comment. At data point 2, he made two comments. At data point 3, he made three comments and asked one question. At data point 4, he made two comments and asked one question, and at data point 5, he made two comments. After reaching high team agreement on the status of implementing adult modeling with the SGD, the team was poised to rate their confidence in whether Hector's performance was a valid measure of his learning.

Step 2: Dialogue About Trends in Fidelity and Efficacy Data

After reviewing both data sources collected over a 3-week period, team members talked about their impressions of the data. Although the levels of fidelity of implementing the support were consistent with the team's goals, the graph of Hector's use of the device showed his progress was not what the team had expected. The team engaged in some dialogue and generated a list of possible reasons why the support was not increasing his participation (measured by his device use), including the following:

- There had not been a long enough period of modeling to make a difference
- Adults were modeling but classmates were not
- The reading group was held just after lunch, which was a low energy time of the day for Hector
- Maybe the measure of participation should include Hector sharing information in response to direct questions (independently, without other prompts)

The BA facilitator polled the group to see whether team members were leaning toward the support as effective or ineffective. All group members signaled "ineffective."

Step 3: Determine Efficacy

Given the unified response from the team to the polling in Step 2, the BA facilitator moved the group to register formal levels of agreement. All group members rated themselves at a 2 or 3, signaling their agreement that the support was ineffective.

Step 4: Determine Action

The team agreed to return to Phase 3 with three adjustments to the support plan: 1) adults and classmates would model use of the device, 2) the whole class would be led in an after-lunch "alerting" activity by the OT, and 3) the data collection would include responses to direct questions (sharing information, independently) as measures of Hector's participation.

Activity B: Review and Take Action on CASTS Recommendations Not Yet Explored

Decisions about the CASTS recommendations not yet explored (i.e., those not yet in Phase 2) include initiating or delaying the exploration of the recommendation.

Step 1: Review CASTS Recommendations Status Summary Sheets

The team reviews and discusses the status of the CASTS recommendations implemented thus far, using the prioritization form depicted in Figure 7.2. The BA facilitator notes the status of implementation and polls the team for agreement with the status ratings (e.g., complete, in progress, not initiated).

Step 2: Dialogue About CASTS Recommendations Not Yet Explored

The team engages in dialogue about the recommendations not yet explored, taking into consideration fidelity of implementation and student efficacy data. The potential benefits of initiating Phase 2 activities with these recommendations are discussed.

Step 3: Determine Action

The team decides which action will be taken for the unexplored recommendations—initiate or delay.

Phase 4 Examples of Activity B

Josie was a fifth-grader with Rett syndrome who used facial expressions and eye pointing to communicate by selecting messages from an E-tran display. When her team conducted a status review of the CASTS during Phase 4, they found that two recommendations had not yet been explored and described—using 18-point font for all written text and conducting a systematic exploration of different symbol positions on the E-tran. A high level of fidelity had been achieved for the Phase 3 recommendations, and yet Josie was not demonstrating an increase in initiation using the E-tran. Rather than concluding that Josie was unable to communicate, the team agreed to initiate both unexplored recommendations.

Marcus was a student with Down syndrome who used a combination of spoken words and a DynaVox MT-4 SGD to communicate about both social and academic topics. During Phase 4, the team reviewed the student and team supports that were recommended by the CASTS. The team found that all of the student supports had been moved through Phases 2 and 3 and that one team support remained untried—rotating roles during instructional planning meetings. The SLP facilitated all team meetings, the special education teacher took notes, and the paraprofessional monitored time. The team reviewed Phase 3 data that showed team members were implementing student supports with high fidelity and there were significant improvements in Marcus's membership, participation, communication, and learning of grade-level core academics. Given these results, the team decided to delay initiation of Phase 2 exploration of rotating team roles.

Activity C: Review Status and Decide Next Steps for Professional Development

As the team proceeds to Phase 4 with a support, some might assume that professional development to increase team members' skills is complete. This may not be the case. A formal review of the status of professional development recommended during the CASTS is needed. Decisions about professional development include 1) discontinuing presentations or workshops on the topic and maintaining team members' skills through monitoring for continued fidelity; 2) continuing developing team members' skills to achieve fidelity and specifying the format (e.g., coaching, modeling) best suited for the team's needs as well as specifying the expectations for fidelity (e.g., which team member needs to develop which skills in order to achieve the desired level of fidelity); 3) initiating professional development in content areas recommended from the CASTS; or 4) adding newly identified professional development to support the implementation of recommendations from the CASTS, as needed.

Step 1: Check Fidelity

Check the fidelity data to see if all team members have achieved the desired level of fidelity for implementing all supports. If team members have achieved the fidelity levels, then the team may recommend to discontinue presentations or workshops on the topic and to maintain skills through continued monitoring of fidelity (which may take the form of occasional probes and completion of fidelity checklists). If this is not the case, then proceed to Step 2. If this is the case, then proceed to Step 3.

Step 2: Identify Professional Development Needs

Identify the discrepancies in team performance and needed supports in areas in which professional development has already been initiated. The BA facilitator leads dialogue about the team members' needs for continued professional development (e.g., What are the new skills that need to be evidenced? What form of professional development is needed to assist this team member to improve his or her implementation of the supports?). Develop a plan for increasing fidelity through modeling, coaching, consultation, and so forth, as discussed in Chapter 8.

Step 3: Review CASTS Recommendations

Review the CASTS professional development recommendations to see what has yet to be provided and/or may be needed in order to initiate exploring new supports. Prioritize the professional development content and format according to the steps described in CASTS (Chapter 6). Implement professional development.

Step 4: Examine Best Practice Rating Scales and Efficacy Data

Examine results from the BA Best Practices Rating Scales (Appendix A) and the Student and Team Outcomes Survey (Appendix 7.1) in the areas of intermediate outcomes (collaborative teaming) and ultimate outcomes (membership, participation, and learning) to see if additional or refresher training is needed in these areas.

Step 5: Update Professional Development Status

Summarize findings and recommendations by updating the professional development plan and reprioritizing the content and format needed to increase declarative and procedural knowledge of student and team supports (as described in Chapter 6).

Phase 4 Example of Activity C

Luisa was a sixth-grader with a label of IDD who did not use her voice to communicate. Several recommendations were made during the CASTS to explore supports for use of a SGD.

Step 1: Check Fidelity

A review of the fidelity data revealed that two team members—the SLP and the special education teacher—had both achieved their level of fidelity for implementing the AAC support plan. The general education teacher, paraprofessional, and OT had not yet achieved their individually determined levels of fidelity.

Step 2: Identify Professional Development Needs

The two team members who had achieved their level of fidelity on the support plans had attended the recommended workshops, and the other team members had not. Given this information, the role of the BA facilitator was not to chastise the team members who did not attend the workshops, but rather to recommend a plan of action. The BA facilitator chatted with the team about possibly starting with an after-school workshop, lead by the SLP and special education teacher, focused on practical use of the AAC device within academic lessons in the general education classroom. They proposed a plan to then increase their fidelity through modeling and coaching from the two more knowledgeable team members. They reasoned that this would be more cost effective than attending an additional workshop; however, administrative support would be needed to provide substitutes to relieve the SLP and special education teacher for the training.

Step 3: Review CASTS Recommendations

The BA facilitator systematically reviewed the status on the CASTS recommended professional development. That status check revealed that some professional development recommendations had been completed and others had not.

Step 4: Examine Best Practice Rating Scales

The BA facilitator examined results from the BA Best Practices Rating Scales to see if additional or refresher training was needed in these areas. When reviewing the outcome data that had been collected quarterly on student and team outcomes, there was evidence that Luisa's membership and participation had both increased significantly. Team members reported they were presuming her competence; however, reports on team member collaboration, specifically instructional planning meetings, had not shown consistent improvement. The BA facilitator recommended that the team receive additional coaching on how to run effective and efficient meetings.

Step 5: Update Professional Development Status

The team summarized its findings and recommendations by updating the professional development status and reprioritizing the content and format needed to increase declarative and procedural knowledge of student and team supports (as described for CASTS in Chapter 6). The team agreed to the professional development identified during these steps and prioritized it in a revised professional development plan.

Activity D: Rate Team Member Confidence in Student's Performance as Evidence of Learning

The comprehensive review of implementing CASTS recommendations is grounded in the origins of the BA Model—to move students from merely having access toward learning the general education curriculum within the general education classroom. This activity asks team members to rate the level of confidence in the student's demonstrated performance as an authentic measure of his or her learning only after the team has confirmed fidelity of implementation and efficacy of the supports provided.

This part of Phase 4 is conducted after the team reports that many supports for the team and the student are demonstrating efficacy. Within this activity of Phase 4, teams are seeking to find out if team members agree that the student's performance is evidence of learning the general education curriculum. Team members have not answered this question thus far. Presuming the student is competent has lead the team to explore, implement, and document the efficacy of supports that foster membership, communication, and participation in the general curriculum as provided in the context of the general education classroom. With these basic indicators of access in place, team members are likely to experience higher confidence in their ability to educate this student with IDD. If team members are still reporting (via the quarterly Student and Team Outcomes Survey) that the student is well below proficient relative to grade-level expectations and they have low confidence in their ability to teach this student, then the team is not yet ready to address this question. The BA facilitator guides the team through the following three steps.

Step 1: Identify the Curriculum Area
Team members first specify in which curriculum content area they have greatest confidence regarding the conditions described previously.

Step 2: Dialogue About Impressions of Student Performance
The BA facilitator guides team members to dialogue about their impressions of the student's demonstrated performance in this curricular area and why they think it is representative of the student's learning. The BA facilitator will use the team member ratings of student performance from the Student and Team Outcomes Survey that is collected quarterly as a source of data for this conversation. Team members should cite specific student work samples and instructional activities in which the student has been successful with efficacious supports.

Step 3: Rate Team Members' Confidence in Student Performance as Evidence of Learning
The BA facilitator explains the rating rubric and asks team members to identify the rating that best represents their confidence level with the student's demonstrated performance as evidence of learning.

Rating

- 4 = The efficacious supports are provided with fidelity almost always. We are *highly confident* that this work represents the student's learning because we have ensured supports for all of the student's areas of need in order for him or her to be a member, participate, and learn.
- 3 = The efficacious supports are provided with fidelity most of the time. We are *moderately confident* that this work represents the student's learning

because we have ensured supports for most of the student's areas of need in order for him or her to be a member, participate, and learn.

2 = The efficacious supports are provided with fidelity some of the time. We are *minimally confident* that this work represents the student's learning because we have ensured supports for some of the student's areas of need in order for him or her to be a member, participate, and learn.

1 = The efficacious supports are provided with fidelity rarely. We are not at all confident that this work represents the student's learning because we have not ensured supports for the student's areas of need in order for him or her to be a member, participate, and learn.

Phase 4 Example of Activity D

Hector was a first-grade student with autism who did not use spoken words to communicate and whose reported visual acuity was 20/80. His first language was Spanish, although his mother was bilingual and used both English and Spanish at home.

The CASTS recommendations for student supports that were explored, implemented with high fidelity, and found efficacious included the following:

- Read directions aloud to Hector and underline key information in directions
- Reduce visual complexity by blocking or other techniques
- Use visual magnification devices for text that is not enlarged
- Provide visual step-by-step scripts to support Hector's understanding and completion of multistep instructions
- Use adapted furniture (e.g., tilt easel, wiggle cushion)
- Provide scheduled sensory and movement breaks
- Scribe Hector's dictated responses from his SGD
- Fill in Hector's responses to multiple-choice items on a worksheet or test
- Use AT and AAC for writing and in all academic work
- Administer tests at a time of day that takes into account Hector's health status or learning style
- Expand the number of conversational turns by Hector using his SGD
- Explore Unity software and other core vocabulary on his SGD
- Use modeling to increase Hector's use of the SGD by providing communication boards to classmates and adults
- Explore bilingual capacity of the SGD

CASTS recommendations for team supports that proved efficacious included the following:

- Plan for Four Blocks (literacy framework) during each weekly instructional planning meeting
- Prepare materials prior to the activity in which they are needed

- Complete to-do tasks in a timely manner
- Regularly attend team meetings and notify BA facilitator of planned absences
- Rotate roles during instructional planning meetings
- Identify enduring understandings in general education lesson

After reaching high team agreement on the status of the CASTS recommendations, team members were poised to rate their confidence in Hector's performance as a valid measure of his learning.

Step 1: Identify the Curriculum Area

Team members decided that they would first evaluate whether Hector's demonstrated performance in silent reading comprehension was evidence of authentic learning because they felt Hector was a full-time member and actively participating in that instructional block of the day. The team had the highest agreement regarding the fidelity and efficacy of those supports and had allocated much instructional planning time to implementing those supports with the general education teacher as the primary instructor.

Step 2: Dialogue About Impressions of Student Performance

The following excerpt of dialogue occurred during two team meetings prior to rendering their confidence ratings.

- *Susan, the BA facilitator and special education teacher:* "Let's talk about what we are seeing in terms of Hector's performance and how we might judge whether these observations represent authentic learning and/or Hector's learning potential."
- *Frank, the general education teacher:* "Before we all focused on Hector's use of his AAC device, I would say that I had no evidence at all for what Hector was learning when he looked at books. I wanted to believe that his interest in books and his intensive focus during silent reading was an indicator that he was doing more than looking at pictures, but when I asked him questions about what he read, he just wasn't giving me anything back. Now, when I ask him a question about the characters or the plot, and he uses his device to answer, I can say, 'Wow, he really was reading and understanding that book!'"
- *Marisol, the SLP:* "When I did Hector's evaluation at the beginning of last year, I wrote that he had no valid or reliable yes or no response, so it did not seem logical to program his AAC device with vocabulary from the books he was reading. I couldn't imagine that he could communicate if he didn't even give yes or no answers appropriately. I don't think one thing has made a difference. I think we have been consistently and systematically giving him AAC supports throughout the day and we keep telling him, 'Hector, I know that you know this.' Now I'm even wondering if perhaps he's outgrown his current device and needs one with a greater variety of messages on it."
- *Sylvia, Hector's Mom:* "Since he was 2 years old, Hector has been fascinated with books. He even takes them into his bed at night and piles them

carefully around him when he sleeps. Some people told me that behavior was a compulsion or that he was sort of perseverating on lining up the books. I didn't really have anything to back me up, but I just kept on reading to him. Even though I felt a little silly, I did what you said and used paper communication boards that you sent home to talk about the story we were reading. Now, when it's time for bed he gets the book and the boards and climbs up on my lap."

- *Jonathan, the paraprofessional:* "I do agree that Hector has made leaps and bounds in his communication, but I still wonder if maybe I am overcueing him or providing a little too much verbal and physical support when he does his comprehension questions. What do you think? You all have a chance to observe me, and maybe you can tell if you think it's really his own work?"

- *Priscilla, the OT:* "I, too, was concerned about that question. I think the key here is that Hector is demonstrating silent reading comprehension with all of us, not just with you, Jonathan [the paraprofessional]. I think that's one way we can evaluate whether Hector's performance is 'real'— are we seeing him perform the same in different situations with different people? For me, he's really met that test."

Step 3: Rate Team Members' Confidence in
Student Performance as Evidence of Learning

Following this and similar conversations, team members used the rubric for rating their confidence—four members rated their confidence at a 4 (highly confident), and two members rated their confidence at a 3 (moderately confident). Thus, the team was ready to report to the ALT that the supports it was providing were efficacious, that they should be sustained, and that Hector's performance was indeed a valid representation of his learning.

CHALLENGES TO SUCCESS IN PHASE 4

The challenges to successfully completing Phase 4 include 1) incomplete records regarding the implementation of supports during Phases 1–3, 2) differences of opinion among team members about the efficacy of a particular student or team support, 3) ascribing a lack of efficacy of a support to an inherent deficit within the student, 4) lack of adequate time for the BA facilitator to synthesize data and support Phase 4 activities, and 5) attempts by the team to sustain an effective practice without the necessary administrative support.

Incomplete Records

If a team arrives at Phase 4 and has not kept adequate records of its activities during Phases 1, 2, and 3, then team members will not have adequate documentation for making good decisions during Phase 4. Use of a BA binder or electronic portfolio (see Chapter 5) is one way to help keep track of the various documents and data sources (see Chapter 8) that the team will need to review in Phase 4. If the required data are not available, then the team needs to be cautious about relying on anecdotal evidence to make decisions. In case this happens, the team would be well advised to return to the beginning of Phase 3 and develop a systematic plan for collecting the necessary fidelity of implementation and efficacy data prior to making decisions during Phase 4.

Reconciling Team Member Judgments About Efficacy

Reconciling team members' conflicting judgments about what constitutes efficacy is another challenge to implementing Phase 4 of the BA Model. All three authors of this book have witnessed the conflict that arises when team members do not share a unified view of the meaning behind particular student behaviors or performance. This situation arises most commonly when the student does not yet have a consistent and reliable means of communication. For example, James was a high school student with autism and a label of IDD who did not use his voice to communicate other than saying "hi" and "bye" when prompted by an adult. He had been exposed to the Picture Exchange Communication System (PECS) and sign language earlier in his educational career, but he had no effective means of communication at the time of his team's initiation of the BA Model. His educational program consisted of self-help and other functional skills that were taught in community-based environments (e.g., a pet store, restaurants, grocery stores) and in a general education culinary arts class. His educational team decided to use the BA Model to improve his membership, participation, and learning of general education curriculum.

During CASTS, it became clear there were differences of opinion about many aspects of James's educational program, including the following:

- James's inherent abilities
- The value of AAC for a student with James's measured cognitive ability
- Whether an appropriate education consisted of a focus on functional skills, academic learning, or some combination of both
- The communicative meaning of James's behaviors

At the conclusion of the CASTS, all team members registered a high level of agreement with exploring the use of an SGD with James. At the end of Phase 2, there was also a high level of team agreement that the use of an SGD with James showed promise and merited further implementation in Phase 3. When the team reviewed fidelity, efficacy, and student performance data in Phase 4, however, it became apparent that two team members could draw very different conclusions after looking at the same videotape of James communicating or reviewing the same student performance data.

When James selected different messages on his SGD during a small-group discussion (e.g., "Could you tell me more about that?" "I like that idea." "Anything else?"), the special education teacher interpreted the selections as random and lacking intent. In contrast, the SLP viewed the same behavior as evidence that James was increasing his initiations and demonstrating clear intent and meaning.

The BA facilitator's role in resolving this dilemma was not to force either team member to change his or her mind, but rather to shift the team's attention to return to Phase 3. The BA facilitator supported the team to create shared expectations about, "What counts as evidence that James's selections on his SGD are representing his learning?" Reframing the disagreement from personal perspectives of the meaning of James's behavior to considering evidence of his performance opened up a dialogue about what it looks like when students are learning to use their SGDs. This allowed the team to create benchmarks of James's communication growth over time and acknowledged the many variables that are involved in such a determination. The team then returned to Phase 3 to collect more data with a shared understanding and shared expectations for what team members would document.

Ascribing Lack of Efficacy to Student Deficits

Ascribing a lack of efficacy of a support to an inherent and unalterable student deficit is the third challenge to implementing Phase 4 successfully. For example, a team may support a student to use a particular SGD with high fidelity, and the student may not use that device to give the correct answers on a spelling test. The team may be tempted to conclude that the student does not know and may never learn third-grade spelling words rather than 1) examining other factors that may have contributed to the student's lack of use of the SGD on that particular day, 2) considering other possible supports and instructional approaches to foster use of the SGD, or 3) fostering other ways for the student to demonstrate learning. Overcoming this challenge relies on teams presuming students' competence and encouraging one another to ask themselves, "What else could account for this situation?"

Beyond Access Facilitator's Time Constraints

The lack of adequate time for the BA facilitator's essential leadership role is another challenge to effectively and efficiently engage in Phase 4. Just as in the CASTS, the BA facilitator needs to devote time to leading the team through a careful consideration of student and team performance data and discussion of sustaining effective supports over the long run. If the BA facilitator has competing priorities due to other responsibilities outside or within the school, such as an increasing caseload of students with IDD, then he or she will lack the time necessary to adequately support the BA team in a Phase 4 review process. When a team does not have the time or effective guidance from the BA facilitator to review and reflect on the hard work to date, then members may experience frustration and increased conflict regarding student and team performance.

Trying to Sustain Efficacious Practices without Administrative Support

Administrative support is essential to the successful implementation of Phase 4 in providing the BA facilitator and team members the time and supports needed to engage in thoughtful review and reflection of Phase 3 documentation. This book's first two authors had occasion to work with a team that tried valiantly to sustain effective practices without the necessary administrative support. In this case, one member of the team registered high agreement with all of the CASTS recommendations, yet consistently missed team meetings, failed to follow through with agreed-on responsibilities, and missed scheduled instructional sessions with the student. During Phase 3, other team members took on the recalcitrant team member's responsibilities to implement the supports with fidelity and efficacy. These team members, however, found themselves falling further behind in fulfilling other responsibilities. Within a few short weeks, several team members expressed that they were "burned out" using the BA Model, reporting that it was "too much work" and a crisis situation was reached.

Phase 4 of the BA Model provided a way of dealing with this situation. The team was achieving high fidelity of implementation with a particular constellation of supports, but only because team members were picking up the slack caused by one team member not fulfilling his responsibilities. Despite that team member's lack of participation, the student was learning more than ever before with the implementation of the appropriate supports. At this point, the other team members should have referred the dilemma—with supporting evidence—to the ALT. Under the existing circumstances, the team was unable to sustain the student supports over time without the participation of the other team member. The other team members' desire to avoid conflict merely delayed it, to the detriment of the team and the student. With administrative support, there could be clarification of expectations of all team members and a plan for addressing the reasons the wayward team member was not engaged.

DEALING WITH CHANGE

During Phase 4, some teams may experience frustration when there is a discrepancy between currently available organizational and systems-level supports and what they are learning is necessary for supporting a student's membership, participation, and learning of the general education curriculum in the general education classroom. If one or more team members do not yet demonstrate the professional skills or commitment necessary for high fidelity of implementation, then conflict may arise. And if the supports the team has implemented do not prove to be efficacious, then they may experience disappointment expressed as, "After all this hard work, you mean we aren't 'done' yet?" As Pat Mirenda said so eloquently in her foreword, using the BA Model is not "for people who either want quick fixes or who are squeamish about tackling difficult challenges head on." The BA facilitator and the ALT can help the team to deal productively with each of these emotions.

Even as the BA facilitator or ALT addresses these Phase 4 challenges head on, an effective BA facilitator understands the importance of and spends energy on shoring up the foundations of effective team collaboration through celebrating good work, nurturing individual and team relationships, and paying attention to each team member's needs in order to influence their commitment to teamwork. Jorgensen (2006) suggested that an inclusion facilitator (much like a BA facilitator) consider three elements of each team member's identity when planning how best to support that person through a difficult change process: 1) the team member's bottom-line values, 2) the team member's concerns about inclusive education, and 3) the team member's personality type. Imagine one team member whose bottom-line values are rooted in authority, whose level of concern about inclusive education is centered on how much time he or she will have to spend planning over the weekend, and whose personality type is a high-level achiever.

Contrast this team member with another who is passionate about social justice, whose concerns are less about the Model's effect on self than on students, and whose personality type is a helper (Jorgensen, 2006). The strategies that the BA facilitator and ALT utilize to support diverse team members are as diverse as the team members themselves.

CONCLUSION

After engaging in Phase 4 activities, team members have high confidence in the next steps they need to take in order to support the realization of the BA Model's ultimate indicators—enhanced membership, participation, and learning of general education curriculum in the general education classroom for students with IDD. Concluding Phase 4 activities does not signal that the student and team have arrived at a final destination; rather, it results in furthering shared understanding among all team members about what has worked so far and provides a direction for continued work toward common goals. Chapter 10 describes the roles and activities of ALT in implementing and sustaining effective student and team supports over time.

REFERENCES

Jorgensen, C.M. (2006). Transforming hearts and minds: The inclusion facilitator's role as a change agent In C.M. Jorgensen, M. Schuh, & J. Nisbet, *The inclusion facilitator's guide* (pp. 65–102). Baltimore: Paul H. Brookes Publishing Co.

Administrative
Leadership Team

S hared leadership through the activities of a leadership team is an essential element of successful implementation and sustainability of a variety of innovative educational reforms and practices such as PBIS, RTI, urban school reform,
and inclusive education (Artiles, Kozleski, Dorn, & Christensen, 2006; Burns &
Ysseldyke, 2005; Jorgensen, Schuh, & Nisbet, 2006; Katzman, Gandhi, Harbour,
& LaRock, 2005; Kozleski & Smith, 2005; Villa & Thousand, 2005; Warren et al.,
2004).

Consistent with the effectiveness of leadership teams in educational reform
and improvement efforts, a BA ALT (see Figure 10.1) supports implementation of
the BA Model and its sustainable use over time. This chapter begins by defining
membership on the team and critical dispositions needed by ALT members. Then,
it describes the ALT functions and activities that are related to 1) starting the BA
Model, 2) implementing the BA Model with fidelity, 3) acting on referrals from
BA teams during Phase 4, and 4) promoting sustainable use of the BA Model over
time. We will provide examples of 1) challenges that the ALT might encounter,
2) how those challenges might be addressed, and 3) the ALT's role in helping BA
teams through the change process.

MEMBERSHIP ON THE
ADMINISTRATIVE LEADERSHIP TEAM

Based on their role in the school or school district, members of the ALT are positioned to provide a variety of supports to BA teams, such as 1) leveraging resources and coordinating efforts across school initiatives, 2) clarifying BA team
member job roles and responsibilities, 3) addressing scheduling and space issues,

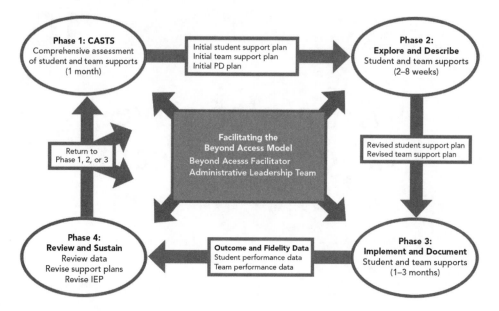

Figure 10.1. Facilitating the Beyond Access Model. (From McSheehan, M., Sonnenmeier, R.M., & Jorgensen, C.M. [2009]. Membership, participation, and learning in general education classrooms for students with autism spectrum disorders who use AAC. In D.R. Beukelman & J. Reichle [Series Eds.] & P. Mirenda & T. Iacono [Vol. Eds.], *Augmentative and alternative communication series: Autism spectrum disorders and AAC* [p. 427]. Baltimore: Paul H. Brookes Publishing Co.; adapted by permission.) (*Key:* CASTS, Comprehensive Assessment of Student and Team Supports; IEP, individualized education program; PD, professional development.)

4) mediating interpersonal conflicts, 5) providing clarification on policy and legal issues, and 6) assisting BA teams to solve challenging problems.

The ALT is composed of the following individuals: 1) the building principal, 2) the building-level special education administrator (if one exists), 3) the district-level special education administrator, 4) the special education teacher whose caseload includes students with IDD, and 5) an in- or out-of-district consultant who functions as the primary facilitator of the BA Model.

Principal

The building principal has long been recognized as a key in promoting inclusive education or any other kind of significant change in educational philosophy or practice (Riehl, 2000). Principals' roles are multifaceted and include 1) leading the school mission under the direction of the superintendent; 2) supporting accountability to standards and other educational outcomes; 3) maintaining communications with families, the school board, and the broader community; 4) developing and managing operating budgets; 5) overseeing facilities operations, including technology; 6) hiring and supervising personnel; 7) developing the school schedule; 8) addressing student conduct problems; and 9) mediating personnel difficulties (Hale & Moorman, 2003). At one time or another, each of these job roles may be required to support BA teams to implement the BA Model with fidelity, address difficulties as they arise, and support the Model's sustainable use over time.

Building- and District-Level Special Education Administrators

The building-level special education administrator (if one exists) and the district-level special education administrator also play key roles on the ALT. These professionals have in-depth knowledge of special education law and policy and can provide key support to BA teams when they need clarification of legal issues, when resources in the special education budget are required, and when teams need support to adopt and sustain evidence-based practices.

Special Education Teacher

In Chapter 5, we described the key role that the special education teacher plays on the BA team. This individual serves as the liaison between a BA team and the ALT. The special education teacher is intimately familiar with the philosophical and practice foundations of the BA Model, works on a daily basis with BA team members and the students the team supports, and shares his or her professional content expertise with the ALT when it considers issues relating to implementing BA Best Practices. The special education teacher is also aware of interpersonal dynamics on each BA team, including the relationship between school-based team members and students' families.

Beyond Access Facilitator

The last member of the ALT is the BA facilitator. Although this individual may not have a formal job title called "BA facilitator," he or she serves a vital function for BA teams and the ALT. As described in Chapter 5, the BA facilitator may be a school employee (e.g., a special education teacher, an administrator, a related services provider, a curriculum coordinator with expertise in educating students with IDD) or an outside consultant. His or her skills as a professional developer, mediator, coach, and facilitator are critical to BA teams, and his or her participation on the ALT is crucial when the team addresses difficulties with implementing or sustaining the use of the BA Model.

DISPOSITIONS OF THE ADMINISTRATIVE LEADERSHIP TEAM MEMBERS

Three dispositions are essential for each member of the ALT to promote success in supporting the use and sustainability of the BA Model: 1) strong inclusive values; 2) strengths-based views of educational team members, including parents/guardians; and 3) willingness to address conflict. In addition, team members must value data in decision making.

Inclusive Values

Inclusive values are reflected in the BA Best Practices (see Appendix A). Many of the challenges to implementing the BA Model are related to the Model's philosophy that all students with IDD are presumed competent to learn general education curriculum content and are valued members of and participants in age-appropriate general education classrooms. When members of the ALT hold those inclusive values and transmit them to BA teams, they support a shift from asking, "Should this student be included?" to, "What supports does the student need in order to be a member, participate, and learn?" The BA value of inclusive education emphasizes that difficulties are viewed not as problems with inclusive education per se, but with its implementation.

Strengths-Based Perspective

Just as students with IDD are presumed competent to learn, members of BA teams are viewed from a strengths-based perspective; that is, they are presumed competent to learn and apply the BA Best Practices with ongoing professional development and administrative support. Just as the BA Model emphasizes that student learning is not evaluated unless and until appropriate and adequate supports are provided to them, the same value is applied with team members. If the SLP does not currently have the skills to support a student's use of AAC, then a strengths-based approach would suggest that it is the responsibility of the ALT to provide the professional development and coaching that the SLP needs in order to adopt new AAC practices. If a paraprofessional does not accurately and consistently implement the instructional supports that were planned by the other team members, then a strengths-based approach would suggest that the paraprofessional needs additional training, time to prepare materials, and coaching from a professional team member in order to do his or her job well.

Is there a point at which the ALT must determine that a particular team member is not demonstrating a minimum level of competence and ought to be reassigned? Obviously, the answer is yes. Even when operating from a strengths-based perspective, the ALT is ultimately accountable for assuring that BA team members are qualified to do the job for which they were hired and are meeting the requirements of students' IEPs.

Willingness to Address Conflict

The third essential disposition for ALT members relates to their willingness to address conflict within their own team or in the BA team. Because the BA Model itself consists of a variety of strategies and processes that support teams to develop shared understanding and to solve their own conflicts, those conflicts that are brought to the ALT are usually complex and resist easy solutions. Although not all members of the ALT need to be expert mediators, the team as a whole must be able to draw from their own or outside expertise to help BA teams address conflict. This willingness to address conflict calmly and skillfully is just as important as finding money for supplies or adjusting the school schedule to create common planning time for teams.

Valuing Data in Decision Making

Using objective data about student performance is one of the key elements in modern approaches to monitoring the effect of school reform initiatives and to providing professional development and support for teachers. In fact, one of the core principles contained in the National Staff Development Council's (NSDC; 2001) *Standards for Staff Development* requires using student data to establish priorities for adult learning, to monitor progress or growth in teacher skills, and to sustain continuous improvement. The ALT's attention to the right kinds of data to inform decision making during BA Model implementation is an essential disposition to success. Monitoring team results from the CASTS will assist with describing which instructional areas need improvement and how to differentiate the needed professional development and support across team members. This same attention is needed when monitoring for implementation of the BA Model activities. Use of data will position the ALT for both effectiveness (making the right decisions) and efficiency (acting on decisions in an organized and timely manner).

ADMINISTRATIVE LEADERSHIP TEAM FUNCTIONS AND ACTIVITIES

The functions of the ALT include the following:

1. Provide initial support and resources for a team to begin using the BA Model.
2. Support and monitor fidelity of implementation of the BA Model through Phases 1, 2, 3, and 4.
3. Address Phase 4 referrals from the BA team.
4. Support sustainability of the BA Model by addressing broader school reforms.

Table 10.1 depicts these ALT functions and related activities. Each will be described more fully in the next section.

Initial Support for Start-Up

The ALT engages in five activities related to BA Model start-up, including 1) guiding the decision about whether a team will use the BA Model, 2) establishing ALT membership, 3) providing the team (including parents/guardians) with an orientation to the Model, 4) ensuring that the student's team has weekly instructional planning time, and 5) establishing ALT monthly meetings.

Deciding Whether to Use the Model

Obviously, before the BA Model begins to be used in a school, no BA ALT exists, although other leadership teams may exist to support other initiatives (e.g., PBIS, RTI). The impetus for using the BA Model may come from any member of a student's IEP team or a school administrator. The *decision* to more formally explore using the BA Model with a student/team must include school administrators, with input from the members of a student's IEP team, including parents/ guardians.

A short (e.g., 2 hour) informational meeting is scheduled for the student's team members, including the student's parents/guardians, the special education teacher, a general education teacher, related services providers, the principal,

Table 10.1. Functions and activities of the Beyond Access (BA) Administrative Leadership Team (ALT)

Functions	Activities
Provide initial support and resources for BA Model start-up	Provide orientation to the BA Model
	Establish ALT membership
	Poll for team member buy-in
	Provide weekly instructional planning time for team
	Establish ALT regular meeting schedule
Support fidelity of implementation of the BA Model through Phases 1, 2, 3, and 4	Gather, analyze, and reflect on fidelity of implementation data
	Take corrective action
Address Phase 4 referrals from the BA team	Review and discuss referrals at monthly ALT meeting
	Formalize decisions to act or not act on particular referrals
	Notify student team of decisions
	Provide supports or intervene as necessary
Support sustainability of the BA Model— for a student team	Reconduct Comprehensive Assessment of Student and Team Supports (CASTS)— tailored to include "lessons learned" from initial implementation of BA Model
	Specify recommendations for sustainability
	ALT and student team develops action plan for sustainability
	ALT and student team implements action plan and monitors progress

building- and/or district-level special education administrators, and a BA facilitator (if one is involved at this stage). The person initiating the meeting might share written materials about the Model ahead of time. A presentation about the Model is made at the meeting, and adequate time for dialogue is provided.

Toward the conclusion of the meeting, the team is polled to see if they agree on a decision to use the BA Model, using the levels of agreement depicted in Chapter 5. The administrator(s) leading the meeting confirm with all team members their commitment to learning and implementing new practices with the goal of continuous improvement in the student's educational program. We recommend that the decision to use the BA Model rates a Level 1 or 2 agreement by all team members. Any team members who are polled at a 3, 4, 5, or 6 are invited to express their concerns and additional dialogue ensues. If all team members are then at a Level 1 or 2 of agreement, then the school administrators schedule a meeting to discuss their final decision and inform the members of the student's team when they will communicate that decision.

If the team or the administration does not have strong agreement for using the Model, then we do not recommend using it at this time. Perhaps additional information or dialogue is necessary, and the decision can be revisited at a later date.

Establishing the Administrative Leadership Team Membership

Once the decision is made to move forward with implementing the BA Model, it is important to establish the membership of the ALT and ensure the members gain a thorough understanding of the BA Model and the role of the ALT. The ALT may review written information about the BA Model, including the expectations regarding time and resources, and engage ALT members in dialogue to answer all questions about implementing the Model.

Orienting the Team to the Beyond Access Model

Orientation to the BA Model will require a minimum of a day-long workshop or working session. Once again, materials to be read prior to the orientation session are shared with all team members. The orientation session consists of information on the following topics: 1) history of the BA Model, 2) BA research, 3) BA Best Practices, 4) Model components, 5) team collaboration, 6) professional development, and 7) role of the ALT.

An effective BA orientation 1) addresses all team members' questions and concerns; 2) describes all four phases of the Model; 3) provides details about the CASTS; and 4) clarifies the roles and responsibilities of the team members, BA facilitator, and ALT. It is important to communicate the membership of ALT to the student's team members to assure them that administrative support for implementing the BA Model exists from the very beginning. The team is informed that they will have a weekly, 45-minute to 1-hour instructional planning meeting, and the time and location are specified.

Establishing Weekly Instructional Planning Meetings

A critical role of the ALT is to provide a 45-minute to 1-hour instructional planning time that accommodates all team members' schedules. This can be a challenge for the ALT in schools where instructional planning is not already built into team members' schedules. Nevertheless, it remains one of the most important elements of the BA Model. Designing, implementing, and evaluating supports for students with the most complex educational needs simply cannot be done by one team member alone or by many team members working in isolation. Often, the ALT must make changes to the school schedule to create this time. Some general education teachers have several "prep periods" each week. At the elementary level, these prep periods may coincide with times that students are in arts, technology, or health and physical education classes. Although the optimal situation would be that all general education teachers involved in a student's educational program attend the weekly instructional planning meeting, it may not be feasible because of scheduling constraints. The majority of schools that have used the BA Model are able to schedule time for this weekly meeting for the BA facilitator, general education classroom teacher, paraprofessional, special education teacher, and key related services providers (e.g., SLP, OT). Attendance by other specialists (e.g., PT, ESOL [English Speakers of Other Languages] teacher, reading specialist, behavior specialist) is dependent on the needs of the student.

Creative solutions to potential problems with some team members' attendance at the weekly planning meeting can be found. For example, one BA team had difficulty with attendance by the paraprofessional at the entire meeting because she was responsible for escorting the student off the school bus. Rather than consider the situation "her problem," the team rotated that job so that any team member would only have to miss the last 10 minutes of their weekly meeting once every 2 months. They valued the contribution of the paraprofessional and accommodated their schedule to ensure her participation.

Scheduling Monthly Administrative Leadership Team Meetings

The final activity coordinated by the ALT is establishing a monthly ALT meeting. All members of the ALT attend this meeting, and the agenda consists of 1) updating student and team activities (provided by the team's special education teacher and/or the BA facilitator, 2) discussing data that were collected regarding fidelity of implementation of the Model, 3) addressing specific referrals to the ALT from the BA team, and 4) talking about considerations for sustaining effective use of the BA Model.

Fidelity of Implementation of the Beyond Access Model

The overarching goal of the BA Model is to improve the quality of the instruction and supports provided to a student to learn the general education curriculum within the general education classroom. The BA Model is intended to positively affect the quality of student learning that is related to the quality of the implementation of instruction and supports provided by team members to the student. One of the roles of the ALT is to ensure that the BA Model is being implemented with a high degree of fidelity so that if there are successes or struggles, stakeholders can take a critical look at what they have actually done and what they may want to change. Fidelity is critical to achieving the same results that were achieved during the research or model demonstration phase of a particular educational practice. It is widely acknowledged that even when educators are provided with high-quality professional development during the initial roll-out of an innovation, variations in implementation are bound to occur (Fullan, 2008). Thus, it is prudent that administrators monitor for and take corrective action to ensure a high degree of fidelity of implementation of the BA Model.

The examination of the overall fidelity of implementation of the BA Model involves three broad areas of focus.

1. Are the components and activities of the BA Model being implemented?
2. What are the areas of team members' practice that are consistent with or deviate from the BA Model (i.e., implementation of components, activities, or the BA Best Practices)?
3. What factors encourage or hinder full implementation of the BA Model?

It is the responsibility of the ALT to ensure that these questions are being asked and that any concerns with implementing the Model are being addressed on a regular basis.

In order to effectively monitor and support fidelity of implementation of the BA Model, ALT members must 1) have working knowledge of the BA Model,

2) have an active presence in classrooms where teams are implementing the BA Model, 3) engage in regular communication with team members, 4) examine the status of implementation of each phase of the BA Model on a regular basis, 5) identify activities that address the areas of concern, and 6) evaluate the outcomes of changes made.

Becoming Familiar with the Beyond Access Model

The ALT begins to ensure the fidelity of implementation as soon as the decision is made to use the BA Model and ALT membership is established. The ALT needs to have a working knowledge of what implementing the BA Model entails to support team members throughout the process and to answer any questions they might have. ALT members learn about the BA Model from reading articles and resource materials, from the BA facilitator, and from discussions with school administrators who have implemented the BA Model in their schools.

Having an Active Presence in the Classroom

Members of the ALT need firsthand knowledge of how each phase of the BA Model is being implemented by the student's team members. This is best accomplished by ALT members having an active presence in weekly team meetings and in the classroom. This will look different depending on the individual ALT member and the team members implementing the BA Model. Some administrators are very "hands on" and participate in all classrooms in their buildings; others may need to develop a presence within the classroom. The disposition of nonjudgmental observation is essential. The goal is to gather information that will support and improve implementing the BA Model, not for evaluation or supervisory purposes.

An observation protocol can be used to summarize ALT members' observations during a classroom visit related to implementing the BA Model. Figure 10.2 depicts a form for recording ALT observations related to the primary BA indicators of students' membership, participation, communication, and learning. There is also a place on this observation form to note any areas of concern for consideration at the next scheduled ALT meeting.

Engaging in Regular Communication with Team Members

In addition to having a presence in the classroom, it is crucial for ALT members to engage the team members in regular communication. This should include both informal conversations to get a sense of how implementation of the Model is going, as well as more formal conversations, such as providing feedback to team members present during a classroom observation. Feedback can be provided immediately following the observation (if possible) at a scheduled team meeting or at some other convenient time. Engaging in these types of conversations supports an open dialogue during which questions can be asked and dilemmas that may not have been obvious during the observation may be raised. Such communication also provides assurance to team members that they have administrative support for implementing the Model.

Examining the Status of Implementation of Each Phase of the Model

The ALT is also responsible for ensuring that each step of each phase of the Model is implemented with fidelity. The checklist presented in Appendix 10.1 is a tool for documenting and evaluating the degree to which the activities within each phase of the Model have been implemented.

Supporting and Monitoring Fidelity of Implementation of the Beyond Access Model: Class Observation Monitoring Form (page 2 of 3)

Beyond Access Model fidelity indicators	Level of implementation
Is there evidence of the target student's membership in the classroom?	☐ None ☐ Partial ☐ Full
List examples of evidence of student membership.	
Is there evidence of the target student's active participation in the classroom activities observed?	☐ None ☐ Partial ☐ Full
List examples of supports in place for student participation.	
Is there evidence of the student's learning of the general education curriculum?	☐ None ☐ Partial ☐ Full
List examples of supports in place for student learning.	
List examples of the student's demonstration of learning.	
Areas of concern to discuss at the next administrative leadership meeting	

Supporting and Monitoring Fidelity of Implementation of the Beyond Access Model: Class Observation Monitoring Form

Instructions

Complete this form following the activities instructions given in Chapter 10 for supporting and monitoring fidelity of implementation of the Beyond Access Model.

Student: _____ Teacher: _____ Grade: _____

School: _____ Date: _____

Observer: _____ Time spent observing: _____

Primary instructor

☐ Teacher ☐ Specialist ☐ Educational assistant

☐ Other (list): _____

Activity/lesson

Grouping

☐ Whole class
☐ Small group
☐ Independent

Beyond Access Model fidelity indicators	Level of implementation
Is there evidence that the primary instructor presumes the student's competence to learn (holds high expectations)?	☐ None ☐ Partial ☐ Full
List examples of presumed competence.	

Figure 10.2. Supporting and Monitoring Fidelity of Implementation of the Beyond Access Model: Class Observations Monitoring Form. (Full-size, three-page version included on the accompanying CD-ROM.)

The ALT may identify a point person—such as the BA facilitator—with primary responsibility to monitor the implementation within each phase. Any challenges to implementing a particular phase of the Model are brought to the attention of the ALT for discussion. Likewise, any concerns raised by ALT members based on in-class observations are also brought to the ALT for discussion. The following questions are helpful in determining changes that might need to be made.

1. Is the BA facilitator and/or special education teacher guiding the target student's IEP team through this phase of the BA Model as intended? Does the BA facilitator and/or special education teacher have the supports needed to do this? If not, what is needed?

2. Are all team members implementing BA Best Practices in the areas recommended by the CASTS? Do all team members have the supports needed to do this? If not, what is needed?

3. In what ways do the team's practices align with or deviate from the intent of the BA Model?

4. Have all team members received the professional development needed to implement this phase of the BA Model as intended? If not, what is needed?

5. What factors encourage implementing the BA Model as intended?

6. What factors hinder implementing the BA Model as intended?

Through the recursive process of asking these questions regularly (at least quarterly), the ALT monitors the fidelity of implementation of the BA Model. Responses to the questions will help the ALT collaborate with the student's team to identify additional supports needed to effectively implement the BA Model.

Identifying Activities to Address the Areas of Concern

After the ALT has examined areas of concern and factors contributing to the success of or difficulty with implementing the BA Model, they are ready to ask, "What changes need to be made to improve the fidelity of implementation of the BA Model?" Brainstorming is one strategy the ALT can use to identify changes. Once the ALT has a list of possible actions, members can prioritize the one or two solutions that are most likely to improve fidelity of implementation. The ALT will then develop a plan for implementing the change(s), a set of criteria by which to determine whether the change(s) are effective in improving fidelity of implementation of the BA Model, and a time line for evaluating the outcome of the change(s) made.

Evaluating Outcomes of Changes Made

By the specified time line, the ALT will revisit the weekly team meetings and classroom to make additional observations regarding the implementation of the BA Model, with specific attention to the criteria for the actions established in the previous step. Additional information may also be collected through informal interviews with team members regarding the changes made. All of the data collected are then reviewed by the ALT to determine whether the changes addressed the concerns previously raised or if additional changes are needed.

Phase 4 Referrals from the Beyond Access Team

Monitoring for fidelity of implementation of the BA Model components and activities increases ALT awareness of the successes and challenges experienced by a student's team as they implement the Model. From within the student's team there may also arise questions or concerns that require some administrative input. When these occur, the student's team may make a formal referral to the ALT to make them aware of the situation or to request action within a certain time line.

Although formally scripted in Phase 4, the student's team may make a referral to the ALT at any point during use of the BA Model. In Chapter 9, the referral process is described for continuing implementation of supports with action required from the ALT. A similar process can be used for addressing challenges as they arise for a student's team. The following are examples of how the ALT addresses referrals from a BA team.

Clarifying Team Member Roles

Clarifying team member roles and responsibilities is a common referral to the ALT. Although BA teams will clarify team member roles as part of Phase 2, there may be some role confusion as the team tries to design and implement specific student supports and instructional strategies. To clarify roles and responsibilities, a representative from the ALT may facilitate a dialogue with team members regarding specific responsibilities that need to be fulfilled in order to effectively plan and provide the necessary supports and instructional strategies to the student. Once there is a comprehensive list of all of the responsibilities to be fulfilled, the ALT member may then facilitate a dialogue of which team member(s) have or would likely develop the knowledge and skills needed to fulfill each responsibility. The product is an individualized job role chart that specifies the primary job roles of each team member (see Chapter 5). Because this process includes input from each of the team members, it contributes to shared understanding among team members regarding their own and others' roles and responsibilities. The roles and responsibilities chart may then be posted where the team holds its weekly planning meeting as a tool for assigning specific tasks to individual team members.

Scheduling and Staffing that Promote Team Collaboration

Team collaboration is another type of referral to the ALT. Fostering a culture of team collaboration entails much more than simply adjusting the school schedule so that general and special education teachers have common planning time, although that is a necessary first step. Because every school is different, the following are examples from a variety of schools and school districts that illustrate some actions that ALT members have taken to foster team collaboration.

- At a large urban elementary school, the ALT allocated every team supporting a student with IDD to have 1 hour of scheduled planning time per week, and all team members were expected to attend.

- The ALT supported the hiring of a "roving paraprofessional" to support students while students' paraprofessionals attended team planning meetings.

- The ALT supported the building principal and team members to rotate the job of "getting Tyrone off the bus" so that no one team member had to miss the last 15 minutes of an early morning team meeting as the buses arrived.

- The ALT worked with district-level administrators to assign special education teachers with expertise related to students with learning disabilities to grade-level teams, with a plan for one special education teacher for every four grade-level classrooms. Special education teachers with expertise related to students with IDD filled the role of inclusion facilitators of students across multiple grades (Jorgensen et al., 2006).

- The ALT supported building principals in a rural school district to use professional development funds to enable students' teams to have several half days of collaborative planning time during the school year when the 1-hour weekly planning time was not sufficient to accomplish a particular recommended task (e.g., to create several units worth of graphic organizers using Kidspiration software). Team members who attended received professional development hours toward their 3-year recertification requirement.

- With support from the ALT, a building principal met with his department leaders to clarify the expectation that high school teachers who had a student with IDD in their classes would meet weekly with the school's special education teacher to share upcoming lesson plans so that the student's team would have the necessary information in time to make adapted materials that supported this student's full participation and learning in general education classes.

- The ALT developed a districtwide practice that all staff attend four day-long professional development workshops throughout the school year. Mornings were devoted to a keynote presentation related to one of the district's long-term improvement initiatives, and during the afternoons, school-based teams were provided with time to meet to do curriculum mapping and instructional planning.

- Based on a plan initiated by the special education teacher, the central office administrators in one BA district gave strong support to a districtwide Learning Circle for Inclusive Education. The Learning Circle started in 2006 with eight teachers who met monthly to just "talk about inclusive education." It expanded to include staff and administrators from all five towns that are part of the large school district. They now have a web site and lending library and are responsible for planning the agenda for one of the district's professional development days.

Helping Teams Resolve Conflict

There is likely to be conflict as teams engage in change. A key role of the ALT is to provide support for actions that will decrease conflict to enhance team collaboration. In some situations, this may mean engaging in mediation; in other situations, it may mean providing the time and processes for team members to identify their common interests, areas of concern, and possible solutions to those concerns. Often, there are multiple actions to resolve conflict.

Securing Additional Resources

When teams do not have the resources they need to adequately implement students' educational programs, it is the responsibility of the ALT to make every possible effort to provide those resources by deploying existing resources or using creative strategies to acquire additional ones. The five strategies that have been most successful for BA schools are as follows.

1. Exploring the use of instructional technology by using free or trial versions of software
2. Utilizing resources of AAC and AT manufacturers for equipment and training
3. Writing grants for instructional materials or technology resources
4. Partnering with universities or other organizations in model demonstration efforts that provide access to tangible resources
5. Budgeting for or reorganizing to provide additional staff resources

Sustain the Beyond Access Model

Sustainability for the BA Model at either a team or school level should consider lessons learned from sustainability of other efforts, such as Schoolwide Positive Behavior Support (SWPBS) or RTI. Sustainability addresses continued implementation and monitoring of BA Model components and activities, individualized and integrated with other school improvement efforts to the extent necessary to maintain effectiveness for students and teams. Sustaining the Model with one student's team may differ from sustaining it within the context of larger school reform activities.

Team-Level Activities

A team that is interested in continuing to use the BA Model across multiple years can redo the CASTS process at the end of a school year to prepare for the following year, or do so at the beginning of the next school year, which will allow the team to reflect on the progress made and the challenges that remain. Teams may find it helpful to tailor the CASTS activities (e.g., the questionnaire, interviews) with specific questions about insights from engaging in the structures, processes, and activities of the BA Model. As the CASTS findings are reported to a team experienced with the BA Model, recommendations can be explored that will specifically address the strengths and struggles reflected in the context of that school and that team working together for that particular student.

As new members join a team, it is important to engage the start-up activities listed in this chapter. New team members will need an orientation to the Model and will need a chance to rate their level of agreement with participating in the BA Model effort. Skipping such formalities may result in fractured ownership within the team, leading to individual frustration, problems with implementation, and team conflict.

School Reform Activities

The following section presents a synthesis of our work with the BA Model and others' work in educational systems change to situate the BA work within a larger context of existing school reform efforts.

Leading Inclusive Values

Bill Henderson, longtime principal of the O'Hearn School in Boston, a fully inclusive school since the mid-1980s, described "champions of inclusion" who have helped make it more possible for students who have disabilities to participate in meaningful ways with their peers in a wide range of activities. "Although the quality of inclusive education does indeed depend on many factors related to whole school change and improvement, it is important to acknowledge the people who really make it happen" (Henderson, 2006, p. 7).

Henderson emphasized that

> The salient characteristics of champions of inclusion do not depend upon advanced degrees and training. Although in many instances, special skills are certainly required, in most cases it is the accompanying positive beliefs, attitudes, and behaviors that are most significant. Indeed it is common for those who have been identified as champions of inclusion to state that what they are being recognized for is really quite ordinary. (2006, p. 12)

An example of a BA school's efforts to lead inclusive values was reflected in a simple, one-sentence statement as part of their district mission statement. It read, "Granite State Elementary School is a community of learners where all students are welcomed into the mainstream of general education with the supports and services necessary for the success of all." ALT members within this school demonstrated these values in a variety of environments and situations, including the following:

1. Providing regular updates about the rationale for and outcomes of inclusive educational practices to the school board and PTA, in interviews with local media, at faculty meetings, and within their own professional organizations
2. Embedding inclusive education knowledge and skills into staff members' individual professional development plans and performance evaluations
3. Addressing inclusive education practices through professional development events
4. Treating students as valued members of the school community
5. Establishing school honors that acknowledged diversity of student gifts and talents
6. Incorporating inclusive values into school traditions and customs

Hiring Staff with Beyond Access Values, Dispositions, and Skills

One role of the ALT is to identify dispositions, knowledge, and skills that are related to the provision of inclusive best practices. This information can come from a variety of sources such as 1) the BA Best Practices; 2) the list of team member skills presented in Chapter 5; 3) practice guidelines from professional organizations such as TASH (http://www.tash.org/), the American Speech-Language-Hearing Association (http://asha.org), and the American Occupational Therapy Association (http://aota.org); and 4) books such as *The Inclusion Facilitator's Guide* (Jorgensen et al., 2006) and *The Paraprofessional's Guide to the Inclusive Classroom: Working as a Team, Third Edition* (Doyle, 2008).

In the interview process, prospective employees might be asked the following questions:

- What are your beliefs about inclusive education?
- What does our school's mission statement mean to you?
- What experiences have you had teaching and supporting students with IDD in inclusive general education classrooms?
- In your past job, describe your role on collaborative teams for students with disabilities?
- What are your thoughts about No Child Left Behind legislation and other standards-based reforms for students with IDD?
- How have you collaborated with families of students with IDD with respect to their children's educational program, home life, or community participation?
- What volunteer or service activities have you been involved with that relate to children or adults with disabilities?
- What college coursework or in-service training have you had related to inclusive education, differentiated instruction, Universal Design for Learning, positive behavior supports, curriculum modification, facilitating social relationships, augmentative communication, AT, and futures or transition planning?
- What professional journals do you read on a regular basis? What professional organizations do you belong to? What professional conferences have you attended in the last 3 years?
- Do you have examples of lesson plans or other materials that reflect your skills in inclusive practices?

Providing Ongoing Professional Development
Related to Inclusive School Climate and Practices
The professional development that forms the foundation of the BA Model is consistent with the standards for high-quality professional development proposed by the NSDC (http://www.nsdc.org). For example, the NSDC proposes that all staff development be grounded in the goal of improving the learning of all students. They recommend that adults are organized in learning communities whose goals are aligned with those of the school and district, that skilled school and district leaders guide continuous instructional improvement, and that resources are dedicated to support continuous adult learning and collaboration. Each of these standards is reflected in the BA Model. BA teams are small learning communities that learn to use the Model together and utilize multiple sources of data to assess the

fidelity of the Model's use and to evaluate student learning. The BA facilitator and BA ALT guide the Model's use and support continuous instructional improvement through iterative engagement with Phases 1–4 of the Model, and both the BA team and the ALT act to secure the human and material resources necessary to use the Model with fidelity and to improve students' membership, participation, and learning. Although one-time workshops may be offered as part of a BA team's professional development plan, the Model shifts the emphasis from this type of learning to a greater emphasis on job-embedded professional development that occurs when teams use the Model with fidelity. Table 7.1 presented in Chapter 7 depicts one school's professional development plan. The role of the ALT is to support the implementation of the plan with resources, monitor its implementation, and support the team to revise it at regular intervals.

Nurturing Partnerships with External Critical Friends
The last type of resource that is available to a school's BA ALT is establishing a relationship between the school and an external "critical friend" (e.g., a faculty member from an institution of higher education that is receiving state or federal grants, private foundation support) to investigate and/or develop new practices for educating students with IDD (Olson, 1994). These public and private projects typically work in local schools, providing professional development, technical assistance, and tangible educational products such as software or hardware free of charge to the local school in exchange for the opportunity to learn from the experiences of the school's staff. Schools participating in the original BA Model Demonstration Project, for example, were provided with weekly onsite technical assistance, professional development workshops, model instructional materials, and other resources as they participated in the development and evaluation of the BA Model. Information for local schools interested in becoming associated with one of these projects can be obtained from two primary sources: the Association of University Centers on Disabilities (http://www.aucd.org) and its state-level organizations and the Office of Special Education Programs in the U.S. Department of Education (http://www.ed.gov/about/offices/list/osers/osep/index.html).

CONCLUSION

Knoster, Villa, and Thousand (2000) adapted a model of systems change copyrighted by Dr. Mary Lippitt of Enterprise Management Ltd. and related it to inclusive education, acknowledging the key roles of five elements: vision, professional skills, incentives, resources, and action plan. Jorgensen added an additional element to the model—reflective practice (York-Barr, Sommers, Ghere, & Montie, 2005). According to this model of complex change, if vision is missing, then confusion results. If team members do not have the necessary skills or lack self-efficacy, then they become anxious. If educators do not have time for reflection to think deeply about their work, then they can become stagnant and their creativity suffers. If incentives are not provided, then team members resist change. If resources are scarce, then people become frustrated. And if there is no action plan, then the entire enterprise makes a false start or people get caught on a treadmill and fail to move forward.

The activities of the ALT are consistent with this model and with our experience using the BA Model in schools. The ALT draws on its knowledge of effective systems change when it provides leadership and resources during the initial start-up of using the BA Model, provides resources that support teams to implement the Model with fidelity, takes action on referrals during Phase 4, and supports the Model's sustainability over time. When the ALT is effective, all elements of the change model can work together to promote enhanced membership, participation, and learning for students with IDD.

REFERENCES

Artiles, A., Kozleski, E., Dorn, S., & Christensen, C. (2006). Learning in inclusive education research: Re-mediating theory and methods with a transformative agenda. *Review of Research in Education, 30*(1), 65–108.

Burns, M.K., & Ysseldyke, J.E. (2005). Comparison of existing response-to-intervention models to identify and answer implementation questions. *The California School Psychologist, 10,* 9–20.

Doyle, M.B. (2008). *The paraprofessional's guide to the inclusive classroom: Working as a team* (3rd ed.). Baltimore: Paul H. Brookes Publishing Co.

Fullan, M. (2008). *The six secrets of change.* San Francisco: Jossey-Bass.

Hale, E.L., & Moorman, H.N. (2003). *Preparing school principals: A national perspective on policy and program innovations.* Washington, DC: Institute for Educational Leadership.

Henderson, B. (2006). Champions of inclusion. Making the extraordinary ordinary. *International Journal of Whole Schooling, 3*(1), 7–12.

Jorgensen, C.M., Schuh, M.C., & Nisbet, J. (2006). *The inclusion facilitator's guide.* Baltimore: Paul H. Brookes Publishing Co.

Katzman, L.I., Gandhi, A.G., Harbour, W.S., & LaRock, J.D. (Eds.). (2005). *Special education for a new century.* Cambridge, MA: Harvard Education Press.

Knoster, T.P., Villa, R.A., & Thousand, J.S. (2000). A framework for thinking about systems change. In R.A. Villa & J.S. Thousand (Eds.), *Restructuring for caring and effective education: Piecing the puzzle together* (2nd ed., pp. 93–128). Baltimore: Paul H. Brookes Publishing Co.

Kozleski, E.B., & Smith, A. (2005). *On...transformed, inclusive schools: A framework to guide fundamental change in urban schools.* Retrieved April 5, 2008, from http://urbanschools.org/pdf/TransformedSchools.pdf?v_document_name=Transformed%20Schools

National Staff Development Council. (2001). *Standards for staff development.* Retrieved October 11, 2008, from http://www.nsdc.org/standards/index.cfm

No Child Left Behind (NCLB) Act of 2001, PL 107-110, 115 Stat. 1425, 20 U.S.C. §§ 6301 *et seq.*

Olson, L. (1994, May 4). Critical friends. *Education Week,* 20–27.

Riehl, C.J. (2000). The principal's role in creating inclusive schools for diverse students: A review of normative, empirical, and critical literature on the practice of educational administration. *Review of Educational Research, 70*(1), 55–81.

Villa, R.A., & Thousand, J.S. (2005). *Creating an inclusive school* (2nd ed.). Alexandria, VA: Association for Supervision and Curriculum Development.

Warren, J.S., Edmonsen, H.M., Griggs, P., Lassen, S.R., McCart, A., Turnbull, A.P., et al. (2004). Urban applications of schoolwide positive behavior support: Critical issues and lessons learned. In L. Bambara, G. Dunlap, & E. Schwartz (Eds.), *Positive behavior support: Critical articles on improving practice for individuals with severe disabilities* (pp. 376–387). Austin, TX: PRO-ED.

York-Barr, J., Sommers, W.A., Ghere, G.S., & Montie, J.K. (2005). *Reflective practice to improve schools: An action guide for educators.* Thousand Oaks, CA: Corwin Press.

Checklist for Documenting Fidelity of Implementation

Checklist for Documenting Fidelity of Implementation

Instructions

Complete this form following the activities instructions given in Chapter 10 for supporting and monitoring fidelity of implementation of the Beyond Access Model.

Student: _____   Grade: _____

School: _____

Person completing checklist: _____

Dates of review: 1. _____   Circle phase(s) currently implemented: 1   2   3   4

2. _____   1   2   3   4

3. _____   1   2   3   4

4. _____   1   2   3   4

(Key: N/A = not applicable, N = not implemented, P = partially implemented, F = fully implemented)

Beyond Access (BA) Model start-up activities	Level of implementation		
Host initial BA Model overview session with individualized education program (IEP) team	N/A N	P	F
Gain formal agreement among team members to implement the model	N/A N	P	F
Establish Administrative Leadership Team (ALT) membership	N/A N	P	F
Establish ALT monthly meetings	N/A N	P	F
Provide the team (including parents/guardians) with an orientation to the BA Model	N/A N	P	F
Schedule a weekly 45- to 60-minute instructional planning time for the IEP team	N/A N	P	F

Checklist for Documenting Fidelity of Implementation (page 2 of 7)

Phase 1: Comprehensive Assessment of Student and Team Supports (CASTS) activities	Level of implementation		
ALT and student's team monitor and reflect on their dispositions toward the BA Model work (see Chapter 6)	N/A N	P	F
BA facilitator reviews student's educational records	N/A N	P	F
BA facilitator gathers and reviews student, team, and school artifacts	N/A N	P	F
BA facilitator administers written questionnaire and Student and Team Outcomes Survey to team members	N/A N	P	F
BA facilitator reviews BA Best Practices Rating Scale and reflects on discrepancies with current team practices	N/A N	P	F
BA facilitator observes student throughout a whole day at school	N/A N	P	F
BA facilitator visits the student's home and interviews parents/guardians	N/A N	P	F
BA facilitator observes a team meeting	N/A N	P	F
BA facilitator interviews all team members	N/A N	P	F
BA facilitator conducts follow-up interviews as necessary	N/A N	P	F
BA facilitator synthesizes and summarizes all CASTS findings	N/A N	P	F
BA facilitator develops draft CASTS recommendations	N/A N	P	F
BA facilitator shares findings and recommendations with team	N/A N	P	F
BA facilitator gains team members' agreement with the findings	N/A N	P	F
BA facilitator gains team members' agreement with the recommendations	N/A N	P	F

Appendix 10.1. Checklist for Documenting Fidelity of Implementation. (Full-size version included on the accompanying CD-ROM.)

Phase 2: Explore and Describe activities	Level of implementation			
ALT and student's team monitor and reflect on their dispositions toward the BA Model work (see dispositions listed in Chapter 7)	N/A	N	P	F
Team explores and describes student and team supports				
Step 1: Team confirms and prioritizes recommendations (for student and team support) to explore and describe	N/A	N	P	F
Step 2a: Team determines the specific conditions that will guide the exploration of a particular recommendation	N/A	N	P	F
Step 2b: Team decides what key BA indicators will be used to check the effect of the trial recommendation	N/A	N	P	F
Step 3: Team determines if the individuals involved in trying out the recommendation have the capacity for implementation	N/A	N	P	F
Step 4: Team initiates the exploration of the recommendation for the determined period of time	N/A	N	P	F
Step 5: Team makes adjustments in the implementation of the recommendation if immediate positive results are not observed	N/A	N	P	F
Step 6: Team engages in discussion of and reflection on BA indicators	N/A	N	P	F
Step 7: Team continues to make adjustments to the conditions under which they are exploring the recommendation	N/A	N	P	F
Step 8: Team members share their impressions about the effect of the recommendation	N/A	N	P	F
Step 9: Team formally decides on the action for an explored recommendation	N/A	N	P	F
The supports are explored and described in a way that maintains high expectations and presumed competence of the student's abilities	N/A	N	P	F
Professional development is implemented to enhance team members' knowledge and skills in areas specifically needed to explore and describe the supports during Phase 2	N/A	N	P	F

*The Beyond Access Model: Promoting Membership, Participation, and Learning for
Students with Disabilities in the General Education Classroom
by Cheryl M. Jorgensen, Michael McSheehan, and Rae M. Sonnenmeier*

Phase 3: Implement and Document activities	Level of implementation			
ALT and student's team monitor and reflect on their dispositions toward the BA Model work (see Chapter 8)	N/A	N	P	F
Fidelity of implementation				
Step 1: Team formalizes support description into a checklist	N/A	N	P	F
Step 2: Team identifies conditions for implementation	N/A	N	P	F
Step 3: Team identifies their capacity for implementation	N/A	N	P	F
Step 4: Team initiates implementation with fidelity documentation	N/A	N	P	F
Step 5: Team adjusts implementation of the support and fidelity documentation as needed	N/A	N	P	F
Step 6: Team discusses and reflects on fidelity documentation	N/A	N	P	F
Step 7: Team adjusts implementation of support and fidelity documentation based on Step 6	N/A	N	P	F
Step 8: BA facilitator summarizes data collected	N/A	N	P	F
Step 9: Team makes a decision regarding continued implementation of the support	N/A	N	P	F
Team collects efficacy (outcome) data quarterly using the Student and Team Outcomes Survey	N/A	N	P	F

*The Beyond Access Model: Promoting Membership, Participation, and Learning for
Students with Disabilities in the General Education Classroom
by Cheryl M. Jorgensen, Michael McSheehan, and Rae M. Sonnenmeier*

(continued)

Checklist for Documenting
Fidelity of Implementation *(page 6 of 7)*

Phase 4: Review and Reflect activities *(continued)*	Level of implementation			
Review status and decide next steps for professional development				
Step 1: Team makes a fidelity check regarding professional development activities	N/A	N	P	F
Step 2: Team identifies professional development needs	N/A	N	P	F
Step 3: BA facilitator checks CASTS recommendations for professional development	N/A	N	P	F
Step 4: Team examines indicators from BA Best Practices Rating Scale	N/A	N	P	F
Step 5: Team updates professional development status	N/A	N	P	F
Rate team member confidence in student's demonstrated performance as evidence of learning				
Step 1: Team identifies the curriculum area	N/A	N	P	F
Step 2: Team engages in a dialogue about impressions	N/A	N	P	F
Step 3: Team members rate confidence in student's demonstrated performance as evidence of learning	N/A	N	P	F
ALT activities	**Level of implementation**			
ALT develops a working knowledge of the BA Model	N/A	N	P	F
ALT monitors and reflects on dispositions toward the BA Model work (see Chapter 10)	N/A	N	P	F
ALT holds monthly meetings	N/A	N	P	F

Checklist for Documenting
Fidelity of Implementation *(page 5 of 7)*

Phase 4: Review and Reflect activities	Level of implementation			
ALT and student's team monitor and reflect on their dispositions toward the BA Model work (see dispositions listed in Chapter 9)	N/A	N	P	F
Review data and decide if Phase 3 supports are efficacious and sustainable				
Step 1: Team reviews data	N/A	N	P	F
Step 2: Team engages in a dialogue about trends in the fidelity and efficacy data	N/A	N	P	F
Step 3: Team determines efficacy	N/A	N	P	F
Step 4: Team determines action for supports deemed not efficacious: improve fidelity, adjust support, or discontinue	N/A	N	P	F
Step 5: Team determines action for supports deemed efficacious: continue without ALT intervention, continue with ALT consideration, or put on "hold" until ALT can intervene	N/A	N	P	F
Referrals are made to the ALT with team input	N/A	N	P	F
Review status and take action on CASTS recommendations not yet explored				
Step 1: Team reviews and discusses CASTS status summary sheets	N/A	N	P	F
Step 2: Team discusses potential benefits of initiating Phase 2 activities with these recommendations	N/A	N	P	F
Step 3: Team decides which action will be taken for the unexplored recommendations: initiate or delay	N/A	N	P	F

Checklist for Documenting
Fidelity of Implementation *(page 7 of 7)*

ALT activities *(continued)*	Level of implementation		
ALT monitors fidelity of implementation of the BA Model	N/A	N	P	F
ALT has an active presence in classrooms where teams are implementing the BA Model	N/A	N	P	F
ALT engages in regular communication with team members	N/A	N	P	F
ALT examines the status of implementation of each phase of the BA Model on a regular basis	N/A	N	P	F
ALT identifies activities that address the areas of concern	N/A	N	P	F
ALT evaluates the outcomes of changes made to address areas of concern	N/A	N	P	F
ALT completes monthly review of student team referrals	N/A	N	P	F
ALT identifies action to address referrals (barriers to implementation) and address them in a timely fashion	N/A	N	P	F
ALT addresses sustainability of BA Model practices for student's team	N/A	N	P	F
ALT integrates BA Model practices with schoolwide reform efforts	N/A	N	P	F

Summary *(Review ratings and identify areas of concern to be addressed by ALT)*

Afterword

After reading this book, we anticipate a variety of reactions from readers, such as, "This is exactly what I have been looking for to help me support students with IDD to learn in a general education classroom" to "I can't imagine how this process could be managed." As we have worked with teams who have had those same reactions, we have found it helpful to take to heart the work of Michael Fullan, former Dean of the Ontario Institute for Studies in Education of the University of Toronto, who is an international authority on education reform who has consulted with schools around the world for more than 30 years. His insights into the change process speak directly to the likely team experience in using the BA Model (Fullan, 2008).

An implementation dip is normal. When BA teams experience an initial decrease in their effectiveness, they can be assured that this is temporary and even necessary as they question their current practices, devote energy and time to learning new practices, and move from innovation to sustainability.

Behaviors change before beliefs. When teams first begin using the BA Model, they are told, "Just for now, put aside your judgment about whether your students who experience IDD can learn general education curriculum content while you explore and implement supports that might help them do just that." This recommendation acknowledges that deeply held beliefs take a long time to change and only do so when people have new experiences that contrast with those beliefs.

The size and prettiness of the [change] planning document is inversely related to the quantity of action and student learning. We admit that the outline of information to be included in a CASTS report as described in Chapter 6 can be very comprehensive, detailed, and in Fullan's words, "pretty." A CASTS report or any other BA document may not need to be this comprehensive, however, *as long as students achieve the desired outcomes of membership, participation, and learning.* The research done thus far on the BA Model has found that improved student and team outcomes have occurred in teams that have implemented the Model with high fidelity (including producing comprehensive and "pretty" documents). What we do not yet know is how much of which BA components are most highly related to these positive outcomes.

Shared vision and ownership is more an *outcome* of a quality process than it is a *precondition*. The BA Model is, at its heart, a model of professional development that leads to behavior change. Its four iterative phases reflect an understanding of adult learning theory and the process of change where there are no a priori conditions to be met, other than agreement to use the Model with fidelity. We expect that team members will not share a common vision and ownership until they have learned and practiced the Model over time, and this insight may reassure them when they become anxious about the slow pace of change.

We also have found it helpful to share with new BA teams a reflection that was written by a BA facilitator who supported two students' teams to use the Model. Laurie Lambert began her educational career as a paraprofessional, supporting individual students with IDD who were included at least part-time in general education classrooms. After receiving her special education certification, she became her school's inclusion facilitator. She represents one of the hundreds of dedicated educators we have met over the years who work tirelessly to ensure that students with IDD are welcomed as valued members of their general education classrooms and school communities, who support them to be full participants in the same educational and social routines of their classmates, and who presume their competence to learn.

REFLECTIONS ON USING THE BEYOND ACCESS MODEL IN AN ELEMENTARY SCHOOL BY LAURIE LAMBERT

As with any school, there were certain challenges to overcome when making the steps to full inclusion. At my K–4 elementary school in southeast New Hampshire, these challenges most often took the form of preconceived notions concerning the need for students with significant disabilities to focus on life skills training rather than on learning academic content.

Another challenge was implementing positive behavior supports for students to participate in classroom activities. This was discussed in numerous team meetings, yet there seemed to be little follow through in the general education classroom. This resulted in behaviors that generated the claims that the learning of classmates was interrupted by the behaviors displayed by students with significant disabilities. Thus, pull-out services often became the topic of meeting discussions.

The BA Model appeared to be the life preserver I had been looking for to fully include students with significant disabilities in the general education curriculum. I was intrigued the moment I first read about it. The BA Model promoted full inclusion for students with significant disabilities by using teaming and supports for membership, participation, and learning within the general education classroom. They offered ongoing technical assistance to all team members and guided us through the paradigm shift of pull-out services to push-in services.

To begin the process of implementing the BA Model at our school, the school principal, special education director, another team member, and I attended an informational workshop about the BA Model. Each of us saw the amazing potential of using a model that focused on using the least dangerous assumption of presuming competence philosophy as an avenue to fully include students with significant disabilities within the general education classroom and by the prospect of actually teaching them the general education curriculum. We were totally hooked! Although I knew there would be some struggles in helping the rest of the team commit to full inclusion, I knew that I had the support of the administration. Therefore, any reservations I had were greatly reduced.

During the first couple of months of implementing the BA Model, our team went through the typical norming-storming-forming process of becoming an effective team. The BA Model helped provide us with a framework to run effective meetings and hold each other accountable for the accommodations and modifications that we planned as a team. Some team members struggled with shifting their paradigm of life skills training to incorporating the philosophy of least dangerous assumption of presuming competence as part of their everyday practice. Although we met some resistance, we continued to encourage trying the suggestions before dismissing them. When team members allowed themselves to try the suggestions, they suddenly saw how successful the student was in the general education classroom.

The first crystallizing moment for our team came during a morning meeting time. Previous to applying the least dangerous assumption for presuming competence principles, Kevin, a third-grader with autism, would do some alternate morning work at his desk rather than joining the rest of the class on the floor for morning message, calendar, and so forth. This happened mostly because some of the team members thought the information was too difficult for him and that he did not seem to be paying attention. The BA project staff from the University of New Hampshire encouraged us to presume that Kevin was competent and have him participate in morning meeting time. After a lengthy discussion at a team meeting, we all agreed to give this a try for 2 weeks. Kevin did join the morning meeting time, albeit lying on his beanbag chair rather than sitting on the floor.

During morning meeting, the teacher had a daily morning message that she used as language activity in which she would either misspell words for students to edit or indicate that some words were left out by using a blank to have the students use their strategies to figure out the unknown words. On the Wednesday of the second week of supporting Kevin, the teacher had written a sentence with a couple of missing words.

"Today is _____ _____."

She waited for hands to raise to fill in the blanks. No one. She asked again. No one. She provided some clues and hints. Still no one. On the third try, Kevin got up off his beanbag chair, walked up to the easel, pointed to the two blanks and said, just as clear as day, "Early release." Stunned, the teacher asked him to repeat what he said. Once again, he said, "Early release." Kevin was absolutely correct!

Well, I guess he was paying attention, even though he did not necessarily look as though he was. From that point on, each and every team member knew Kevin was capable of working in the general education curriculum.

There are two important parts of the BA Model that were particularly help-ful in promoting the positive changes that we saw. The first was the BA teaming model. This was probably the single most important piece to further our goal of teaching the general education content to students with significant disabilities. The BA Model showed us how to use an agenda to keep our discussions focused and productive. This agenda system also helped hold all of us accountable for the accommodations and modifications that we volunteered to do.

Team members taking turns fulfilling specific roles within each meeting was another aspect of this type of agenda system. This way each and every member took a turn being the facilitator, the recorder, the timekeeper, and so forth. This helped enlighten all of the team members to what each role entailed. This re-sulted in an increased awareness and willingness to be a vital, active part of the team.

The technical assistance that supported our use of the least dangerous as-sumption to presume competence was the second part of the BA Model that was instrumental in helping our team through this paradigm shift. BA project staff came into our meetings, showed us how to run them effectively, offered expert-ise in providing accommodations and modifications, and then went into the class-room to assist with follow through of the planned lessons. The more we followed through with our team meeting plans and the more we applied the least danger-ous assumption of presuming competence, the more progress we saw in the stu-dent in all areas. This technical assistance was ongoing throughout the school year and helped us to become more skilled at teaching and supporting students with significant disabilities in the general education classroom, which resulted in the learning of academic content by our students.

The BA Model does require a significant amount of meeting time dedicated to instructional planning. We scheduled an hour each week to accomplish this task. It was difficult freeing up all of the team members so that they could attend meetings. We were able to work through this with the support of our principal, by scheduling our meetings to begin a half-hour before school and run a half-hour into the school day. This way coverage for the classroom was only needed for a half-hour per week during a time that is typically taken up with attendance, lunch count, and morning work anyway. This worked well for us.

Some team members definitely struggled with doing things differently. Just sticking to an agenda of instructional planning during our team meetings was tough. It seemed that there was always an attempt to put instructional planning time on the back burner to talk about behavior. The BA Model helped us ac-knowledge that both topics were important but needed to be discussed at differ-ent times. So, we began to schedule separate meetings to discuss behavior. Then a funny thing happened—the more we modified lessons that included the stu-dent in the general education curriculum and provided consistent positive behav-ior supports, such as an effective communication system and self-regulation tech-niques, the fewer behavior problems we saw. Soon, we were not having any separate meetings concerning behavior because this student was totally engaged in all aspects of his classroom.

Shifting everyone's notion of who is responsible for teaching the student was another struggle in using the Model. Previous notions were that the special edu-cation teacher was the only person responsible. The BA Model helped the team realize that each team member had a role and a responsibility to the academic and social progress of this student. We became better organized and supportive team members. The classroom teacher adjusted her lesson planning times so that she was a week ahead in order to bring those plans to our team meeting and give us the time to modify the lessons accordingly. We took turns modifying books so that it did not always fall on one person's shoulders. This helped the paraprofessional feel involved in the teaching of this student rather than a bystander. The more she saw the rest of the team implement accommodations and modifications, the better she became at it and was able to successfully follow through. As a result of this improved coordination of planning, my role as an inclusion facilitator became one of guiding the entire team through the process of including students rather than being the only person responsible for every single portion of the student's program.

In conclusion, the BA Model helped guide us through using the principles of least dangerous assumption of presuming competence in order to fully include our students in the general education curriculum. As a result, we saw improved learning of academic content, fewer disruptive behaviors, and improved socialization for our students. As a team, we became more organized, better skilled at implementing accommodations and modifications, and incredibly supportive of each other. All of this resulted in a better educational environment for our students and a positive working environment for us all.

REFERENCES

Fullan, M. (2008). *The six secrets of change*. San Francisco: Jossey-Bass.

Beyond Access
Best Practices
Rating Scale

Appendix A. Beyond Access Best Practices Rating Scale. (Full-size version included on the accompanying CD-ROM.

Beyond Access
Best Practices Rating Scale

BEYOND ACCESS

This document is designed to offer schools a set of best practice indicators related to educating students with intellectual and/or other developmental disabilities (IDD) within the general education classroom. These best practices form a framework to guide planning for student and team supports. Completing the rating scale will allow schools and educational teams to evaluate their current performance in each area and determine targets for improvement.

The best practice indicators are divided into nine areas that affect education for students with IDD within the general education classroom. It is intended that schools address each of the nine areas over a period of time.

1. High expectations and least dangerous assumption of presumed competence
2. General education class membership and full participation
3. Quality augmentative and alternative communication (AAC)
4. Curriculum, instruction, and supports
5. Team collaboration
6. Professional development
7. Ongoing authentic assessment
8. Family–school partnerships
9. Special and general education reform

The Beyond Access (BA) facilitator will complete the rating scale as one of the activities of Phase 1 of the BA Model—the Comprehensive Assessment of Student and Team Supports (CASTS). A summary of the findings from the rating scale will be presented as part of the CASTS summary. As part of the CASTS recommendations, the BA facilitator guides the team in identifying possible best practice areas for professional development and will develop an action plan with support from the Administrative Leadership Team (ALT) to address priority areas.

Instructions

- Complete the BA Best Practices Rating Scale as part of the CASTS process.

- Critically review and reflect on all of the data collected during the CASTS (i.e., review of records, interviews, observations) regarding current student and team performance in each of the nine best practice areas.

- Read and consider each indicator carefully. Rate the level of evidence present regarding each best practice indicator using the following scale—no evidence, partial evidence, or adequate evidence. This document is designed to assist schools in improving services offered to all students—it is not designed to be punitive.

- Review the ratings. For any indicator with less than adequate evidence, circle a priority rating using the following scale: 1: immediate priority; 2: near future priority; 3: future priority.

- Summarize the ratings in each best practice area. Share the summary with the educational team as part of the CASTS findings meeting.

- Engage the educational team and ALT in a process to identify priority areas for exploration.

The Beyond Access Model: Promoting Membership, Participation, and Learning for Students with Disabilities in the General Education Classroom by Cheryl M. Jorgensen, Michael McSheehan, and Rae M. Sonnenmeier Copyright © 2010 by Paul H. Brookes Publishing Co. All rights reserved.

Beyond Access
Best Practices Rating Scale *(page 2 of 14)*

BEYOND ACCESS

1. High Expectations and Least Dangerous Assumption of Presumed Competence

Description: The inherent value and dignity of students with IDD is respected. All students with IDD pursue the same learner outcomes as students without disabilities. When students do not currently demonstrate content knowledge or skills, the principle of least dangerous assumption of presuming competence applies, and all aspects of their educational programs continue to reflect high expectations.

Indicators	No evidence	Partial evidence	Adequate evidence	Priority rating
1.1 Person-first language is used.				1 2 3
1.2 Language regarding the student's functioning or developmental level is not used; rather, descriptions of the student focus on abilities and needs.				1 2 3
1.3 Annual goals on the student's individualized education program (IEP) reflect content standards from the general education curriculum.				1 2 3
1.4 Predictions are not made that the student will "never" acquire certain knowledge or skills.				1 2 3
1.5 People speak directly to the student rather than through a paraprofessional or other person.				1 2 3
1.6 People use age-appropriate vocabulary and inflection when talking to the student.				1 2 3
1.7 In order to respect privacy, staff discuss the student's personal care, medical needs, and other sensitive issues out of earshot of other students and only with those who need to know.				1 2 3
1.8 The student works on the same grade-level content standards as typically developing peers with appropriate supports.				1 2 3
1.9 The student's individual discipline and behavior intervention plan relies on teaching appropriate skills (punishers or aversives are not used).				1 2 3

The Beyond Access Model: Promoting Membership, Participation, and Learning for Students with Disabilities in the General Education Classroom by Cheryl M. Jorgensen, Michael McSheehan, and Rae M. Sonnenmeier Copyright © 2010 by Paul H. Brookes Publishing Co. All rights reserved.

Indicators	No evidence	Partial evidence	Adequate evidence	Priority rating
2.9 There are no places or programs just for students with disabilities.				1 2 3
2.10 Students with disabilities are proportionally represented in classes, courses, clubs, and extracurricular activities.				1 2 3
2.11 The student's name is on all class lists, lists of groups put on the board, job lists, and so forth.				1 2 3
2.12 The student receives the same materials as students without disabilities, with supports (i.e., accommodations, adaptations) provided as necessary.				1 2 3
2.13 The student participates in classroom and school routines in typical locations (e.g., the Pledge of Allegiance, lunch count, jobs, errands, eating lunch in the cafeteria).				1 2 3
2.14 The student rides the same school bus as his or her peers without disabilities.				1 2 3
2.15 The student attends classes with other students, arriving and leaving at the same time.				1 2 3
2.16 The student participates in classroom instruction in similar ways as students without disabilities (e.g., whole-class discussions, at the board, in small groups, when called on by the teacher).				1 2 3
2.17 The student participates in school plays, field trips, and community service activities.				1 2 3

---

2. General Education Class Membership and Full Participation

Description: Students with IDD are members of age-appropriate general education classes in their neighborhood schools. These students have access to the full range of learning and social experiences and environments offered to students without disabilities. Students with IDD actively participate in the general education instruction in the general education classroom as provided by the general education teacher, with supports from special education and related services in the form of specially designed instruction and supplementary aids and services provided as needed.

Indicators	No evidence	Partial evidence	Adequate evidence	Priority rating
2.1 The student is on the roster of and formally a member of an age-appropriate general education class.				1 2 3
2.2 The student attends the school he or she would attend if he or she did not have a disability.				1 2 3
2.3 The student progresses through the grades according to the same pattern as students without disabilities.				1 2 3
2.4 The student marches at graduation at the average age at which other classmates without disabilities graduate.				1 2 3
2.5 The student receives a diploma when he or she is discharged from special education.				1 2 3
2.6 The student learns in outside-of-school, age-appropriate, and inclusive environments after the age of 18 and before he or she receives a high school diploma or is discharged from special education.				1 2 3
2.7 Related services are delivered primarily through consultation in the classroom.				1 2 3
2.8 Related services are delivered in typical, inclusive environments.				1 2 3

Beyond Access
Best Practices Rating Scale *(page 5 of 14)*

Indicators	No evidence	Partial evidence	Adequate evidence	Priority rating
2.18 The school is physically accessible.				1 2 3
2.19 The school accommodates the student's sensory needs.				1 2 3
2.20 The student's individual behavioral goals are aligned with the schoolwide behavioral rules.				1 2 3
2.21 The student's individual behavior supports and interventions are similar to ways that students without disabilities are supported.				1 2 3

3. Quality Augmentative and Alternative Communication

Description: Students with IDD are provided with accurate and reliable AAC supports and services that enable them to communicate about the content of the academic curriculum and in social situations with adults and age-appropriate classmates. Discrepancies in communication performance with age-appropriate classmates are used to inform the design and provision of AAC supports and services.

Indicators	No evidence	Partial evidence	Adequate evidence	Priority rating
3.1 The student has a means to communicate at all times.				1 2 3
3.2 The student has a means to communicate for a variety of purposes, including voice output/ speech-generating devices (SGDs).				1 2 3
3.3 Although the student may have multiple ways of communicating, a primary means of communication is identified, as needed, for demonstrating speaking, reading, writing, and listening.				1 2 3

Beyond Access
Best Practices Rating Scale *(page 6 of 14)*

Indicators	No evidence	Partial evidence	Adequate evidence	Priority rating
3.4 The student's communication system is programmed with messages to demonstrate learning of age-appropriate general education academics, commensurate with his or her age-appropriate classmates.				1 2 3
3.5 AAC systems are provided to enable the student to communicate for the purposes of self-determination and futures planning.				1 2 3
3.6 Supports are provided to enable the student to communicate for the purpose of self-determination and futures planning.				1 2 3
3.7 The student, his or her family members, and classmates without disabilities participate in selecting messages programmed into the AAC system.				1 2 3
3.8 When acting as a facilitator, people clearly engage in a support role, not actively participating in the content of the interaction between the student using AAC and his or her conversational partners.				1 2 3
3.9 When conversing with the student as a conversational partner, classmates and adults utilize information provided by facilitators to converse directly with the student, not with the facilitator.				1 2 3
3.10 Training and support to use the AAC system is provided to the student in the contexts and routines in which the student will communicate.				1 2 3
3.11 Training and support to use the AAC system is provided to the team, including classmates, in the contexts and routines in which the student will communicate.				1 2 3
3.12 AAC supports take into consideration the communicative functions of challenging behavior.				1 2 3

Indicators	No evidence	Partial evidence	Adequate evidence	Priority rating
Instruction…				
4.4 Reflects principles of Universal Design for Learning:				1 2 3
4.4a To support recognition learning and provide multiple, flexible methods of presentation.				
4.4b To support strategic learning and provide multiple, flexible methods of expression and apprenticeship.				
4.4c To support affective learning and provide multiple, flexible options for engagement.				
4.5 Reflects the learning styles of all students in the class by the use of visual, tactile, and kinesthetic materials and experiences.				1 2 3
4.6 Prioritizes the use of research-based strategies for increasing student achievement, such as:				1 2 3
4.6a Identifying similarities and differences.				
4.6b Summarizing and note taking.				
4.6c Reinforcing effort and providing recognition.				
4.6d Giving homework and providing opportunities for practice.				
4.6e Using nonlinguistic representations.				
4.6f Using cooperative learning.				
4.6g Setting objectives and providing feedback.				
4.6h Generating and testing hypotheses.				
4.6i Asking questions, and providing cues and advance organizers.				
4.7 Is provided in multiple formats such as individual, pairs, small groups, and whole class.				1 2 3

Indicators	No evidence	Partial evidence	Adequate evidence	Priority rating
3.13 A variety of funding sources and streams (e.g., Medicaid, private insurance, school funding) are utilized to acquire and maintain assistive technology (AT) and AAC systems and to support training of the student, his or her family, classmates, and support personnel.				1 2 3

4. Curriculum, Instruction, and Supports

Description: Students with IDD can learn the general education curriculum and can learn (some of) it via general education instruction. Consistent with Response to Intervention (RTI), curriculum and instruction are designed to accommodate the full range of student diversity. Accommodations supplement universally designed instruction and are provided to facilitate engagement in general education instruction for all students. Instructional groupings include students with IDD. Additional (more intensive) supports and modifications are provided to facilitate engagement in the general education curriculum via general education instruction as needed. Individualized or pull-aside instruction is provided to students with IDD only as a last resort to enable them to make progress within the general education curriculum. Students learn functional or life skills within typical routines in the general education classroom or other inclusive activities and environments.

Indicators	No evidence	Partial evidence	Adequate evidence	Priority rating
Curriculum is…				
4.1 Based on common content standards for all students.				1 2 3
4.2 Presented in a variety of accessible formats including written information at appropriate reading levels and in formats as indicated on the student support plan (e.g., video, picture/symbols, actual objects, demonstrations, orally).				1 2 3
4.3 Individualized through the development of personalized performance demonstrations for some students.				1 2 3

Beyond Access
Best Practices Rating Scale *(page 10 of 14)*

BEYOND ACCESS

Indicators	No evidence	Partial evidence	Adequate evidence	Priority rating
4.15 Reflects benchmarks similar to those of students without disabilities.				1 2 3
4.16 Reflects evaluation methods similar to those of students without disabilities.				1 2 3
4.17 Allows the student to receive grades that reflect "personal best" achievement and improvement.				1 2 3

5. Team Collaboration

Description: General and special education teachers, related services providers, and parents/guardians demonstrate shared responsibility by collaborating in the design, implementation, and evaluation of students' educational programs. Teams develop discipline-specific skills, enhance communication skills, and utilize meeting structures and team processes for effective collaboration.

Indicators	No evidence	Partial evidence	Adequate evidence	Priority rating
5.1 The roles and responsibilities of all teachers and staff reflect the commitment and skills needed to teach and support all students, including those with disabilities.				1 2 3
5.2 Special education staff work within the general education classroom as coteachers, team teachers, small-group instructors, or one-to-one support teachers for all students in the class.				1 2 3
5.3 The roles and responsibilities of special education teachers, paraprofessionals, and related services providers, reflect the provision of supports and services to students to enable them to participate in and benefit from the general education curriculum and to teachers to enable them to effectively teach heterogeneous classes.				1 2 3

Beyond Access
Best Practices Rating Scale *(page 9 of 14)*

BEYOND ACCESS

Indicators	No evidence	Partial evidence	Adequate evidence	Priority rating
Supports...				
4.8 Are provided within the general education class and other typical environments to enable the student to participate in and benefit from the general education curriculum and other inclusive learning opportunities and activities.				1 2 3
4.9 Are defined by the student's support plan and may include:				1 2 3
4.9a Physical, emotional, and sensory supports.				
4.9b Adapted materials; AT and AAC.				
4.9c Personalized performance demonstrations.				
4.9d Personalized instruction.				
4.9e Individualized grading and evaluation plans.				
4.10 For behavior challenges consider the student's sensory needs.				1 2 3
4.11 For behavior challenges are designed after completing a functional behavioral assessment (FBA).				1 2 3
4.12 For individual student behavior challenges focus on teaching a new skill that replaces the function of an inappropriate behavior.				1 2 3
4.13 Are consistent with a schoolwide positive behavior philosophy.				1 2 3
Evaluation and grading...				
4.14 Includes criteria for judging success that reflects:				1 2 3
4.14a General education curriculum standards.				
4.14b Personalized IEP goals and objectives.				

Indicators	No evidence	Partial evidence	Adequate evidence	Priority rating
5.4 There is collaborative planning time during the day for general and special education teachers and related services providers to ensure all parties are familiar with the lesson content and appropriate supports are provided for the student.				1 2 3
5.5 Teams use formal processes for: 5.5a Conducting meetings. 5.5b Solving problems. 5.5c Making decisions. 5.5d Evaluating their own effectiveness.				1 2 3
5.6 There is a team in place for teachers to discuss and problem-solve learning and behavioral concerns for individual students.				1 2 3

6. Professional Development

Description: Professional development is job embedded, including workshops, onsite coaching, mentoring, and reflective practice. It is provided for general and special education staff together, with team members learning alongside one another, and is linked to improved educational outcomes for students with IDD.

Indicators	No evidence	Partial evidence	Adequate evidence	Priority rating
6.1 Teams use reflective practice strategies and structures to engage in job-embedded learning and professional growth.				1 2 3
6.2 General and special education staff attend professional development events together.				1 2 3
6.3 General education staff identify learning about students with disabilities in their professional development plans.				1 2 3

Indicators	No evidence	Partial evidence	Adequate evidence	Priority rating
6.4 Regular review of student learning data informs the content and format of district, school, and individual professional development plans.				1 2 3
6.5 PD is designed and delivered using principles of UDL.				1 2 3
6.6 Teams learn how to identify and utilize supports that facilitate the learning of all students.				1 2 3
6.7 Team members have adequate expertise in conducting FBA, designing behavioral interventions plans, and creating behavioral supports and crisis management plans to assist classroom teachers.				1 2 3

7. Ongoing Authentic Assessment

Description: Authentic, performance-based assessments are conducted within typical activities in inclusive environments for the purpose of identifying students' learning and communication styles, preferences and interests, academic strengths and weaknesses, and need for support.

Indicators	No evidence	Partial evidence	Adequate evidence	Priority rating
7.1 Present level of performance statements on the IEP reflect the: 7.1a Student's talents, abilities, skills. 7.1b Student's learning styles. 7.1c Student's preferences. 7.1d Supports that the student needs to learn well.				1 2 3
7.2 Assessment reports reflect the student's abilities and needs rather than deficits and weaknesses.				1 2 3

Beyond Access
Best Practices Rating Scale *(page 14 of 14)*

BEYOND ACCESS

9. Special and General Education Reform

Description: Administrators provide leadership to align general and special education reform and improvement with respect to the creation of a community of learners that is inclusive of learners with IDD.

Indicators	No evidence	Partial evidence	Adequate evidence	Priority rating
9.1 The values of diversity and inclusion are evident in the school's mission statement.				1 2 3
9.2 General and special education administrators promote the values and benefits of inclusive education: 9.2a At meetings. 9.2b In school improvement plans or annual reports. 9.2c In school newsletters or web sites. 9.2d In conversations.				1 2 3
9.3 General and special education personnel participate together in schoolwide improvement and reform efforts that benefit students with and without disabilities.				1 2 3
9.4 The school has three to five established behavioral rules that describe expected social behavior for all students.				1 2 3
9.5 The schoolwide behavioral expectations are taught and rewarded for all students.				1 2 3
9.6 The student's discipline for a specific infraction is comparable with other students' discipline.				1 2 3

The Beyond Access Model: Promoting Membership, Participation, and Learning for Students with Disabilities in the General Education Classroom by Cheryl M. Jorgensen, Michael McSheehan, and Rae M. Sonnenmeier
Copyright © 2010 by Paul H. Brookes Publishing Co. All rights reserved.

Beyond Access
Best Practices Rating Scale *(page 13 of 14)*

BEYOND ACCESS

Indicators	No evidence	Partial evidence	Adequate evidence	Priority rating
7.3 If the student has difficulty communicating, then assessment tools and strategies are chosen accordingly.				1 2 3
7.4 Teachers and related services providers use ongoing dynamic assessments instead of discrete, one-time assessment tools.				1 2 3

8. Family–School Partnerships

Description: Families and schools are engaged in partnership to create quality inclusive educational experiences for students with IDD. Families are connected to resources for developing their own leadership and advocacy skills.

Indicators	No evidence	Partial evidence	Adequate evidence	Priority rating
8.1 Family priorities are reflected in annual goals on the student's IEP.				1 2 3
8.2 Families acknowledge teachers' efforts on behalf of their children.				1 2 3
8.3 Families know about resources for building their own leadership and advocacy skills relative to their children's education.				1 2 3
8.4 Families attend case management meetings or planning meetings on a regular basis.				1 2 3
8.5 Families have input and receive regular information about their children's social behavior.				1 2 3
8.6 Individual behavioral interventions reflect the family's culture.				1 2 3

The Beyond Access Model: Promoting Membership, Participation, and Learning for Students with Disabilities in the General Education Classroom by Cheryl M. Jorgensen, Michael McSheehan, and Rae M. Sonnenmeier
Copyright © 2010 by Paul H. Brookes Publishing Co. All rights reserved.

Beyond Access
Best Practices
Action Plan

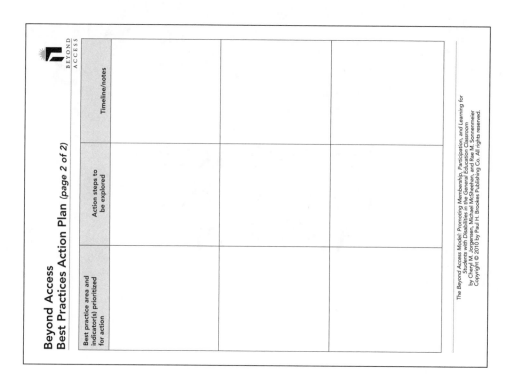

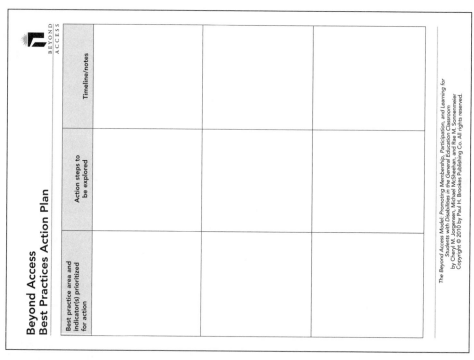

Appendix B. Beyond Access Best Practices Action Plan. (Full-size version included on the accompanying CD-ROM.)

Index

Page numbers followed by *f* indicate figures; numbers followed by *t* indicate tables.